CW01312515

HOW TO AVOID A PHD
(PENALTY FOR HARDWORKING DUMMIES): WISHING I WERE AN AUTODIDACT

Tamara I. Hammond

authorHOUSE

AuthorHouse™
1663 Liberty Drive
Bloomington, IN 47403
www.authorhouse.com
Phone: 833-262-8899

© 2022 Tamara Ionkova Hammond. All rights reserved.

No part of this book may be reproduced, stored in a retrieval system, or transmitted by any means without the written permission of the author.

Cover Designer: Ivana Georgieva

Published by AuthorHouse 11/10/2022

ISBN: 978-1-6655-7526-3 (sc)
ISBN: 978-1-6655-7527-0 (hc)
ISBN: 978-1-6655-7525-6 (e)

Library of Congress Control Number: 2022920788

Print information available on the last page.

Any people depicted in stock imagery provided by Getty Images are models, and such images are being used for illustrative purposes only. Certain stock imagery © Getty Images.

This book is printed on acid-free paper.

Because of the dynamic nature of the Internet, any web addresses or links contained in this book may have changed since publication and may no longer be valid. The views expressed in this work are solely those of the author and do not necessarily reflect the views of the publisher, and the publisher hereby disclaims any responsibility for them.

*For my talented and reliable American husband Ernie, who,
unlike his country, kept his promises to me, and to whom
I dedicate this book with love and appreciation*

Acknowledgements

Many special thanks to my grandson Triston for his Toltec wisdom, love, and help during my work, and for brightening my life.

Many profound thanks to my daughter Tammy for her enlightening information, and to her husband, Peter, for his hard work.

Many genuine thanks to my American friends and family, who inspired me to write this book, and who will always have my love and gratitude.

Many heartfelt thanks to my Bulgarian friends and family, whose support and encouragement are essential in my expatriate life.

Many sincere thanks to my friends around the world for their care, communication, and networking.

Many whole-hearted thanks to my book-cover designer, Ivie, for her creativity and profound understanding.

Contents

Acknowledgements vii
Introduction.. xi

Chapter 1   The Failure of Mainstream Media to Counter-Balance the Three Estates of Power: A Short History of the Corruption of the Forth Estate 1

Chapter 2   The Critics of the Media Are the Fifth Estate: The Rise of Dissident Indie Media as Opposition to the Fourth Estate 18

Chapter 3   The Regulatory Capture of the Four Estates of Power by Neoliberal Robber Barons: The Crime Bill of 1994, The Telecommunication Act of 1996, the 1999 Repeal of Glass-Steagall Act, the Patriot Act of 2001, and the Great Reset of 2020 36

Chapter 4   The Role of Academia in Supporting the Status Quo: From Walter Lippmann and Edward Bernays to Barak Obama and Sheryl Sandberg, the Propaganda Wheel is Always Well-Greased.. 54

Chapter 5   Academic Dissidents: The Glaring Absence of Noam Chomsky, Cornell West, and Chris Hedges from the Mainstream Media 71

Chapter 6   The Infiltration and Co-option of Genuine Movements: Neutralizing Opposition through Corruption and Violence from the Black Panthers and the NOW to #BLM and #MeToo 87

Chapter 7	The Climate Change Disaster: From the Oil Industry Sabotage to the New Green Deal Profiteers, No One Has the Wellbeing of Species in Mind	104
Chapter 8	The Dissident Indie Media: If They Can See Through Propaganda, We Can Too	124
Chapter 9	Never Trust Politicians, Mainstream Journalists and Academics: They Are the Ruling Class	143
Chapter 10	Ignorance is Propaganda's Best Friend: Challenging and Investigating The Official Narrative Is the Only Way to Educate Yourself and Others	160

Conclusion 177
The Tale of The Stairs 179
Bibliography 185

Introduction

This book is a continuation or rather rebuttal of my 2011 book titled How to Obtain a PhD, about hard-working dummies chasing the American Dream. In my subsequent book with the same acronym for PhD (Penalty for Hardworking Dummies), I argue that incredibly naïve thinkers and intellectuals fall victims of the educational system and propaganda in America including the author of this book. I was heavily brainwashed by a sophisticated industry called "People Relations" founded by Edward Bernays in the 1920s that is even more effective today. In my case, after 15 years in academia and a Doctorate degree, I finally broke free from the neoliberal ideology that kept me hostage for quite some time. Yet, in the first book I deciphered some important aspects of the propaganda and was able to see through it. For example, the financial predatory lending for profit, the food and drug fraudulent industry, and the two-party system that works for the same elites, among others were obvious to me from the beginning. Paradoxically, as I delved into my academic studies, I was swayed away from my critical perspective as I was emersed in the deliberate promotion of corporate agenda in the complete absence of opposite views.

Fortunately, thanks to dissident figures such as Eugene Debs, Howard Zinn, Noam Chomsky, and independent journalists such as Chris Hedges, Glenn Greenwald, Matt Taibbi, Max Blumenthal, Aaron Mate, and Caitlin Johnstone among others, I reexamined and challenged the propaganda imposed on everyone by equally mercenary academia and media. In addition, whistleblowers and heroes who risk their freedom and comfortable lives to reveal the truth about our government's unconstitutional spying on its citizens and carrying out illegal military actions, lifted the veil of secrecy and shed a light on the grim reality of corporate tyranny. To celebrate my liberation from the manufactured consent among corporate controlled media and academia, I decided to share my newly acquired enlightenment with everyone eager to know the truth. More importantly, I wish I were an autodidact instead of investing more than a dozen of years in ridiculously expensive institutionalized boot camp called higher education. I argue that the goal of the business model of higher education is to enslave future employees through enormous debt and to condition them to work around the clock in low-paying, precarious jobs for decades in order to pay back their student loans. Any massive investment in formal education precludes the quest for learning the truth while simultaneously delays unbiased research by years. As an autodidact, I could have stumbled upon the truth significantly sooner if I weren't wasting time digesting the mandatory ideology of mendacious mythology designed to maintain the status quo.

This astonishing delay in my discovery of the truth illustrates how powerful the industry of propaganda is, strengthened by the network of mass media, academia, and think tanks working for the real owners of Americans – large corporations driven by profit. The exploitation of the majority of Americans by a handful of super rich multi-billionaires is both facilitated and obscured by mass media because their very few owners control the official narrative. Through very sophisticated mechanisms of propaganda that constantly disseminate the illusion of freedom, democracy, and meritocracy, the myth is perpetuated *ed nauseum*. More outrageously, the media sell to the public absurd ideas such as endless wars, individual responsibility for institutional failures, and social injustice presented as meritocracy. At the same time, the incessant propaganda conditions the public to accept the denial of basic human rights such as healthcare, living wages and higher education as undeserved luxuries. More importantly, the persisting system driven by greed, which prioritizes profit above human health and existence leads to the devastation of life on earth and cannot be sustained anymore.

Fortunately, people are waking up to the sobering facts of climate emergency and the independent new media both inform people and organize their resistance against their extinction. Demonstrated in organizations such as Extinction Rebellion founded in November 2018, as well as Sunrise youth movement in the US from 2017, citizens' outrage cannot be suppressed anymore. The opposition is especially embraced and led by the younger generations who are educated by new independent media and have avoided the massive propaganda by choosing not to watch TV or mainstream digital media. Although constantly growing, the awareness of Americans about the exploitative and deadly system that benefits only a few moguls and denies everyone else a decent life, still lags behind the world's response. Only since 2019 there was a shift in public opinion, and as of 2021, two-thirds of Americans believe global warming is both real and caused by humans.[1] The change is driven by the mainstream media who finally decided to support the ideas for green energy for profit, thus breaking the silence they maintained about what they knew since the 1970s. To paraphrase Greta Thunberg, the teenage environmental activist from Sweden, people are not evil or lazy, they just didn't know the scientific facts about our dire situation.

Sadly, as history teaches us, most of the genuine movements get co-opted by special interests, and perhaps unwittingly, they are neutralized by the very powers they fight. The environmental movements are not immune from being co-opted in government cabinets that work covertly against their ideas. By the time this book is published, many of the movements and independent media outlets could be disempowered or corrupted. This recently happened to the Sunrise movement as its leaders were neutralized in 2020. By given a fake seat to the government table they are compelled to accept incremental changes with generous promises for future betterment.[2] The predominant bad actors here are the corporations whose financial interest leads to gross inequality and extinction of the civilization, with the help of their accomplices, the media and academia, who willingly deceive and misinform the public in order to preserve their privileges and high social status. Although a drop in the ocean, every dissenting voice is important, because the solution lies within the many populations who have the power of the numbers and could use it to force governments to change the direction towards extinction.

As many authors who had succumbed to the propaganda and wasted many years before they could see the light, I credit my awakening to the digital independent media outlets too many to be listed here. Nevertheless, I will mention a few journalists besides the ones already stated such as Whitney Webb, Ben Norton, Alan Macleod, Richard Medhurst, Jackson Hinkle, and filmmakers Oliver Stone, Peter Joseph, Abby Martin, and Eleanor Goldfield. Moreover, whistleblowers such as former secret services analyst Eduard

---

[1] Zoe Strozewski, "Ten Percent of Americans Don't Believe in Climate Change, 15 Percent Unsure: Poll," *Newsweek*, Oct. 26, 2021. https://www.newsweek.com/10-percent-americans-dont-believe-climate-change-15-percent-unsure-poll-1642747

[2] In 2020, Varshini Prakash, the founder of Sunrise Movement, became a member of Biden's Climate Task Force.

Snowden, who is currently in exile abroad, and Julian Assange who has been incarcerated for the past three years, revealed to the world international government corruption and illegal measures. Since the propaganda machine constantly calls for censorship in social networks, disseminating the truth often is left to comedians such as Jimmy Dore, Sabby Sabs, Lee Camp, Graham Elwood, Katie Halper, and so on, who are proud descendants of counterculture icons like Lenny Bruce and George Carlin.

In light of the recent pandemic, the international consensus of multiple governments on violating basic human rights is alarming but expected because like the US federal branches they work for the same global tech and pharmaceutical corporations. Although the pandemic exacerbated the economic instability of the western world, accelerated in the first decades of the 21st century, it was not the cause of this crisis, only the catalyst of it. The pandemic was indeed used for enriching the billionaire class globally. Similarly, as corporation-run institutions, most countries mimicked the economic pattern of widening the gap between rich and poor while benefitting a tiny minority at the top. Moreover, the pandemic was used to implement authoritarian measures such as lockdowns, vaccine mandates, and heavy travel restrictions. The synchronized propaganda disseminated through every major media outlet in the world is designed to inflict fear and division in world populations in order to control them. However, massive protests, strikes and demonstrations are pervasive around the world. These global opposition waves resemble the civil movements in the 1960s that brought significant progressive changes in multiple countries, especially in the US. Therefore, my hope is that new positive changes are again possible. I strongly encourage people to study the facts and take a stand against the current policies of exploitation, violation of human rights, and destruction of life on earth. More importantly, I believe in and promote the optimistic message that it is not too late for actions, although it would require massive coordination and solidarity among all progressive people globally.

Finally, I would like to explain some of the terms I use repeatedly throughout the book. The term "fourth estate" represents the established or mainstream media, and the "independent new media," or the "fifth estate" signify the alternative media and are used interchangeably. The term "fourth estate" was coined by Edmund Burke in 1787 as a symbol of the fourth branch of power, the press, whose main function is to hold accountable the other branches of power, namely the executive, legislative, and judicial.[3] The fifth estate is defined by scholar Arthur Hayes as the "critics of the press" and emerges because of the failure of the fourth estate to play its proper role of challenging power.[4] The first, second and third estates of power, are supposed to be independent from the fourth estate in democratic societies. Increasingly, the three main brunches integrate with the mainstream media, which now belong to the ruling class by virtue of their wealth and privileges. Because these undemocratic phenomena and their consequences remain unreported by the press, I analyze the dynamics of power and corruption in western societies and more specifically in the US. As Matt Taibbi describes the invisible role of propaganda coupled with censorship in the inculcation of Americans, "It is subtle, idiosyncratic process that you can stare at for a lifetime and nonetheless not see."[5] I know I didn't see it for nearly 15 years. Therefore, I hope that my work will contribute to the uneasy process of illuminating the current informational eclipse and will help disperse the myths that keep the public oblivious of its own ignorance.

---

[3] Julianne Schultz, *Reviving the Fourth Estate,* Cambridge, UK: Cambridge U Press, 1998, 49.
[4] Arthur S. Hayes, *Press Critics Are the Fifth Estate,* Westport: Praeger Publishers, 2008, 2.
[5] Matt Taibbi, *Hate, Inc: Why Today's Media Makes Us Despise One Another,* New York, London: OR Books, 2021, 11.

Chapter One

The Failure of Mainstream Media to Counter-Balance the Three Estates of Power: A Short History of the Corruption of the Forth Estate

> *Nearly every war that has been started in the past 50 years has been a result of media lies.*
>
> -Julian Assange, 2011

Although the monopolization of the mass media started in the early 1970s, the Communication Act of 1994 was an important milestone in the destruction of free media. The Act eliminated the cap on nationwide station ownership and limitations on cross media ownership, which caused a massive consolidation of media and the domination of the newspapers, airwaves, TV, and the Internet by a handful of corporations. It allowed cross ownership for unlimited number of news outlets. As a result, the media owners were reduced from several hundreds to five corporations currently.[6] The goal is very clear: the fewer the owners, the easier it is to control the narrative and eliminate competition. Ben H. Bagdikian, who is famous for obtaining and delivering the Pentagon papers during his tenure at *The Washington Post*, explains the

---

[6] As of 2020, the media owners are Disney, Comcast (joined by GM), Murdoch's News Corporation, AT&T, and Viacom.

process in his book *The New Media Monopoly: A Completely Revised and Updated Edition with Seven New Chapters* (2004).[7] Bagdikian reveals that there were fifty dominant media companies when the book was first published in 1983.[8] By contrast, by the seventh edition of the book in 2004, all media outlets from newspapers to magazines to book publishers, motion picture studios, and radio and television stations in the United States were owned by five corporations: Time Warner, the Walt Disney Company, Murdoch's News Corporation, Viacom, and Bertelsmann.[9] In 2021, after several new mergers and buyoffs, the owners of the media are still five: Disney, News Corporation, Comcast (joined by GM), Viacom, and AT&T. According to Bagdikian, "This [ownership] gives each of the five corporations and their leaders more communications power than was exercised by any despot or dictatorship in history."[10] As a consequence, these entities set the tone for the public discourse and decide what is acceptable and what is unacceptable for public opinion and what is considered important. While the companies Bagdikian names the "big five" compete in a limited fashion, they all share assets when it is mutually beneficial, thereby making them business partners with each other. Bagdikian further explains the danger of the media monopoly in their unanimous promotion of the status quo:

> Modern corruption is more subtle. Today, or in recent times, advertisers have successfully demanded that the following ideas appear in programs around their ads: All businessmen are good or, if not, are always condemned by other businessmen. All wars are humane. The status quo is wonderful. Also wonderful are grocery stores, bakeries, rug companies, restaurants and laundries. Religionists, especially clergy, are perfect. The American way of life is beyond criticism.[11]

Similarly, digital media's monopoly of five giants including Microsoft,

---

[7] Ben H. Bagdikian, *The New Media Monopoly: A Completely Revised and Updated Edition with Seven New Chapters*, Vienna, Torino, Bari, and Oldenburg, Nov. 15, 2006. First published in 1983 by Beacon Press.
[8] Ibid., 16.
[9] Ibid., 6.
[10] Ibid.
[11] Ibid., 235.

Amazon, Apple, Google, and Meta,[12] control the entire news dissemination by imposing both direct and subtle censorship. In fact, given that in the Age of Information people turn to their digital social networks for news, Silicon Valley controls the newsfeed of billions of viewers. Moreover, even the traditional news outlets provided by cable TV, are often viewed on You Tube (owned by Google), which allows the channel to promote mainstream news while limiting independent sources through their corporate-friendly algorithms. In this manner, unelected billionaires in Silicon Valley control the flow of news using discretion in deciding what programs get exposure. The algorithms work in a predictable way: they are oriented to maintain the status quo and to bring enormous profits through the unpaid labor of millions of users who create content, but more importantly, through selling their collected data to companies who target them based on their likes and preferences. Since the corporate power of the advertising companies is also concentrated, Silicon Valley really has to worry about very few mega sponsors: Wall Street, big pharma, the oil industry, and the military industrial complex.

Edward Herman and Noam Chomsky summarize this invisible control in their book *Manufacturing Consent: The Political Economy of Mass Media*, explaining the five filters of mass media: ownership, advertisement, elite experts, flak, and common enemy.[13] The first already discussed filter, ownership, reached its maximum concentrated monopoly after the 1996 Telecommunication Act. The second filter, advertisement, not only pays for the expenses of the media outlets but it allows them to profit from selling their audiences to the advertisers as products. Because collecting data from users is unconstitutional, media corporations collaborate with the government and sell this information to them as well as to private corporations. Former NSA contractor and whistleblower Edward Snowden revealed in 2013 that Microsoft, Apple, Amazon, Google, and Facebook were sending private citizens' data directly to the government since their inception.[14] Because of their cooperation in spying on regular citizens, they were allowed to become the giants they are now. Consequently, infringing citizens' privacy is protected by the government and the anti-trust laws are not enforced on these corporations.

---

[12] The digital companies are listed chronologically by their foundations: M-1975, App-1976, Am-1994, G-1998, F-2004 (renamed Meta in 2022).

[13] Edward S. Herman, and Noam Chomsky, *Manufacturing Consent: The Political Economy of Mass Media*, New York: Pantheon Books, 1988.

[14] *BBC News*, "Edward Snowden: Leaks that Exposed US Spy Programme," July 1, 2013.

Even more effectively, using digital media, the government manufactures peoples' consent for invading countries such as Afghanistan and Iraq where we maintained military presence since 2001 and 2003 respectively. With the relentless pro-war propaganda in mainstream media and especially through omission, the media is complicit in the unconstitutional, violent policy of breaking international laws. For example, the media's failing to report the USA bombing of ten countries currently on a daily basis, or the importance of approving the bloated military budget increasing every year undermines people's resistance to war and precludes anti-war demonstrations. Even after deciding to withdraw from Afghanistan in 2021 after 20 years, Congress approved almost unanimously an increased annual budget of $768B – an amount greater than the combined budgets of the next ten countries. Instead of questioning and challenging such bi-partisan agreement, the media failed to report the controversy of a seemingly opposition party's enthusiasm to give such enormous military power to a president accused of treachery and therefore, impeached twice. Such controversies, unreported or underreported by the media, prove their loyalty to the ruling class, in direct conflict with the main duty of the fourth estate – to keep the powerful accountable.

The third filter – elite experts is illustrated in the daily news. William Arkin, a military analyst for more than 30 years, explains in his 2021 book *The Generals Have No Clothes* that we are bombing "at least ten countries on any given day" in the Middle East and Africa.[15] According to Arkin, because of secrecy, the real toll of solders and private contractors who died in the "global war on terror" are thousands more than the official number 11,000.[16] Moreover, the cost of war paid by the American people, was more than $6.5T by 2020, twice the cost of annual healthcare for all Americans.[17] Arkin resigned from NBC in 2019, publicizing his resignation letter, which went viral on the Internet. Arkin made a statement that the result of the "so called war on terror" is more terrorists and more violence because these countries are "no safer than 18 years ago."[18] Arkin further explains that he feels out of sync with the network and his expertise less valued because he

---

[15] William Arkin, *The Generals Have No Clothes: the Untold Story of Our Perpetual Wars*, New York: Simon and Schuster, 2021, 6. The countries are Iraq, Afghanistan, Pakistan, Palestine, Syria, Libya, Yemen, Somalia, Nigeria, and Sudan.
[16] Ibid., 9
[17] Ibid., 11.
[18] Arkin," Must Flee TV," *Harpers Magazine* March 2019. The resignation letter was dated Jan 4, 2019 and went viral on the Internet.

was confronted by the overwhelming presence of generals and politicians with pro-war points of view. Arkin defines them as "highly partisan formers who masquerade as analysts" who were glorifying and advocating for wars without being challenged.[19]

The fourth media filter – flak, causes fear of retaliation for deviation from the mainstream narrative. It is evident in the profound failure of the media to complete its role of balancing the first three estates of executive, judicial, and legislative powers of the government. The punishment for disloyalty in journalism could be very serious – it varies from losing access to power to *ad hominem* attacks to firing to physical elimination. The most extreme example is Julian Assange, the founder of Wikileaks, who was arrested in 2019 and contained in high security prison in Belmarsh, London, for exposing war crimes of the US government. He is the only journalist sentenced under the Espionage Act of 1917, which sets a dangerous precedent for the free press everywhere in the world. Other examples of flak against reporting include Phill Donahue who was fired from MSNBC for his anti-war views,[20] and Pulitzer Prize winning Chris Hedges who was fired from the NYT for actively opposing the war in Iraq.[21]

Finally, the last filter – a common enemy – is related to the promotion of endless wars. The persistent push by the media for renewing the cold war with Russia is done for the sole purpose of justifying the enormous military budget. Another target for a cold war pushed by the media is China because of its rising economic power. Shortly after the US withdrawal from Afghanistan, the media sharply increased their anti-Russian propaganda campaign in anticipation of a new hot war, which actually happened in February and still continues currently. The process of media warmongering has a specific goal – besides justifying the inflated military budget, it distracts people from their immediate financial, social, and health problems. It allows the mainstream media to ignore pressing issues facing Americans such as lack of universal healthcare in the middle of a pandemic, loss of jobs, stagnant wages, and food/rent insecurity, and focus on promoting perpetual wars instead. Controlling

---

[19] Ibid.
[20] Amy Goodman, *Democracy Now*, "Legendary Talk Show Host Phil Donahue on the Silencing of Antiwar Voices in U.S. Media," Nov. 11, 2014. https://www.youtube.com/watch?v=Ac7S-QHekio
[21] Julianna Forlano, "Chris Hedges on The Reason He Lost His Job at The New York Times," *Act.TV*, Oct. 29, 2020. https://www.youtube.com/watch?v=Dnee-FGcT4s

the masses through fear of the enemy, the virus, and so on, is an old-tested tactic that always works.

Furthermore, in implementing Bernays's propaganda model, which dictates that the masses should be unaware of the source of their influencers, the audience is overwhelmed with carefully selected images and rhetoric by unknown agents. In his 1928 book *Propaganda,* Bernays wrote:

> The conscious and intelligent manipulation of the organized habits and opinions of the masses is an important element in democratic society. Those who manipulate this unseen mechanism of society constitute an invisible government which is the true ruling power of our country. ...We are governed, our minds are molded, our tastes formed, our ideas suggested, largely by men we have never heard of.[22]

In this blatant admission, the father of People Relations exposes the doctrine to which Americans have been subjected to for a century. In agreement with Bernays's guidance, very few people are familiar with the name of the author of this meticulous propaganda. Bernays proved his point by remaining anonymous after his two most successful People Relations campaigns: influencing women to smoke in the 1930s and a military coop executed by the CIA in Guatemala in the 1950s which opened the door for American United Fruit Company. The term" banana republic" is widely used to depict corporative intervention in foreign countries, mainly Latin American, and merciless exploitation of its population. American corporations use bribery of the corrupt elites of developing countries to allow them to sell their products at no benefits to the local population. As prescribed by the father of People Relations, no one links the concept with its successful creator behind the scenes, Edward Bernays. Likewise, the notorious tobacco industry's push to extend their customers to women, is not associated with Bernays as intended by careful design. As part of his strategy, Bernays deliberately took measures to disconnect his name from his clients, tobacco and fruit corporations. However, Bernays legacy has been and is still used widely by the media and education on the public to its harmful ends. In fact, it is now used more openly by these institutions.

---

[22] Edward L. Bernays, *Propaganda,* Liveright: Horace, 1928, 9.

For example, during the 20th century, the secret services needed to infiltrate the media and recruit certain journalists to convey their agenda on military intervention, and the Cold War with Russia in the news. As revealed by Pulitzer Prize winning journalist Carl Bernstein in 1977, the CIA recruited more than 400 journalists from prestigious news outlets such as the *New York Times*, the *Washington Post, Time Magazine, Newsweek*, and SBC among others. In an operation titled "Mockingbird," whose goal was to sway public opinion about issues perceived negatively, the secret services infiltrated the newsrooms and carried their agenda for decades.[23] In contrast, the contemporary mainstream media do not have to work covertly with the secret services; they could be agents of these organizations openly, receiving internships as is the case of the CNN's host Anderson Cooper who started his career as an intern for the CIA.[24] Another examples are former NSA director James Clapper, former CIA Director Michael Hayden, and present Secretary of State Antony Blinken, who are all paid contributors for the CNN.

In addition, as previously articulated by NBC military analyst William Arkin, generals, secret agents and other guests who do not disclose their ties to special interests are disguised as experts. They are frequently speakers on mainstream programs such as CNN, NBC, and FOX News, among others, and the news anchors do not reveal their conflict of interest, which is never discussed when introducing them to the public. Among the news reporters is Phil Mudd, former head of the FBI and a CIA agent with a title "senior intelligent analysts" for the CNN. In a segment with anchor Jim Acosta, Mudd is given a large platform to promote his secret services organizations and to curry favorable public opinion. More recently, in the fall of 2022, Matt Taibbi, a journalist, former writer and editor of *The Rolling Stones,* and co-host of the *Useful Idiots* with Katie Helper, describes the controversial symbiosis between mass media and the government agencies in his podcast:

> Mudd – who is supposed to be both retired from law enforcement and a member of the media now – then went on about how difficult things are for FBI agents now that unredacted warrant was out, releasing names and robbing agents of their birthright anonymity…"

---

[23] Carl Bernstein, "The CIA and the Media," *Rolling Stone,* June 27, 2007.

[24] Ben Norton, "CNN and 60 Minutes host Anderson Cooper, a Scion of the Vanderbilt Oligarch Dynasty, Worked in CIA Headquarters for Two Summers," *The Gray Zone,* Feb. 25, 2020.

Taibbi muses over the blatant involvement of the secret services in delivering the news and the huge platforms of millions of viewers given to them to defend their profession. Without challenging their opinion, or given alternative worldviews, the news anchors are fawning to power and completely abandoning their duty to hold government officials accountable. Taibbi writes that this is not incidental, but rather the normal practice in current mainstream media:

> Watching, I found myself wondering, "what *is* this?" There was no pretense of separateness between the CNN employees, and the spot's purpose appeared to be let a senior CIA/FBI counterintelligence official whine about the reaction to the Trump raid, stoke fear, and compare Americans to Al Qaeda. It felt less like news than something out of a dystopian novel like *Fahrenheit 451* or *We* and this is essentially on air round the clock.[25]

It is unfathomable to imagine such free press violations conducted by a country that claims to be the world's leading democracy. Therefore, the visible alliance between the media and the military industrial complex warrants public consent for perpetual wars while silencing the voices for peace. The institutional structure of the media defines their reporting strictly within the limits of the interests of the institutions that control them.

The most damaging effect of this censorship is the subtle inculcation of reporters who learn very quickly what kind of reporting is rewarded and what is retaliated. According to Taibbi, he learned from Herman and Chomsky's 1988 book that the propaganda model is perfectly concealed from both the public and the media professionals:

> The key to this deception is that Americans, every day, see vigorous debate going on in the press. This deceives them into thinking propaganda is absent. *Manufacturing Consent* explains that the debate you are watching is choreographed. The range of argument has been artificially narrowed long before you get to hear it.

---

[25] Matt Taibbi, "Sweeps Week on FBI TV!" *TK News by Matt Taibbi,* Aug., 16, 2022.

> This careful sham is accomplished through the constant, arduous policing of a whole range of internal pressure points within the media business. It is subtle, idiosyncratic process that you can stare at for a lifetime and nonetheless not see.[26]

Taibbi's analysis is congruous with Bernays's postulates about obscuring the propaganda techniques and goes even further than that by describing the internalizing of the doctrine by its purveyors and believing it instead of being cynical about it. More recently, we witness an increased and outrageously open censorship on the Internet expressed in regular purges of accounts accused of "misinformation" about important topics. For example, during the Covid pandemic of 2020, doctors, medical experts, scientists, and public figures were banned, shadow banned, demonetized and simply deleted from their platforms without evidence, explanation, or debate with their accusers. The term "misinformation" widely ranged from political views to medical reporting to other issues that deviated from the mainstream narrative. Worst of all, the regulatory action remained behind the scenes and was never revealed to the victims of anonymous censorship including algorithms and other techniques for eliminating unapproved opinions. A notorious example is Pulitzer Prize winning journalist Glen Greenwald, who was prohibited by his employer, the *Intercept,* a company he co-founded, from exposing an important information about corruption committed by then presidential candidate Biden. Greenwald resigned in protest from his very lucrative position; however, such an act of principle is very rare among journalists.

More conspicuous violation of the first amendment are acts of banning public figures from giant platforms such as Twitter, including a sitting president Trump in January 2021. Most importantly, anti-war and anti-establishment journalists were permanently banned from Twitter for their criticism of the US imperialism, worker exploitation, and pandemic measures such as Dr. Robert Malone, and journalists Dan Cohen, and Kit Klarenberg, among others. The most damaging effect of such anti-constitutional censorship is the fact that they have been supported and justified by prominent press members, politicians, public figures, and the general public.

The most common argument that the network is private and has the right to censor does not apply here because the tech companies who practice

---

[26] Taibbi, *Hate, Inc: Why Today's Media Makes Us Despise One Another,* New York, London: OR Books, 2021, 11.

censorship are working in close relationship with the government. Through multi-billion contracts with the Pentagon and other federal institutions, tech monopoly effectively works for the government. For example, Microsoft was awarded a $10B contract with the Pentagon in 2019, which was challenged in 2021 by Amazon.[27] Similarly, Google acquired a renewal of their contract with the Department of Defense in 2021, which replaced the old cloud program JEDI with a new, titled JWCC.[28] According to the Google Cloud CEO Tomas Kurion's own words, "The JWCC may be used by the Department to store personnel records, analyze recruitment, keep medical records, or implement advanced cloud solutions beyond storage or basic analytics."[29] In addition, these giant digital networks function as a public utility because of their massive memberships. For example, nearly 60 percent of the purchases in the US in 2021 have been done through Amazon.[30]

Similar to the traditional media outlets, a series of mergers and buyoffs consolidated the already monopolized tech companies. For example, former Facebook, now Meta, bought in 2012 the growing competitive platform Instagram, and international messaging service company WhatsApp in 2014. In terms of the level of both consumer use and cooperation with the government, digital companies hosting networks of this caliber should be considered a public utility; therefore, should be subjected to government regulations and prohibited from arbitrary censorship. The alternative should be breaking them down by enforcing existing anti-trust laws. The giant digital company Meta with almost 3B users, is practicing anti-constitutional censorship and banning undesirable speech, de-platforming users, closing accounts, and shadow-banning dissenting voices. All this suppression of speech prompted the creation of new independent platforms that host popular journalists with huge followings. Once deprived of making a living through arbitrary punitive measures of demonetizing on the conventional digital titans, namely You Tube, Twitter, and Meta, these censored programs find alternative platforms such as Substack, Rokfin, and Patrion where they depend solely on their subscribers.

The concentration and monopolization of the digital giant corporations,

---

[27] Jordan Novet, "Pentagon Asks Amazon, Google, Microsoft and Oracle for Bids for New Cloud Contracts," *CNBC*, Nov, 19, 2021.
[28] Tomas Kurion, *Inside Google Cloud,* "Update on Google Cloud's Work with the Government," Nov. 11, 2021.
[29] Ibid.
[30] PYMNTS.com. March 14, 2022.

Microsoft, Apple, Google, Meta, and Amazon didn't stop at reducing ownership to five entities. They continued with media cross-over ownership by buying different mediums. For example, in 2013, Jeff Bezos purchased *The Washington Post,* one of the most influential newspapers in the nation. More recently, in April 2022, the wealthiest person in the world, Elon Musk, was considering buying Twitter, one of the most popular digital networks. Although Musk self-proclaimed as a free speech absolutist, this is very unlikely because such principle would run against his own interest of maintaining his enormous wealth. Musk's means of wealth include exploitation of workers, using government contracts to spy on people while enriching himself, promoting military intervention in third world countries to appropriate their resources, and tax payers' funding for his space travel projects that will not benefit regular people, just a few eccentric billionaires.

The alarming increase of censorship and massive propaganda inflicts multiple damaging effects on the public. Perhaps the most harmful is evident in the lockstep of the global governments during the pandemic in the last couple of years. The synchronized draconian measures implemented by most countries including lock-downs, mandatory vaccinations and masks demonstrated once again the power of media when monopolized. There are different ways to practice censorship. As Chomsky said in an interview in 2022, referring to the unpublished Introduction to George Orwell's *Animal Farm,* self-censorship is assured in western democracies through a long process of attending prestigious schools where aspiring individuals learn that certain opinions and way of thinking are beneficial for their careers while others are counter-productive.[31] According to Chomsky, there is a filtering system that starts in kindergarten that selects for obedience and subordination.[32]

In the age of technology, this is still true; however, there are more modern and direct ways to practice censorship besides the discussed methods of de-platforming and closing accounts. For example, self-proclaimed fact-checking agencies, employing former and current government figures, issue warnings and punish users for "violating the rules of the network." It is very arbitrary and non-transparent process because the particular content that is considered offensive is never specified, neither the exact rules broken by the user are

---

[31] Thijmen Spakel, "Noam Chomsky on the Russia-Ukraine War, the Media, Propaganda, Orwell Newspeak, and Language," *Edukitchen,* podcast from the Netherland, April 26, 2022.
[32] Ibid.

revealed. More concerning are the qualifications of the agents, exacting censorship who are inevitably coming from the military or secret services.

For example, Senate Judiciary Committee asked Google's CEO Eric Schmidt, and the founders Sergey Brin and Larry Page in 2011 to change its algorithm in order to censor the activity on the search engine and to burry dissident content bellow hundreds of pages, and they agreed.[33] Similarly, in 2018, Meta signed a contract for consultation with The Digital Forensic Research Lab, created in 2016 by the Atlantic Council. The latter consists of military contractors and the architects of the Iraq war and many other wars such as National Security Adviser Henry Kissinger, CIA director Michael Hayden, CIA Director Leon Panetta, Secretary of State Colin Powell, Secretary of State Condoleezza Rice, Gen. David Petraeus, and so on. As a result, 800 Meta accounts were purged overnight from Meta on October 11, 2018.[34] Networks such as Google and Meta work with government agencies and think tanks sponsored by corporations and military contractors. Corporate media apparatus works very closely with government agencies such as the Atlantic Council who advise them on their censorship. Therefore, everyone out of this centrist by-partisan pro-war consensus among media is a subject to purge.

In light of the current war in Ukraine, every voice that deviates from the official narrative is suppressed through demonetizing, de-platforming or banning. You Tube, owned by Google, is diligently closing down accounts and speakers who present more nuanced or opposite view of the Russia-Ukrainian conflict including suggestions for peace negotiations. After Putin's invasion in Ukraine in Feb., 2022, the NATO, which functions as an US executive arm, immediately escalated the war by sending weapons and troops to Ukraine and is currently trying to turn this local conflict into a World War III. US House Armed Services Committee member Seth Moullton declared on national TV that this is a US proxy war with Russia and he supports a bill that is funding Ukraine bundled with Covid relief because they are equally important.[35]

The official media narrative is to continue the push for renewed cold war with Russia and to start a hot war disregarding the fact that it could be a full-blown nuclear exchange leading to extinction of humanity. Fomenting anti-Russian rhetoric that goes as far as banning Russian athletes from

---

[33] https://searchengineland.com/wp-content/seloads/2011/09/Eric-Schmidt-Testimony.pdf
[34] Nathaniel Gleicher, and Oscar Rodriguez, *Facebook Newsroom*, October 11, 2018.
[35] Brett Baer, "Lawmakers Consider Linking Ukraine and Covid Funding," Billable Hours, *Fox News*, May 2, 2022.

participating in world tennis cup and cancelling Russian musicians from classical concerts, the media successfully mirror the red scare of the McCarthy era. For example, the US branch of a TV program Russia Today titled RT America, was banned on You Tube and Europe in April 2022 and all the records of the shows deleted. As a result, program creators such as journalist Chris Hedges, comedian Lee Camp, and former governor Jesse Ventura among others found themselves without jobs and their recordings through the years disappeared.

Analogical example of censorship is enforced by a technological company named Newsguard, founded in 2018. The company offers censorship products and hires journalists from the establishment to rate the credibility of the content posted on the Internet. Newsguard became more active in January 2020, when they collaborated with the governments of the US, UK, France, Germany, and Italy before, during and after the pandemic. In the following year, the company rated more than 6,000 news sites, or 95 percent of the online news. Predictably, Newsguard targets anti-war, anti-establishment, and anti-neoliberal creators. For example, Newsguard rated WikiLeaks – the website that never had to retrack information since their inception in 2006, as unreliable. At the same time, the Newsguard's ratings of the CNN and the NYT, two establishment outlets that have been wrong about every war in the last two decades, from the two Iraq wars, to the Afghanistan war, to the war in Palestine, Yemen, Libya, and Syria, are favorable. The curious phenomenon of all western countries acting in a lockstep during the pandemic from 2020 to 2022, could be explained with their common use of a uniform news control through the algorithms provided by Newsguard.

Award winning journalist and author Max Blumenthal exposes convincingly the Newsguard's ties to the government, secret services, and corporate lobbyists on his program, *The Grayzone*.[36] As discussed in an interview, Blumenthal received an email from the company asking him seemingly legitimate questions about his program, regarding its ownership, funding, and recent claims that according to Newsguard were false.[37]

---

[36] Online News Association's Independent Feature Award for his 2002 article, "Day of the Dead", published in Salon; 2014 Lannan Foundation Cultural Freedom Award; 2015 Palestine Book Award by the Middle East Monitor for *The 51 Day War: Ruin and Resistance in Gaza*.

[37] Jimmy Dore, "Pentagon-Backed "Newsguard" Threatening You Tube's Anti-War Voices, "*Rokfin,* May, 2022.

Blumenthal published both the letter from Newsguard and his response on Twitter. Here is an excerpt from Blumenthal's response:

> Do you seriously expect us to grovel for approval from the same tentacle of the national security State and financial oligarchy that has rated CNN as a highly credible news source, and whose board of advisors is a grotesque gallery of corporate propagandists, spooks, documented liars, and war criminals who have never faced a scintilla of accountability for their actions?
>
> Your board of advisors includes Anders Fogg Rasmussen, the former NATO Secretary General who presided over the regime change war that transformed Libya from a prosperous, stable nation into the hellish sight of literal slave auctions and ISIS heavens, describing the murderous mission as a "great success;" former CIA and NSA director Michael Hayden, who oversaw the growth of secret torture and mass surveillance programs in partnership with Dick Chaney; Richard Stengel, the self-proclaimed "chief propagandist" of the State Department; Arne Duncan, the privatization-hungry former Secretary of Education who proclaimed that Hurricane Katrina was the best thing that happened to the education system of New Orleans because it literally wiped out public schools; Tom Ridge, who as DHS secretary deployed color-coded terror alerts (like Newsguard's media's "nutritional labels") to frighten the US public into line with Bush's catastrophic "war on terror;" and John Battelle, co-founder of *Wired Magazine*, which exists as clearinghouse for the military intelligence apparatus and was launched with seed money from Jeffrey Epstein beneficiary Nicholas Negroponte, the younger brother of former director of national intelligence and documented Central American death squad overseer John Negroponte.[38]

Max Blumenthal's thorough response summarizes the hypocrisy of these fact-checkers, and their ties with the government as well as special interests.

---

[38] @MaxBlumenthal, August 15, 2022.

In addition, Blumenthal points out in a different tweet that Board member of Newsguard Jimmy Wales also happened to be the founder of Wikipedia – a site that is completely controlled by its founders while claiming to be "democratic" and accessible to all.[39] Blumenthal explains that his news outlet the *Grayzone* was rated "red" by Wikipedia, considered by Blumenthal "unfit to judge us."[40] These undeniable conflicts of interest render such organizations biased, and reveals their hidden agenda that motivates them to act in the interest of the institutions who sponsor and control them. The increased development of such fact-checking companies with dubious connections is very worrisome and infringes the freedom of speech as it erodes democracy.

More recently, in the beginning of 2022, the media abandoned the coordinated campaign for mandates against Covid 19 and engaged in a new massive propaganda in favor of starting a global war. When Russia invaded Ukraine in Feb., 2022, the event was a response to some 20 years of complicated relations after the disintegration of the Soviet Union in 1991. As a former republic of the Soviet, Ukraine has an important geopolitical role because historically, Russia was invaded twice through Ukraine – in 1812 by Napoleon, and in 1941 by Hitler. The official reason given by the Russian President, Putin, was the continuous extension of NATO in Eastern Europe in violation of the Gorbachev-Baker agreement from the 1990s.

According to the National Security Archive, released in Dec. 12, 2017, thanks to the Freedom of Information Act (FOIA), "Declassified documents show security assurance against NATO expansion to Soviet leaders from Baker, Bush, Genscher, Kohl, Gates, Mitterrand, Thatcher, Hurd, Major, and Woerner."[41] When the Ukrainian president Zelensky, encouraged by the US and the EU made public his intentions to join NATO, the result was expected. The Western press completely ignored these known facts and Putin's warnings since 2014 that Ukraine should remain neutral, and pretended that the tension between Russia and NATO didn't exist. First predicting the

---

[39] Ibid.
[40] Ibid.
[41] Savranskaya, Svetlana and Tom Blanton. Slavic Studies Panel "Who Promised What to Whom on NATO Expansion?" . https://nsarchive.gwu.edu/briefing-book/russia-programs/2017-12-12/nato-expansion-what-gorbachev-heard-western-leaders-early James Baker, then Secretary of State, promised Gorbachev that NATO will not expand an inch east of Berlin, if Gorbachev lets Germany reunite and become a NATO member. There have been 14 Eastern European countries added to NATO since, 3 of them at the Russian border (Lithuania, Latvia, and Estonia), and the Ukrainian President declared that he will join NATO as well.

invasion of Ukraine by Russia and using it as a mobilizing point, the Western media then dangerously escalated a conflict that could have been prevented or retained locally, to a real threat of a World War III. The Western mainstream media quickly replaced the calls for censorship and Covid restrictions with irresponsible calls for the use of nuclear weapons.

The culmination of the increased censorship, propaganda, and authoritarian measures, was the formation of the Department of Homeland Security's Disinformation Governance Board to control the information flow and to impose a uniform official narrative. Independent media and critics of the federal intervention instantly renamed the Disinformation Board "The Ministry of Truth," referring to George Orwell's dystopian novel *1984*.[42] The sarcastic title "Ministry of Truth trended on Twitter for hours, according to the official Wikipedia page of the new Board.

The appointed executive director of the Board, Nina Jankowicz, is presented as a researcher and writer prior to her federal appointment. As an undergraduate, Jankowicz specialized in Russian and political science, and spent a semester in Russia in 2010. In 2017, Jankowicz was a Fulbright fellow in Kyiv, Ukraine, and later served as a disinformation fellow at the Woodrow Wilson Center. Apparently, Jankowicz has been groomed for the position of censor for more than a decade. As revealed by her own tweets, Jankowicz promptly participated in Russiagate campaign promoting the Steele dossier, officially discredited later, and openly showed partisan support for the Democratic party who appointed her. Jankowicz also attacked independent journalists because of their anti-war activism such as Max Blumenthal. Similar to former comedian Zelensky, Jankowicz demonstrated buffoonish attitude by literally singing in praise of censorship on social media. Jankowicz posted on Twitter her own singing performance calling herself "Mary Poppins of disinformation.[43]

Regardless of the entertaining qualities of the puppet figures in charge, the insane aggressive policies of military escalation supported by the media could lead to the extinction of humanity. This troublesome fact renders the need of alternative media more urgent than ever in order to counter the war propaganda. As a result, a myriad of digital hosts banned from

---

[42] In the book, Orwell describes a dystopian dictatorship where there is a constant mass surveillance and strict control of speech by the Ministry of Truth.

[43] Nina Jankowicz, "You can just call me the Mary Poppins of Disinformation," *Twitter*, Feb. 17, 2021.
https://twitter.com/wiczipedia/status/1362153807879303171

You Tube, Meta, and Twitter generated subscribes on platforms such as Subtasks, Rokfin, Patreon, Spotify, and Telegram among others. Although the alternative independent media become measurably popular among the long-starved public for objective, nonprofit-driven information, it is unclear how long they could continue to remain in the public domain given the current drastic measures against free speech.

Chapter Two

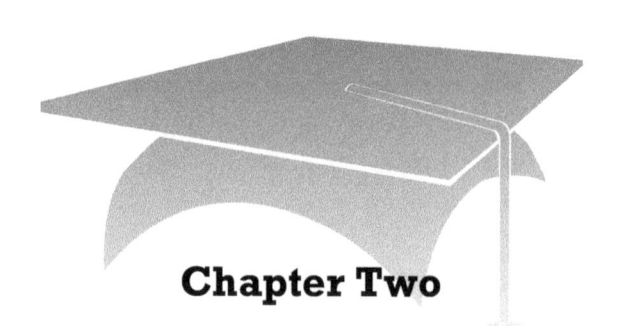

The Critics of the Media Are the Fifth Estate: The Rise of Dissident Indie Media as Opposition to the Fourth Estate

> *These people don't see that if you encourage totalitarian methods, the time may come when they will be used against you instead of for you.*
>
> *~George Orwell, 1945*

There are many alternative media news outlets that are funded exclusively by their subscribers including podcasts and digital platforms. It is not easy to determine which are genuinely reporting the news and which have alternative motives. In general, the rule of thumb is that if the outlet is not sponsored by the government, private billionaires, a monopolistic organization/corporation, or a think-tank representing the ruling class, chances are the outlet is clear of propaganda/special interest. The problem is, the moment genuine dissidents become popular and accumulate massive followings, they become targets of censorship. The next step is to try to bribe them or buy them off after a period of demonetization, in which they become more vulnerable to compromises. In more extreme situations, they are intimidated, threatened, and blackmailed. Either way, it is very hard to fight such methods because these platforms are run by humans who have weak points leading to their breaking, which the powerful exploit. Part of the intimidation are brutal campaigns of punitive actions, which aim at making an example of journalists who refuse to obey the ruling class.

The most notorious case of flak is this of Julian Assange, who exposed the United States' military crimes as well as major corruptions by other governments, large banks, and institutions. As a result, the global powers didn't just quietly make the man disappear but persecuted him for a decade and made sure it was a long, agonizing trial for him. First, the US government, led by the secret services, with the cooperation of some European governments, pressed false criminal charges against him and summoned him in Sweden. Then, they conspired to arrest him and forced Assange to seek a refuge in the Embassy of Ecuador in London, UK. Finally, after seven years confined in the Embassy, and after several failed attempts to assassinate him, in 2017, the US government resorted to overthrowing the president of Ecuador, Rafael Correa, and replacing him with a more US friendly president, Lenin Moreno. In 2019, Moreno revoked Assange's status of political refugee in a sovereign territory and allowed the British police to arrest him. Since then, Assange has been in British custody for three years and suffered torture as he was kept in isolation 23 hours a day and had very limited visits and phone calls. In 2022, a hearing of the Higher Court of London agreed to extradite him to the USA to serve 175 years under the Espionage Act. This sentence is absurd because Assange is an Australian citizen, not a US citizen, and reported facts that were never retracted.

Furthermore, the information published by Wiki Leaks was also published by the *Guardian*, the *New York Times*, the *Washington Post*, and all major newspapers. The mock hearing in London was carefully staged for the purpose of setting a precedent and demonstrating an example of what could be done to anyone who dares to oppose the powerful and expose their crimes. More devastating yet, it presents a threat to all journalists in the world and sets a precedent for persecuting any press member in any country if their reporting is unfavorable to the respective governments. More destructive yet is the deafening silence of the mainstream media anywhere in the world, especially in the West. There is no reporting on the most important case in modern times and there is no outrage for the injustice done to this journalist who won numerous rewards for his excellent reporting, which has never been refuted. Examples of Assange's rewards include:

Gary Webb Freedom of the Press Reward – February 2020.[44]
The Press Project – Person of the Year – 2020.[45]
Gavin MacFadyen Award for Whistleblowers – Sept 2019.[46]
The Danny Schechter Global Vision Award for Journalism and Activism – 2019.[47]
The Willy Brandt Award for Political Courage (Harrison) – October 2015.[48]
Global Exchange Human Rights Award – 2015.[49]
The Kazakhstan Union of Journalists Top Prize – June 2014.[50]
The Brazilian Press Association Human Rights Award – 2013.[51]
New York Festivals World Best TV and Films Silver World Medal – 2013.[52]
Yoko Ono Lennon Courage Award for the Arts – 2013.[53]
Big Brother Award - Italy "Hero of Privacy" – 2012.[54]
Voltaire Award for Free Speech – 2011.[55]
Walkely Award for Most Outstanding Contribution to Journalism – 2011.[56]
Martha Gellhorn Prize for Journalism – 2011.[57]
Sydney Peace Prize - Gold Medal – 2011.[58]
Free Dacia Award – 2011.[59]

---

[44] Joe Lauria, "Julian Assange Wins 2020 Gary Webb Freedom of the Press Reward," *Consortium News,* Feb. 10, 2020.

[45] https://thepressproject.gr/person-of-the-year-julian-assange/

[46] https://www.youtube.com/watch?v=l5ef856QHdQ

[47] "Julian Assange Receives 4th Annual DANNY Award for Journalism," *Defend Wiki Leaks,* June 12, 2019. www.challengepower.info

[48] The award was given to Sarah Harrison, a Wiki Leaks legal defense lawyer and adviser in October 2015. Sarah Harrison: "The award is for those that have been forced into becoming refugees because of their political actions on behalf of us all, and their work for our right to know." www.challengepower.info

[49] https://web.archive.org/web/20150627195622/http://humanrightsaward.org/past-honorees/

[50] Awarded for Julian Assange's outstanding efforts in investigative journalism. www.challengepower.info

[51] http://www.abi.org.br/abi-homenageia-defensores-da-liberdade-de-imprensa-e-de-informacao/

[52] http://www.newyorkfestivals.com/winners/2013/pieces.php?iid=444956&pid=1

[53] http://imaginepeace.com/archives/19347

[54] https://bba.winstonsmith.info/bbai2012.html

[55] http://libertyvictoria.org/node/172

[56] https://www.walkleys.com/board-statement-4-16/

[57] http://www.marthagellhorn.com/previous.htm

[58] http://sydneypeacefoundation.org.au/peace-medal-julian-assange/

[59] http://www.cbsnews.com/news/julian-assange-given-press-freedom-award/

Le Monde Readers' Choice Award for Person of the Year – 2010.[60]
Sam Adams Award – 2010.[61]
Time Magazine - Person of the Year, Reader's Choice – 2010.[62]
Amnesty International UK Media Awards – 2009.[63]
The Economist - New Media Award – 2008.[64]

Despite Assange's enormous popularity and recognition, the US government detained him in London's high security prison Belmarsh and sentenced him to life in prison for the act of exposing the war crimes of the most powerful governments in the world. The mainstream media launched a smearing campaign against Assange and succeeded in covering up the most important assault on press freedom in modern history. For this and other reasons the rise of the independent media continues to turn the tide in favor of the global audiences who are sick and tired of the deceiving subservient reporting of the mainstream media who act as stenographers for the ruling elites.

The most recent prize won by Assange in Feb, 2020, Gary Webb Freedom of the Press Reward, was in memory of the brave journalist Gary Webb, who lost his life because of his investigative reporting on the CIA involvement in the trafficking of cocaine from Nicaragua and supporting the Contras against the Sandinista government.[65] Gary Webb was found dead with two bullet wounds in his head on December 10, 2004, and the police reported it as suicide. After publishing his findings in the *San Jose Mercury News* in 1996, in a series titled "Dark Alliance," Webb was subjected to a smear campaign by the most powerful news outlets such as *The New York Times, The Washington Post,* and *The Los Angeles Times,* who first ignored and downplayed Webb's reporting, then denied his findings. The subversive campaign launched by the media, with the CIA pushing behind the scenes was so strong that the *San Jose Mercury News* succumbed to it. The newspaper retracted Webb's story and demoted the journalist who felt pressed to resign and couldn't find a job

---

[60] http://www.digitaljournal.com/article/301727
[61] http://samadamsaward.ch/julian-assange/
[62] http://newsfeed.time.com/2010/12/13/julian-assange-readers-choice-for-times-person-of-the-year-2010/
[63] https://www.theguardian.com/media/2009/jun/03/amnesty-international-media-awards
[64] https://www.indexoncensorship.org/index-on-censorship-awards-archive/index-on-censorship-award-winners-2008
[65] Ryan Devereaux, "How the CIA Watched over the Destruction of Gary Webb," *The Intercept,* Sept 25, 2014.

for years.⁶⁶ Obviously, Gary Webb was another example made by the ruling class to intimidate every journalist who would dare to challenge the powerful. Fortunately, the scandal was great enough to prompt the dissident press to create a reward in the name of Gary Webb, which was appropriately awarded to Julian Assange in 2020.

Among the many modern dissident journalists who risk their livelihood to report the news and refuse to spread propaganda are Chris Hedges, Caitlin Johnstone, Abby Martin, Whitney Webb, Aaron Mate, Max Blumenthal, Kim Iverson, Natali and Clayton Morris as well as comedians Lee Camp, Jimmy Dore, Russel Brand, Graham Elwood, Sabby Sabs, and Katie Halper among others. In light of the newly manufactured war in Ukraine, some of the dissident reporters who were forced to work at foreign outlets such as Russia Today-America were shut down completely and deleted from You Tube. The banned shows include Chris Hedges' *On Contact*, Lee Camp's *Redacted Tonight*, and Jesse Ventura's *The World According to Jesse*. Chris Hedges was previously fired from the NYT for his stand against the war in Iraq in 2003, after 15 years of reporting and winning a Pulitzer Prize. Likewise, Governor Jesse Ventura's $1M show on MSNBC was cancelled in 2003 for the same anti-war sentiment expressed by Ventura. Lee Camp's material accumulated in 8 years was deleted from You Tube upon banning the program in 2022. All censored reporters resorted to *Substack, Patreon, Rokfin* and other platforms known for their lack of censorship.

Similarly, doctors who become famous for refusing to falsify medical data and spoke openly against harmful measures during the Covid pandemic were smeared, discriminated, and mocked by mainstream media since 2020. For example, Dr. Robert Malone, former government contractor who worked on the mRNA vaccines for more than 30 years and currently stands against massive mandatory vaccinations, was banned from Twitter and LinkedIn in 2021. Remarkably, Malone gained a million followers on his paid podcast supported by his loyal audience, and was reinstated later on LinkedIn. His book, *Lies my Government Told Me* (2022) describes his career as a doctor and government employer with high clearance for more than three decades.⁶⁷

Another public figure, Robert Kennedy Jr, an environmental lawyer and son of Attorney General Robert Kennedy, was ignored by the mainstream media because he opposed Covid mandates, and there have been attempts to

---

⁶⁶ *Encyclopedia Britannica,* Gary Webb.
⁶⁷ Robert W. Malone, MD, MS, *Lies My Gov't Told Me and the Better Future Coming,* June 7, 2022.

ban his 2021 bestseller book *The Real Anthony Fauci: Bill Gates, Big Pharma, and the global War on Democracy and Public Health*.[68] The book contains serious criticism against unhealthy methods of forced lockdowns, vaccine and mask mandate dictated by profit, and offers more than 1800 footnotes from primary sources in support of Kennedy's research. Despite the fact that the book became an instant bestseller, not a single review was published by the legacy media. Regardless of the mainstream media informational eclipse, the author is continuously interviewed by many independent outlets such as *The Mint Press News, Consortium News, The Joe Rogan Experience,* the *Jimmy Dore Show,* Lee Camp's *Moment of Clarity,* and *Redacted* among other dissident outlets. In an interview with SPIN titled "The Outsider," Kennedy responded to the question about media silence regarding his book:

> We have an establishment that is largely controlled by pharmaceuticals. CNN and all the other major networks rely on pharmaceutical revenues. We have the once independent press like *The Guardian, The Independent* among others, and public television that are now completely subservient to Bill Gates. Gates has put more than $250 million into those independent outlets. So, there's blanket censorship across the media of any criticism of Fauci. One of Fauci's minions, Peter Hotez [from Baylor College of Medicine], who's a regular on CNN, he's Gates-funded, Fauci-funded — he's never identified as that. Virtually every one of the CNN experts [on this issue] is funded by Fauci but they never identify that.[69]

Similarly, Dr. Robert Malone and his wife, scientist Dr. Jill Glasspool, both outspoken critics of the government's Covid response, were ostracized by the medical community and smeared by the establishment media who questioned Malone's credentials although he has a medical degree from the Northeastern University and 30 years in the field of vaccines including mRNA. In an interview with *Desert Review,* Malone explains the role of media in the process:

---

[68] Robert F Kennedy Jr., *The Real Anthony Fauci: Bill Gates, Big Pharma, and the Global War on Democracy and Public Health.* Delaware: Skyhorse Publishing, 2021.
[69] Bob Guccione, Jr., "The Outsider," *SPIN,* Jan 17, 2022.

> The legacy media's strategy has been to personalize this, and to try to use these techniques to delegitimize me, and place me as the stalking horse, the exemplar of what's really a very broad movement, and I really don't like that very much...It's not about me – it's about the ideas and the truth...[70]

Furthermore, Malone describes the silencing of doctors who have been banned from media platforms, discredited, and ridiculed for expressing different views or questioning the official narrative, which contradicted all classical rules for medicine since ancient times:

> Pathologists are strongly discouraged to perform autopsies. All the classic stuff that we have had in our hospital system to ensure safety and effectiveness and appropriateness of medical treatment has been suppressed, all in this blind rush with the logic that anything which would cause vaccine hesitancy is not allowed.[71]

Amazingly, the voices against Covid censorship and medical mandates toned down and quietly transitioned in the background during the newly fabricated warmongering campaign launched by the mainstream media in the early 2022. Although in February 2022 the warmongering campaign reached a crescendo, it didn't start with the war in Ukraine. During the 4-year presidency of Donald Trump, the continuous accusation of collusion with the Russian government and some oligarchs, known as Russiagate, was proved wrong by the FBI's investigation during the president's two impeachment hearings in Congress. However, the Russiagate propaganda was used to lay the foundation for a new Cold War with Russia and to instigate support for a future hot war. Investigative journalist Aaron Mate won an Izzy Award on April 15, 2019 for his rebuttal of the fabricated Russiagate scandal pushed by the media for over four years. Both aims to alienate Russia were dangerous and unsafe given the fact that Russia has nuclear weapons and is not afraid to use them.

Ironically, while the Democrats were campaigning for a war with Russia, the Republicans including former president Trump were cheering for a

---

[70] Justus R. Hope, MD, "Dr. Malone Headwind Interview," *Desert Review*, April 12, 2022.
[71] Ibid.

war against China – another nuclear power country with a strong army of over 2.5 million solders. The ludicrous attacks on these two countries were initiated and supported by the corresponding parties forming a bipartisan call for wars and used to increase the military budget every year under these fabricated threats. The war hysteria led by the mainstream media resembled George Orwell's ominous book *1984* (1945), which describes the logistics of totalitarianism and how the propaganda and mass surveillance could be used instead of physical force to achieve obedience from the population.

The only anti-war voices of reason come from the dissident independent news media. The self-described "left" is equal or worse than the "right" in its militant support for censorship, wars, and neoliberal policies. Historically, the left is associated with anti-war movements, support for egalitarian society and opposition to censorship. In contrast, even the self-identified progressive politicians within the left are uniformly abandoning their progressive policies as soon as they get elected. It is increasingly harder to distinguish the two wings of the same party as they both serve the interests of the military industrial complex, big pharma, oil companies, big tech, and Wall Street. The alternative media or the fifth estate are constantly condemned by the establishment media for criticizing the "left." The fifth estate justifiably calls the useless left the "boutique left," "the lockdown left," and the "establishment left" among other monikers.

As the false claims of both right and left establishment media become more obvious, the ratings of the mainstream media decrease sharply. In desperate search for viewers, they resorted to sensational gory news about war atrocities in Ukraine, many of which turned out to be false. For example, the reports about bombing a hospital in Western Ukraine in the first week of March 2022 was proved to be insinuated by the local militia who were openly Nazi supporters.[72] Other examples include the Bucha massacre also performed by the Azov Battalion.[73] The most consequential falsehood, however, is denying the fact that the Ukrainian president Zelensky refused to announce neutrality for Ukraine days before the Russian invasion, which could have prevented the war. Because Zelensky is a puppet installed by the US, he did what he was expected to do to satisfy both NATO and the US war machines. This crucial fact was only reported by the fifth estate and journalists such as

---

[72] Russel Brand, *Under the Skin*, "You've Been Lied to About Why Ukraine War Begin," March 27, 2022.

[73] "Russian War Report: Kremlin Claims the Bucha Massacre Was Staged by Ukraine," *The Atlantic Council*, April 4, 2022.

Richard Medhurst, Lee Camp, Abby Martin, Aaron Mate, Max Blumenthal, and comedians Jimmy Dore, Russel Brand among others.

Similarly, world renowned scholar Noam Chomsky was severely criticized by the "boutique left" for taking a stand again the war in Ukraine.[74] Likewise, Pulitzer Prize winning journalist Chris Hedges expressed his anti-war view during an interview with *The Analysis*.[75] Hedges reminded the audience that thanks to WikiLeaks we know about the previous lies of the mainstream media that led to both wars in Iraq – 1991 and 2003, and how the latter lasted for almost two decades. Prior to the first Iraq war, the media fabricated consent by staging a false testimony about Saddam's solders throwing babies out of their incubators told by the Kuwait ambassador's 15-year-old daughter Nayirah al-Sabah before Congress.[76] Similarly, the 2003 invasion of Iraq was preceded by a massive media propaganda campaign claiming that Saddam had weapons of mass destruction later proven to be false.[77] The same tactics were used for the war in Syria when the media spread false information accusing president Al Assad of inflicting chemical weapons on his own people.[78]

Back in 2011, Julian Assange warned the world that "Nearly every war that had been started in the past 50 years has been a result of the media lies."[79] The discredited mainstream media continue to use the same lazy tactics and deceive the public with similar false flag stories because they are not held accountable and there are no negative consequences for them when debunked. To the contrary, they get promoted and financially rewarded instead of losing their jobs and never have to retract any of the erroneous information they reported. Because they work for the ruling class, the establishment media do not suffer punishment when they report falsehoods on behalf of their superiors. The public contempt does not affect them since it is immaterial to their lifestyles and careers.

However, the inevitable result from such contempt is the overwhelming success of alternative platforms. For example, Joe Rogan, a comedian and

---

[74] Jeremy Scahill, interview. "Noam Chomsky and Jeremy Scahill on the Russia-Ukraine War, the Media, Propaganda, and Accountability," *The Intercept*, April 19, 2022.
[75] Paul Jay, "Chris Hedges on Russia and Ukraine," *The Analysis News* April 21, 2022.
[76] Amy Goodman and Gonzales, "How False Testimony and Massive US Propaganda Machine Bolstered George H.W. Bush's War on Iraq, *Democracy Now*, Nov. 30, 2018.
[77] Larry King, "CNN Official Interview: Colin Powell Now Regrets UN Speech about WMD," Nov 15, 2020.
[78] Aaron Mate, "At UN, Aaron Mate Debunks OPCW's Syria Lies and Confronts US, UK on Cover Up," *The Grayzone*, April 18, 2021.
[79] https://www.linkedin.com/feed/update/urn:li:activity:6926391630958661633/

martial arts champion, built his massive popularity by holding thorough discussions on topics forbidden by the mainstream media and inviting controversial speakers banned from official public forums. For example, Rogan accumulates 11M viewers each show, whereas the most popular cable news shows, Tucker Carson on Fox News and Rachel Meadow on MSNBC gather 2M to 3M viewers per night. Rogan invites guests such as Dr. Robert Malone, Robert Kennedy Jr., and Bernie Sanders when he was controversial in the past. Malone and Kennedy are currently ignored or mocked by the mainstream media for their criticism of Covid measures. Rogan also invites prominent figures welcomed on the mainstream outlets such as Elon Musk, CNN contributor Dr. Sanjay Gupta, among other conventional celebrities.

Similarly, comedian Russel Brand has 5.5 M subscribers because he reports the news in an indiscriminative way by allowing alternative views and sincere discussions on topics censored by the establishment. Examples include the financial ties between policy makers and big pharma, the military industrial complex, the Wall Street lobbyists, and so on. Curiously, the most popular podcast in the nation, hosted by Joe Rogan, after his interview with Dr. Malone, gained 2 million new subscribers. The benefit was mutual – after exposed to Rogan's 11 million viewers, Malone gained fame as well, and the establishment media could no longer dismiss him or ignore him. For example, the *Business Insider* wrote about Malone in February 2022:

> There are reasons why people are listening to Malone – he is an expert source, and he is asking interesting questions about the vaccines. Malone has served as a consultant to the US government, exploring the best ways to repurpose medicines to fight new viral threats. Malone isn't the raving propagandist that some might like to dismiss him as — one who's wrong about everything that comes out of his mouth.[80]

In contrast, the *NYT* continues to misrepresent Malone on its outlet and published an article that cites "a half a dozen Covid experts and researches" without naming them and undermines his expertise in mRNA vaccines by omitting his 30 years in this specific medical field. According to the *NYT,*

---

[80] Hilary Brueck, "The Rise of Robert Malone, the mRNA scientist, Turned Vaccine Sceptic Who Shot to Fame on Joe Rogan's Podcast," *Business Insider,* Feb 27, 2022.

Dr. Malone also routinely sells himself on the shows as the inventor of mRNA vaccines, the technology used by Pfizer and Moderna for their Covid-19 shots, and says he doesn't get the credit he deserves for their development. While he was involved in some early research into the technology, his role in its creation was minimal at best, say half a dozen Covid experts and researchers, including three who worked closely with Dr. Malone. [81]

In the case of Joe Rogan, after his interview with Malone, the host of the podcast was pressed hard by his employer, *Spotify,* the platform on which he disseminates his program and which pays him seven figures annually. Rogan was forced to make a statement that he will balance his guests with opposite views; however, he privately stated that this is as far as he can go and if further censored, will leave *Spotify*. After all, Rogan is famous enough not to need the platform, whereas *Spotify* needs him. Rogan realizes that his honest approach brought him success and he is not willing to compromise his integrity.

Another investigative journalist and critic of the fourth estate is Whitney Webb, who offers a wealth of information unheard of in the mainstream media such as intelligence, tech surveillance, and civil liberties. Her show, *Unlimited Hangouts* is disseminated on Rokfin and Substack, since she was banned from Patreon. Webb's work involves a thorough investigation of the establishment and the work of the World Economic Forum, their ties with the pharmaceutical companies and the media, and the growing influence of Bill Gates and other billionaires on the media narrative and government policies. Webb first alerted the public about the Johns Hopkins' stimulations in 2019, sponsored by Gates and made the connection with the previous stimulations at Hopkins in 2001, titled Dark Winter. The events will be explored in detail in Chapter 4. Similarly, Webb investigates pharmaceutical companies such as Pfizer, Moderna, and AstraZeneca who rose to prominence during the pandemic as they accumulated enormous profits from their Covid vaccines.

The wide spectrum of topics covered by Webb include titles such as "Technocracy Rising with Patrick Wood," "Sanctions and the End of the Financial Era with John Titus," and "Ukraine and the Specter of Bioterror with Bobbie Martin and Gumby," among others featured on her website and

---

[81] Davey Alba, "The Latest Covid Misinformation Star Says He Invented the Vaccines," *The New York Times,* April 3, 2022.

podcast, *Unlimited Hangout*.[82] Webb is a contributor to the *Mint Press* and *The Last Vagabond,* and she interviews doctors, scientists, former government contractors, and whistleblowers on her podcast. Because of her reporting, which deviates from the orthodoxy of limited views on mainstream media, Webb has been banned intermittently from You Tube, Patrion, Twitter, among other platforms. Despite such measures, Webb accumulated 168,000 followers on Twitter, and tens of thousands of views on You Tube.

Webb's 2022 book, *One Nation under Blackmail,* reveals the near century old relations between the US and the Israeli intelligence and organized crime that gave rise to sexual blackmail that currently entangles all powerful elites from tech, government, and big business.[83] Webb talks about the book in an interview with Robert Kennedy on his podcast, *The Defender*.[84]

In 2019, Webb found out through an article in the UK reputable magazine *Evening Standard,* from January 22, 2001, that Epstein earned his first several millions thanks to his dealings with Bill Gates, Donald Trump, and the owner of Victoria Secret, Les Wexner. The article was deleted when Epstein was first arrested between 2006 and 2007 because in the article, Epstein openly claimed that he worked for the CIA. From this article is evident that Gates knew Epstein closely even in the 1990s – a fact that the mainstream media still ignores and pretends that the two only met in 2011. The *NYT* finally published an article in 2021, with a photo dated from 2011 in Epstein's Manhattan residence where he is standing between Bill Gates and Treasury Secretary Laurance Summers, with Microsoft co-founder Boris Nikolic, and JP Morgan CEO James Staley.[85]

Webb explains the ominous connections between these powerful institutions and the dystopian order they planned for us with the massive harvesting and use of data with the help of artificial intelligence, high technology, medicine, and the media. For example, Webb enunciates how the high tech was involved with the national security for the purpose of spying on the population. In addition, the DNA information is collected by companies such as *23 and Me,* DNA testing agency for ancestry origins, in order to exploit

---

[82] https://rokfin.com/unlimitedhangout
[83] Whitney Alyse Webb, *One Nation under Blackmail: The Sordid Union between Intelligence and Crime that Gave Rise to Jeffrey Epstein,* Barnes & Noble, July 22, 2022.
[84] Robert Kennedy, Jr., "Epstein and Bill Gates with Whitney Webb," *RFK Jr., The Defender - Audacity,* May 22, 2021. https://www.audacy.com/podcasts/rfk-jr-the-defender-podcast-55171/epstein-and-bill-gates-with-whitney-webb-386014851
[85] Emily Flitter and James B. Steward, "Bill Gates Met with Epstein Many Times Despite Past," *The New York Times,* October 12, 2021.

the data. Google, Meta, among other social media networks are sharing DNA data with the government for integrating health services including vaccination status into people's digital profiles. For example, last year, Google teamed up with a new branch of national security, Defense Intelligence Unit, to diagnose disease through artificial intelligence. According to Webb, they claimed at first that their focus is on cancer but later admitted that they'll be using the diagnostic software for Covid in the near future. The reason Google wanted the partnership was to access the data the military had, so this was an operation of data mining. Webb elaborates on the future of this collaboration and says that the vaccine credential initiative will be tied to people's economic status as well. The sponsors of this initiative, are not surprisingly, Microsoft, Oracle, Salesforce, and Mayo Clinic among others.

Webb commented on historian Noah Harari, who is a frequent speaker at the WEF at Davos, and who is very close friends with Zuckerberg and Obama. Harari became notorious with his speech in the 2020 conference, for saying that with the merge of human biology and AI we will enter a digital dictatorship. According to Harari, those who refuse to adapt to the new order and therefore, become irrelevant, will form a "useless class," and it would be better to be exploited than useless.[86] More disturbingly, Webb reveals that the Broad Institute of MIT and Harvard is now chaired by Eric Schmidt, the CEO of Google, who is also the biggest donor to the Broad as he recently endowed $150M to the institute. The goal of the Broad Institute is to merge human biology with high tech machines, in order to implement the digital dystopia that Harari suggested at Davos. Webb warns that the preparation and the pursue of transhumanism is not done for the better conditions of society but merely for control. The powerful symbiosis between academia, science, the government and high tech, possess a serious threat to democracy.

Webb experienced the experimental measures during the pandemic in Chile, Latin America. Because of the synchronized efforts between the West and Chile, she realized that this is a global campaign and cannot be accomplished without the cooperation of corrupt governments who betray their own citizens. Such is the case with Chile, where the system of military control was enforced parallel to the digital passports in the West, similar to any marshal laws adopted in emergency situations. Webb is not surprised because the current president of Chile appointed Pinochet's brother as

---

[86] Yuval Noah Harari, "How to Survive the 21st Century," Davos, Jan., 2020 https://www.youtube.com/watch?v=gG6WnMb9Fho

Finance Minister, and many officials in the government have ties to the past dictatorship of Pinochet. According to Webb, Chile has been used as a test lab for the West, as is the case in 1980s during Pinochet, where the economic school of Chicago imposing neoliberal shock economy and austerity was first implemented.

Another prominent dissident, Abby Martin, an investigative journalist and author of the Project Censored that features story blocked from reporting by the mainstream media, has her program, *The Empire Files* where she reports eclipsed information. Abby Martin had her profile taken down from Wikipedia briefly in 2013, but it was restored later.[87] Incidents such as the described ones are indicative of the intentions of the owners of these digital sites, who block them from their viewers because they cannot fire the dissident reporters. Martin is an outspoken journalist as she demonstrates the consequences of the consolidation of new media in the hands of private corporations, and the increasing censorship exposed with the recent shutdowns of sites in Facebook, Google, and Twitter. More specifically, as a critic of the press, Martin choses to pursue her independent career as a freelance journalist without financial security; and as such she is a member of the digital precariat.[88] Martin explained that *RT America* is the only TV station that would let her report controversial issues that are censored on our national TV; therefore, *RT* is filling a huge gap of information created by the US mass media. Martin added that *RT*'s popularity could be interpreted as a result of the US mainstream media's information blackout.[89] In essence, dissident journalists such as Martin have two opposite choices: to work for a foreign television outlet, or become part of the digital precariat. Martin has done both: she worked briefly for *Russia Today* and *Telesur English;* however, most of the time she remains a member of the independent journalism working on her digital podcast and engaging in numerous crowdsourcing projects.

Martin, who currently has no access to *Telesur English* because the program is closed, appears on various counterculture shows, such as *On Contact* with Chris Hedges, *Activism* with Zain Raza, *America's Lawyer* with Papantonio, *Robust Opposition* with Lauren Steiner, *Jimmy Dore's* show, and so on. During Martin's years on air, she interviewed some prominent dissidents,

---

[87] Abby Martin was interviewed about this event on *RT America* on Jan. 13, 2014. https://www.youtube.com/watch?v=NKI0j18Ylpg

[88] *Precariat* is a neologism, coined by Guy in his 2011 book *The Precariat – the Dangerous New Class,* and means precarious proletariat.

[89] Ibid.

including political figures, scholars, journalists, and reporters. For example, Abby Martin has interviewed scholar and linguist Noam Chomsky, first on *RT* television in 2013, then on her current show, "The Empire Files," in 2015. In addition, Martin interviewed Pulitzer Prize winning journalist Chris Hedges; advocate for civil rights and anticorporate presidential candidate Ralph Nader; Green Party founder and presidential candidate Jill Stein; Governor Jesse Ventura; the founder of the *Zeitgeist* Movement Peter Joseph; and many more important figures shunned by the mainstream media.

Furthermore, Martin was included in the CIA investigation about the meddling of Russia in the 2016 elections. Part of the report accused the television channel *Russia Today*, where Martin had her show, of "fomenting discontent."[90] When interviewed, Martin told the radio host Joe Rogan that she was accused of "reporting on fracking, Occupy Wall Street, corporate greed, Hillary Clinton's war crimes," among other topics that are not popular on mainstream media. This, according to the CIA and some mainstream media, allegedly caused candidate Hilary Clinton to lose the elections.[91] Therefore, Martin was singled out and targeted as a reporter who is doing her job by defending the rights of oppressed and exploited people.

For example, Martin defends Native Americans, whose land has been used for extracting oil and gas against their will, or peaceful protestors such as the participants of the Occupy Wall Street movement. Social groups such as those described above who represent the exploited class have limited spaces where they are portrayed with integrity within the fifth estate by journalists such as Martin, Blumenthal, Mate, and Johnstone among other investigative reporters. In the case of Occupy Wall Street, a large percentage of the demonstrators were part of the digital precariat savvy enough to livestream their movement and to publicize their demands refuting the distorted picture presented by the mainstream media. To counter this bias, Martin co-directed a documentary, *99%-the Occupy Wall Street Collaborative Film* (2013).[92] Other films by Martin include *Project Censored* (2013), *Chevron vs. Amazon* (2016), *Gaza Fights for Freedom* (2019), and *Earth's Greatest Enemy* (2022).

On her podcast, *The Empire Files*, Martin explains that as we put our trust in new media giants such as Google and Facebook, believing that they

---

[90] Joe Rogan Experience # 950 – Abby Martin, April 25, 2017.
[91] Ibid.
[92] Audrey Ewell, Aaron Aites, Lucian Reed, Nina Krstic, Katie Teague, Peter Leeman, Aric Gutnick, Doree Simon, and Abby Martin, dirs., *99%: The Occupy Wall Street Collaborative Film,* doc., 2013, 97 min.

are making our society egalitarian, they betray our hope. She distinguishes between the independent and mainstream news media because the latter are effectively practicing censorship under federal guidance. Therefore, advises Martin, we should take our protests back to the streets, to podcasts, and underground. In this way, by criticizing the mainstream digital media, Martin validates her belonging to the fifth estate; at the same time, she perpetuates her status as a freelance reporter, unemployable by the mainstream press because of her reports on corporate corruption. Currently, Martin is crowdfunding her show and will continue her program; therefore, the sanctions are only a temporary impediment. With her 305,000 subscribers, Martin successfully uses the Internet to raise funds through Patreon, a membership platform demonstrating the positive role of new media in the process of emancipation of all oppressed social groups.

Another independent journalist is Caitlin Johnstone, an investigative reporter from Malborne, Australia. Her political writings can be found on *Medium, Observer,* and Substack. According to her profile in *Scoop Info Pages,* Johnstone is a "100 percent crowdfunded rogue journalist, bogan socialist, anarcho-psychonaut, gorilla poet and utopia prepper, living in Australia with her American husband and two kids." Johnstone, who has 173,000 followers on Twitter, writes about politics, economics, media, feminism, and the nature of consciousness. She is the author of the illustrated poetry book *Woke: A Field Guide for Utopia Preppers.* "[93] Some of her articles include: "The Drivers of Empire Want to Rule as Greek Gods," It Takes a Lot of Education to Keep Us that Stupid," Real Cancel Culture: Notes from the Age of the Narrative Matrix," Anyone Who Supports Going to War over Taiwan is a Crazy Idiot," How Is the CIA Still a Thing?" "Fake Political Parties in a Fake Democracy: Notes from the Edge of the Narrative Matrix," "The US Could've Prevented This War Just by Protecting Kyiv from Nazis," "Ukraine Alone Makes Biden the Worst President in a Long Time," "The Most American Thing that Has Ever Happened," among others.

Since the titles reveal clearly the content, it suffices to comment on the last title: it is about the US Congress voting to cut spending for Covid relief in order to pass military aid for Ukraine. It is what always happens historically, and yet every one acts surprised. Johnstone concludes: "I defy you to find anything more American than Washington decoupling relief for its own citizens from its proxy war funding because it wants to make sure the

---

[93] https://info.scoop.co.nz/Caitlin_Johnstone

proxy war funding actually passes."⁹⁴ Johnstone analyzes global politics with emphasis on the American empire so swiftly because she is cosmopolitan and in an international marriage. For example, here is an excerpt from her article "The Corporations Are the Government:"

> Capitalism hinders progress because it ensures that all mass-scale human behavior will be driven by the pursuit of profit. For example, a huge global issue we have right now is cleaning up the pollution in our oceans. That is an easily solved issue if you take out the profit motive: you don't wait for market forces to find some way to make it profitable, you just get in there and clean it up. But with the profit motive it's almost impossible to conceive of it ever being solved.⁹⁵

In regard to censorship, Johnstone questions the motifs of everyone who supports such a totalitarian measure and reminds us that the answer to bad speech is more speech, not censorship. She concludes with chagrin:

> Obviously, the best way to convince conspiracy theorists to trust their institutions is to have an elite cabal of billionaire mega corporations in Silicon Valley coordinate the blanket censorship of their online speech.⁹⁶

Besides shrewdly evaluating the condition of the modern world, Johnstone is absolutely positive and optimistic about human nature and believes that collectively we can create a better world because we have the potential. She refuses to accept that a tiny evil minority could destroy the divine capacity of our souls and minds. The ending of the article is hopeful:

> So much of what we call spirituality is just the mind searching for things that are already the case. Peace. Freedom. Presence. Boundlessness. Unconditional love. These things

---

⁹⁴ Caitlin Johnstone, "The Most American Thing That Has Happened," May 10, 2022, caitlinjohnstone.com
⁹⁵ Caitlinjohnstone.com Oct. 2, 2021.
⁹⁶ Ibid.

are already here, are already you. Just obscured by the mind's flailing around, trying to create them. [97]

Another reason Johnstone believes that the positive majority can defeat the negative minority is that, "Propagandists are motivated by base desires like power, money, and esteem, so they have no access to their own creative depths like we do." Such insight is the essence of Johnstone's confidence that humanity could continue to create amazing art, books, films, and celebrate the love we have for each other. Despite her sober observations of the corruption, greed, cruelty and violence, Johnstone still admires the beauty of humanity and its potential; a rare outcome for a journalist from the "edge of the matrix."

These discussed above journalists are just a few of many talented independent creators of counterculture content. Because such authors refuse to take money from big corporations or work for them to avoid supporting a corrupt system, they are at the mercy of their subscribers. These individuals rely exclusively on their audiences to make a living, and they mostly succeed in remaining independent, which proves that there is a substantial demand for their reporting. It would be reasonable to assume that the fifth estate is winning the public, which abandons the fourth in droves. Therefore, the conclusion could be drawn that the public is hungry for alternative opinions, it wants a variety of views and is fed up with the uniform consensus and propaganda imposed on them by the mainstream media.

---

[97] Ibid.

Chapter Three

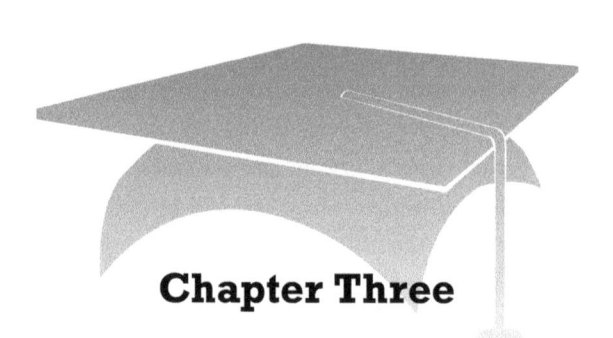

The Regulatory Capture of the Four Estates of Power by Neoliberal Robber Barons: The Crime Bill of 1994, The Telecommunication Act of 1996, the 1999 Repeal of Glass-Steagall Act, the Patriot Act of 2001, and the Great Reset of 2020

> *There are consequences to excessive hope, just as there are to other forms of intemperance. One of these is disillusionment, another is anger, and a third is this book [Listen, Liberal].*
> —*Thomas Frank, 2016*

The initial neoliberal policies that devastated the working and middle class in America were implemented in the 1980s by the Reagan Administration, which was notorious for its union busting actions. Only after destroying the unions, the bi-partisan policies of outsourcing jobs, stagnant wages for more than four decades, and banning collective bargaining was possible. However, it took a Democratic President to pass the most harmful laws such as NAFTA (the North Atlantic Free Trade Agreement), the Crime Bill of 1994, the Telecommunication Act of 1996, and the1999 repeal of the Glass-Stegall Act, which was in place since 1933. Bill Clinton implemented all these anti-worker, anti-democratic policies and the media never mention it when they gush over him and his wife Hilary Clinton who ran for president and lost in 2016. Nevertheless, the next Republican president started a 20-year war supported by the two next administrations, and used it to pass the Patriot Act of 2001. This Act makes it legal to arrest, throw in prison and detained indefinitely any American citizen who can be put on a terrorist list by president's discretion. The wars and the devastating policies were supported by both main parties – Democrats and Republicans – regardless of who was in charge. The military industrial complex benefitted from the perpetuals wars; big business in all fields benefitted from outsourcing production and services to Mexico, China, and India; the private prison industry benefitted from the Crime Bill; Wall Street benefitted from the repeal of Glass-Stegall Act; and the media moguls benefitted from the Telecommunication Act. The permanent losers were regular Americans.

Passing NAFTA was Bill Clinton's first achievement. Bush W.H. tried and failed before Clinton. The bill was presented as expanding the trade market that will bring hundreds of thousands of jobs for the Americans, higher wages and more exports. In reality, it did the opposite. It was a direct blow to the organized labor who opposed it, and allowed the factory owners to move their production abroad in search of cheap labor. It also hurt Mexican farmers who no longer could compete with Western technology. It was a disaster because it turned prosperous cities and towns in the Midwest and throughout the country, which hosted automobile factories, steel plants, textile and paper mills, into abandoned ghost towns.

For example, Danville, Virginia, lost 650 textile plants between 1997 and 2009 as a direct result of NAFTA.[98] Dayton, Ohio, lost 15,000 jobs as large companies such as General Motors, NCR, Mead Paper, Delphi, among others closed their productions and moved abroad.[99] Between 2000 and 2010, Pennsylvania lost 294,000 manufacturing jobs, a decline of 24 percent.[100] Bruceton, Tennessee, closed three large textile plants employing 1700 workers; General Motors in Flint, Michigan, reduced its workers from 80,000 before NAFTA to 7,200 in 2019. From 2000 to 2010, Michigan lost

---

[98] Michael Collins, "The Abandonment of Small Cities in the Rustbelt," *Industry Week*, Oct. 10, 2019.
[99] Ibid.
[100] US Bureau of Labor Statistics.

420,000 jobs; Illinois – 302,000; Indiana – 213,000 for the same period.[101] The few remaining factories were functioning in poor conditions because the owners threatened to move their business abroad if the workers demanded better wages. The passing of NAFTA put an end to the thriving blue color job market but didn't stop there. All the customer service jobs, digital and low-end white color jobs were gradually transferred to India and China. The profit was never better for the production-owners as the wages went down and most of the well-paying jobs were outsourced.

The Crime bill was the second great achievement of Bill Clinton's administration. As was the case with NAFTA, lobbyists from the private prison industry had the attention of the Clinton administration, hungry for wealth and power. Vise President then and current president Joe Biden drafted the bill, worked hard to pass the law and bragged about it. According to his own words:

> The liberal wing of the Democratic Party is now for 60 new death penalties. That is what is in this bill. The liberal wing of the Democratic Party has 70 enhanced penalties… The liberal wing of the Democratic Party is for 100,000 cops. The liberal wing of the Democratic Party is for 123,000 new state prison cells.[102]

As a result of the Crime Bill, the prison population more than doubled in 12 years – it grew from 357,292 in 1970 to 759,100 in 1982. Consequently, a $1,7B for profit organization, Corrections Corporation of America (CCA), was established in the next year, in 1983. 2016 documentary *13th* delineates the role of the media in propagandizing the population in believing that black people are "predatory criminals" and "dangerously violent," as the mass media constantly featured African Americans arrested or behind bars.[103] The Bill cost $30B and imposed mandatory minimum sentence, three strikes that resulted in life sentence, and 60 new capital punishment without parole. Not incidentally, CCA and ALEC (American Legislative Exchange Council), were the main lobbyists for the 1994 Crime Bill. Thus, the growing private prison industry depended on the judiciary and legislative branches to make profit.

---

[101] Collins, 2019.

[102] Naomi Murakawa, *The First Civil Right: How Liberals Built Prison America*, Oxford, 2014, Kindle Edition.

[103] Du Vernay, director. *13th* Doc., 2016.

Increasing the prison population along with longer sentences were directly linked to the industry's profits. Consequently, the bi-partisan harsh policies were caried out throughout the 21st century by the Bush, Obama and Trump administrations. Excessive funding, militarization of the police, increased number of policemen and their lack of accountability escalated the abuse of power. By 2000, there were 2, 015,300 prisoners in the US; 878,400 of them were black.[104] The black male population was only 6.5% in the nation, yet comprised 40% of the prison population.[105]

Furthermore, similarly to the cotton and tobacco industries during the legal slavery, the correctional industry depends economically on the cheap labor of prisoners. Incarcerated workers are paid $1 an hour while they are overcharged for phone calls and hygiene items. In addition, corporations that provide correctional buildings and security systems, receive both government contracts and subsidies. Private companies such as Walmart, JCPenney, Victoria Secret, among others, routinely use cheap prison labor. In addition, prisoners are employed to fight wild fires on the front lines as is the case in California. At this point, the private prison industry is so big and powerful that it is economically risky to try to reform the system. Even more pernicious are the socio-economic measures that prevent former felons from earning a living. They have a great difficulty getting hired, acquiring student loans, borrowing money, or receiving housing assistance and financial help. In this way, mass incarceration destroys former offenders and absorbs them back into the correctional system because other options are not available to them.

According to the documentary, the judiciary system is set up to avoid trials because they are costly. To that end, the courts order excessive bail amounts that keep poor people imprisoned. Instead, they are offered a bargain and remain incarcerated indefinitely without being convicted. According to Senator Charles Rangel, 97% of prisoners accept plea bargain which is, in his words, the worse violation of human rights.[106] Furthermore, felons are stripped off their rights to vote, which excludes them from the social contract. According to academic and civil leader Melina Abdullah, featured in the documentary, "So many aspects of the old Jim Crow are suddenly legal again once you are branded a felon. So, it seems, in America, we haven't really ended racial cast, but simply redesigned it."[107] In short, the Crime Bill

---

[104] Ibid.
[105] Ibid.
[106] Ibid.
[107] Ibid.

of 1994 provided a greenlight for exploitation of poor people's labor, targeting specifically people of color with the purpose of enriching private corporations. The prison system is funded by the taxpayers and costs more than affordable housing without solving crimes and homelessness, and only benefits a few corporations who make profit of human suffering.

Another legislation with long term consequences is the Telecommunication Act signed into law in 1996 by President Clinton. The Act restricted regulations that have been in place since 1934 and made legal cross-ownership and mass media owned by a few individuals. As it led to media concentration, the results today are evident in the entire array of media outlets, which is owned and controlled by five companies. Critics of this trend warned us back then that it threatens the First Amendment as it restricts the marketplace of ideas. For example, First Amendment expert C. Edwin Baker wrote in 2005, "The key goal, the key value, served by ownership dispersal is that it directly embodies a fairer, more democratic allocation of communicative power."[108] Furthermore, other critics argue that media concentration facilitates censorship. According to the *First Amendment Encyclopedia,*

> Some [critics of media concentration] point to Internet censorship in China as one example, noting in particular how Google has cooperated with the government there to block access to some Web sites. Others worry that as the media become increasingly corporate and for-profit, other forms of self-censorship, such as covering only the news that brings in large audiences, will follow.[109]

Among the most prominent critics of media concentration are media analyst and professor Ben Bagdikian, scholar and dissident Noam Chomsky, and most notably, British writer George Orwell. Bagdikian wrote the book *Media Monopoly* back in 1983, warning the public about the threat of the growing concentration of ownership that led to the great control of information and authoritarianism. Chomsky co-wrote with Edward S. Herman *Manufacturing Consent* in 1988, where he described the mechanism of control and filtering unwanted ideas and information. George Orwell explained in his censored Introduction of *Animal Farm* (1945) that although

---

[108] John O. Omachonu and David Schultz, "Media Concentration," *The First Amendment Encyclopedia*, 2009.
[109] Ibid.

the book is about communist totalitarianism, in western democracies the censorship is equally effective without the use of physical power. According to Orwell, there are two ways of controlling the content of information – through media ownership, e.g., media are owned by wealthy people who only allow ideas that support the status quo, and secondly, through education – there is a filtering system, which starts in kindergarten that selects for obedience and subordination. Amazingly, Orwell's introduction is still censored. It was first published in the *Times Literary Supplement* in 1972, and in the 2000 Penguin edition of *Animal Farm* as Appendix.[110] However, the preface is still not attached to the book it belongs.

As Orwell, Bagdikian, and Herman-Chomsky warned us, concentrated media ownership was among the most devastating effects of the Telecommunication Act. The mergers that followed made mass media obedient and uniformly providing the same messages that favor the status quo and glorify the elites. Notoriously, digital mogul Bill Gates, after being hit with a cream pie in the face in 1998, focused on his public image disseminated by the media through investing significant amounts of his billions in positive press. According to *Grayzone,* Gates donated over $300 million to media outlets to promote favorable reporting.[111] Recipients of his cash include US most important news media such as CNN, NBC, NPR, PBS, MTV, *The New York Times,* and *The Atlantic* as well as foreign press including BBC, *The Guardian, The Financial Times, The Daily Telegraph, Le Monde, Der Spiegel, El Pais,* and Al-Jazeera.[112] In addition, Gates funds universities and more specifically, programs in the field of journalism, health, education, and global development. Recipients include Johns Hopkins University, Columbia University, University of California Berkeley, Seattle University, Rhodes University (South Africa), Tsinghua University (China), Pan-Atlantic University Foundation, among others.[113]

However, after the Telecommunication Act, the richest oligarchs can now openly buy major media outlets that set the tone of reporting, without having to bribe them through donations and indirect funding. For example,

---

[110] Emanuel Rosado, "The History Behind Orwell's *Animal Farm* Unpublished Preface," *Medium,* Sept. 16, 2019. https://medium.com/lessons-from-history/the-history-behind-george-orwells-animal-farm-unpublished-preface-bf3b64496463

[111] Alan Macleod, "Documents Show Bill Gates Has Given $319 Million to Media Outlets to Promote His Global Agenda," *Grayzone,* Nov. 21, 2021.

[112] Ibid.

[113] Ibid.

Jeff Bezos bought one of the US most prestigious and influential newspapers, the *Washington Post,* in 2013. Predictably, Amazon's stocks value raised steeply their value and now his corporation is worth more than $1 trillion.[114] More importantly, the *Washington Post* confirmed the legitimate concerns about such conflict of interest by hiring columnists who promoted the right of billionaires to their power and wealth and vehemently opposed higher taxes for the rich. In addition, the editors relentlessly stifle legitimate criticism over wages and working conditions in Bezos' giant company, Amazon.[115] For example, *Washington Post's* star columnist Megan McArdle claimed that Americans want to destroy billionaires' fortunes because of their class envy, featuring a picture of Bezos.[116] In tune with her masters' interests, McArdle previously argued that Walmart's wages are too high, defended Google's monopoly and the cheap way of building houses for profit that caused the notorious fire in 2017 at London's Grenfell Tower, which killed 72 poor residents.[117]

The Fairness Doctrine, implemented since 1940, issued by the FCC (Federal Communication Commission), compelled media outlets to cover adequately controversial issues of public importance, and to afford a reasonable opportunity for contrasting points of view.[118] However, it was repealed by the FCC in 1987. More recently, in 2017, the FCC repealed another pillar of democracy – the Net Neutrality rules, gradually implemented since 2005. These rules include prohibiting internet service providers from using discriminatory filters in order to promote or ban information including slowing down or speeding up the flow of the Internet. Net Neutrality has been disputed ever since by the owners of the tech corporations, which were against such egalitarian rules. It was against their interests to provide Internet services equally to all. They preferred to reward high paying users with high-speed Internet in order to make quick profit. The battle ended in 2017, when the newly elected president Trump appointed Ajit Pai, an open opponent of Net Neutrality, to the position of Chair of the FCC. As a result, the FCC repealed Net Neutrality, despite the strong public support for it. As of 2022,

---

[114] "Amazon – 25 Year Stock Price History," *AMZN-Macrotrends,* https://www.macrotrends.net>charts.

[115] Janine Jackson, "Jeff Bezos Fake News in the Newspaper He Really Owns," *FAIR,* June 4, 2021.

[116] Alan Macleod, "With Bezos at the Helm, Democracy Dies at the *Washington Post* Editorial Board," *Mint Press,* June 18, 2021.

[117] Ibid.

[118] Audrey Perry, "Fairness Doctrine," *First Amendment Encyclopedia,* 2009.

some states such as CA, NJ, OR, VT, and WA took the measure in their hands and passed their own versions of Net Neutrality rules.[119] With the FCC decision to repeal the rules of Net Neutrality, another step backwards was made against democracy and equality. Without Net Neutrality, only wealthy individuals and companies can enjoy quality Internet services, whereas regular people with modest incomes are left behind and discriminated against in the field of digital services, which are prevalent in the 21st century.

The next step in de-regulating was Clinton's historic repeal of Glass-Steagall Act in 1999. The Act was issued in 1933 and successfully regulated the banks since the Great Depression and prevented the markets from serious financial crashes for more than six decades. The Gramm-Leach-Bliley Act in 1999 lifted restrictions against banks offering commercial banking, insurance, and investment services (by repealing key provisions in the 1933 Glass–Steagall Act). In 1999, Laurance Summers, Treasury Secretary appointed by Clinton, endorsed the Gramm-Leach-Bliley Act, which removed the separation between investment and commercial banks. Thus, the Act opened the floodgates for speculations that led to a series of bubbles and finally to the 2008 financial crisis. The story of repealing the Glass-Steagall Act is very informative and revealing about the permanent forces behind the two-party political system that remain constant regardless of which party is in charge.

Academy Award winning documentary *Inside Job* (2010), directed by Charles Ferguson, gives a full picture of the planning, executing and ending of the 2008 global financial disaster architected by a few financial experts with the support of several bi-partisan administrations. It started with Reagan's appointment of Alan Greenspan, Columbia alumnus, as chairman of the Federal Reserve in 1985, who served for unprecedented five terms for 19 years during four administrations: re-appointed by George H.W. Bush, Bill Clinton, and George W. Bush until 2006. Greenspan was a staunch promoter of de-regulation of the banks and supported an economy that thrived on low wages based on worker's job insecurity. After his re-appointment by Clinton for a third term as chair of the Federal Reserve, Greenspan finally succeeded in repealing the Glass-Steagall Act that prevented the economy from crises such as the Great Depression. Thanks to this development, three immediate crises followed: the burst of the 2000 Internet high tech product bubble, the 2007 housing bubble, and the 2008 financial market crash.

---

[119] Jomile Nakataviclute, "What Is Net Neutrality: Its History and Importance," *Nord VPN*, April 26, 2022.

Law Professor in banking and finance Timothy Canova summarizes the financial crisis in his article of 2015:

> As central banks have become increasingly influenced and even captured by large private banks and financial institutions, they have pursued policy agendas that favor those same private interests. The structure of the U.S. Federal Reserve suggests a central bank that has been captured by design and is rife with inherent conflicts of interest in its governance, regulatory, and monetary policy functions. These conflicts are often overlooked because of the myth of central bank independence, which has rested on truncated empirical studies and flawed readings of economic history. Yet, the myth has legitimized the Federal Reserve's policy agenda—particularly beginning in the 1980s when Alan Greenspan became chair of the Federal Reserve—when deregulation, liberalization, and privatization came to serve the private interests of Wall Street banks while creating a boom-and-bust bubble economy. The austerity bias of central banks was also revealed in both the academic work and monetary policy approach of Ben Bernanke, who succeeded Greenspan as Federal Reserve chairman just ahead of the 2008 financial collapse. [120]

Canova's analysis is rarely referenced when the 2008 crisis is discussed. Among the plethora of literature explaining the financial crisis and referring to the Great Depression of the 1930s, economists such as Greenspan, Bernanke, and Henry M. Paulson among others, act completely surprised when such crises occur. For example, Bernanke, who dedicated his career to studying the Great Depression, reacted unprepared to prevent or even soften the impact of the market crash. Similarly, Treasury Secretary Paulson stated on national TV the day before the crash that the US economy is solid and stable. What was obvious even to the layman in economics – that the regulations of the Glass-Steagall Act were implemented specifically because of the 1929 economic crash to prevent future financial disasters, eschewed the high-echelon experts. Another obvious conclusion – that the trickle-down economy

---

[120] Timothy A. Canova, "The Role of Central Banks in Global Austerity," *Global Legal Studies,* 22, No 2, Summer 2015, Indiana U Press, 665.

failed consistently for decades since the 1980s – was escaping the experts' understanding as well. Inversely, economist Canova offers a more thorough and comprehensive view of the 2008 crash:

> Not only was the Federal Reserve's response to crisis a reflection of the domination of Wall Street interests, it also revealed a complete misreading of the lessons from the Great Depression by Bernanke and other mainstream economists. The result has been a flawed "trickle-down" response to the financial crisis, as the Federal Reserve and other leading central banks have provided massive subsidies to financial institutions and markets while relegating other sectors of the economy and society to the pains of austerity. A more balanced economic approach will require reform of central bank governance to include representatives of a wider range of social interests in monetary policymaking.[121]

The economy for the average person still hasn't recovered since. Only the financial sector, big banks such as Goldman Sacks, Citi Group, JP Morgan, among others were bailed out with $700B by the Bush Administration in 2008, and become even bigger, too big to fail, as it was made clear by the following Administrations of Obama, Trump, and Biden. Many people who lost their homes in the housing bubble, people who lost their small businesses during the Pandemic of 2020 – 2022, were never bailed out because they weren't big enough, significant enough, or relevant. Regardless, their tax-payers money was used to rescue the banks, the airlines, the digital monopolists, and the military industrial complex. There was always money for the latter, never for the former. During the pandemic, the pattern of upward transfer of funds to the top one percent reached its highest in US history with the acquisition of $4.6T taxpayers' money.[122]

The next blow to regular people's freedom was done at the turn of the century, in October 2001, after the 9/11th terrorist attack. The passing of the

---

[121] Ibid.
[122] Chase Peterson-Withorn, "How Much Money American's Billionaires Have Made during the Covid 19 Pandemic," *Forbes,* April 30, 2022. https://www.forbes.com/sites/chasewithorn/2021/04/30/american-billionaires-have-gotten-12-trillion-richer-during-the-pandemic/?sh=2b306fabf557

Patriot Act contributed to the destruction of our already feeble democracy and to weakening the constitution. Congress quickly reacted to the attack with voting for the controversial Patriot Act, which was passed with 98 to 1 vote in the Senate and 357 to 66 votes in the House. The Act was signed into law by President Bush, and has been extended multiple times during the next 20 years. The Patriot Act was reauthorized in 2005, extended in 2011, reissued in 2015 under the Freedom Act, reenacted through 2019, and finally expired in March 2020.Through the 10 titles of the Act were extended surveillance powers of the government, seizing tangible property, and arbitrary terrorist list made by the President of suspects who could be arrested and detained indefinitely without a trial. The fact that took Congress roughly a month to draw and pass the Act without any discussion, demonstrates that it was previously considered and prepared. This presumption could be demonstrated in two concrete examples of simulations at Johns Hopkins University with the participation of the same organizations.

An event titled Dark Winter stimulation performed in June 2001 at Johns Hopkins could be linked to the Nine Eleventh follow-up government actions. The event stimulated viral attacks, predicting the real anthrax attacks in September 2001, which were later traced back to the Pentagon.[123] According to Johns Hopkin's University website, operation Dark Winter was performed on June 22-23, 2001, in the Center for Strategic International Studies, where the university hosted a senior level war game examining the national security, intergovernmental, and informational challenges of a theoretical biological attack on the American homeland.[124] Besides the participation of the government officials including National Security Advisor David Gergen, CIA Director R. James Woolsey, FBI Director William Sessions, Secretary of Defense Frank Wisner, among others, there were five representatives from the national press corps (including print and broadcast) who participated in the game and conducted a lengthy press conference with the President. The synchronization between higher education, government, and mass media is impressive. Among the five findings of the stimulation were national security issues caused by civil disorder and breaking down the institutions, disconnection between different levels of government (federal, state, and

---

[123] Whitney Webb, "Invisible Enemies: Parallel between the Anthrax Attacks and Covid 19," *Unlimited Hangouts,* Oct., 2021.
[124] "Dark Winter," John Hopkins, Bloomberg School of Public Health, Center for Health Security. https://www.centerforhealthsecurity.org/our-work/events-archive/2001_dark-winter/about.html

local), overwhelming of the hospitals, dealing with the media on all levels of government and managing of information, and finally, ethical, political, cultural, and legal challenge.[125]

The goal of the simulation seems to be government's preparation to keep the population under control. According to the summary, no concern for saving people's lives and wellbeing was expressed at any time during the exercise.[126] The synchronized efforts and lockstep between government, academia, healthcare industry and media are forecasting and informative in relation to the current events of Covid 19 pandemic. From the first simulated event, Dark Winter in June 2001, which preceded 9/11, the consequences were passing of the Patriot Act, a legislation that kept American population in strict control for nearly 20 years.

Incidentally, an identical stimulation at the same place, Johns Hopkins University, was performed prior to the 2020 Covid outbreak on October 18, 2019, titled Event 201. According to the official side of the event:

> Event 201 was a 3.5-hour pandemic tabletop exercise that simulated a series of dramatic, scenario-based facilitated discussions, confronting difficult, true-to-life dilemmas associated with response to a hypothetical, but scientifically plausible, pandemic. 15 global business, government, and public health leaders were players in the simulation exercise that highlighted unresolved real-world policy and economic issues that could be solved with sufficient political will, jointly propose these financial investment and attention now and in the future.[127]

The three sponsors for Event 201 were Johns Hopkins University, World Economic Forum, and Bill & Melinda Gates Foundation. They proposed seven recommendations, which urged the governments to cooperate with businesses under the euphemism "public-private cooperation." As in the case with the 2001 simulation Dark Winter, the media were assigned an important role. Recommendation number seven articulates:

---

[125] Ibid.
[126] Ibid.
[127] https://www.centerforhealthsecurity.org/event201/about

> Governments and the private sector should assign a greater priority to developing methods to combat mis- and disinformation prior to the next pandemic response. Governments will need to partner with traditional and social media companies to research and develop nimble approaches to countering misinformation. This will require developing the ability to flood media with fast, accurate, and consistent information. Public health authorities should work with private employers and trusted community leaders such as faith leaders, to promulgate factual information to employees and citizens… For their part, media companies should commit to ensuring that authoritative messages are prioritized and that false messages are suppressed including through the use of technology.[128]

The use of technology included algorithms, which effectively censored all messages that deviated from or contradicted the "authoritative" narratives. Flooding the media with "fast, accurate, and consistent" information was easily achieved as news anchors, medical experts, and government officials were eager to obey to the top-down instructions. As was the case with the Dark Winter preparation, the simulation Event 201 in October 2019, which preceded the Covid pandemic from March 2020, led to a number of draconian measures that are still in place in 2022. For example, lockdowns, closing of businesses and schools, mandatory vaccinations and masks are still enforced in 2022, and in some places such as China and Italy, digital passports are required for participation in public life. The digital passports are based on social credit scores generated through medical records, social media activities, and obedience to the ruling class. The consequences for disobedience vary from banning from traveling to restrictions from buying merchandises to freezing financial assets to incarcerating in camps.

In both emergency occasions, a terrorist attack in the former, and a viral respiratory pandemic in the latter, the events were used to control the masses and to transfer funds upward from the public to a handful of oligarchs. For example, as a response to the pandemic, a CARES Act passed by Congress in 2020, released $4.6T by 2021, most of which went to companies such as Microsoft, Amazon, Pfizer, and Moderna, among other pharmaceutical and

---

[128] Ibid.

digital corporations.[129] As a result, these companies more than doubled their wealth and 493 new billionaires were created since Covid 19.[130] For example, Pfizer made $37B in 2021 alone, and is predicted to sell Covid vaccines and Covid pill Paxlovid worth from $98B to $102B in 2022.[131]

In contrast, according to a study from Columbia University, 8 million average Americans fell into poverty in the period between February and September 2020.[132] According to a study from the University of Michigan in 2019, even before the pandemic, the US poverty rate was 18 percent, the fourth highest among 40 countries measured by OECD, only ahead of Romania, Costa Rica, and South Africa.[133] By comparison, countries in Northern, Western and Eastern Europe have poverty rates below 10 percent.[134]

According to *Forbes*, American billionaires gained $1.4T in two years since the pandemic as their wealth totals $4.6T in April 28, 2022.[135] For example, Elon Musk, the founder of Tesla and Space X, increased his wealth more than six times, from $27B in 2020 to $170B in 2022.[136] Similarly, since the pandemic, Amazon owner Jeff Bezos's net worth increased with $80B to over $200B in 2022. Google co-founders Larry Page and Sergey Brin more than doubled their net worth from $40B each to $102B and $99B respectively.[137] Mark Zuckerberg, the owner of digital network Meta gained $35B during the pandemic; Microsoft owner and pharmaceutical investor Bill Gates' wealth increased with $22B.[138]

Such development is not accidental, it is purposely designed because each of these billionaires operated in the digital industry and benefitted from the measures during the pandemic. For example, lockdowns compelled people to order supplies online including food, and many small to medium restaurants, stores, and entertainment businesses were bankrupted as a result

---

[129] Chase Peterson-Withorn, *Forbes,* April 30, 2022.
[130] Ibid.
[131] Julia Kolewe, "Pfizer Accused of Pandemic Profiteering as Profit Double," *The Guardian,* Feb. 8, 2022.
[132] Stefan Sykes, "8 Million Americans Slipped into Poverty amid Coronavirus Pandemic, New Study Says," NBC News, Oct. 16, 2020. https://www.nbcnews.com/news/us-news/8-million-americans-slipped-poverty-amid-coronavirus-pandemic-new-study-n1243762
[133] Poverty.umich.edu "Poverty Solutions," University of Michigan. http://data.oecd.org/inequality/poverty-rate.htm
[134] Ibid.
[135] Peterson-Withorn, *Forbes,* April 30, 2022.
[136] Ibid.
[137] Ibid.
[138] Ibid.

Tamara I. Hammond

of mandatory closure. Decisions to close small restaurants, churches, fitness spaces and shopping strips while huge workplaces like Amazon warehouses, meat processing factures and Tesla auto plants with thousands of workers remained open, were not made for public safety. Instead, they were motivated by profit in favor of big businesses and subsequently, raised questions and resentment. Such selective measures prove intentions to eliminate completion through bankrupting and buying small business. These and other policies demonstrate that all the restrictions were implemented for profit, not for health reasons. The final measure – issuing digital passports has been imposed globally as planned. Besides China, Italy, and some Scandinavian countries, ten of the United Stated require such documentation for daily necessities. The world's response to Covid links pharmaceutical industry, medical institutions such as Oxford, to investors like Bill Gates and Antony Fauci who funded the research of the virus. Similarly, it reveals the connections between organizations like the World Economic Forum to international governments, academic institutions such as Johns Hopkins University, and global media.

One of the controversial measures that disrupted the well-being of global populations and had multiple negative social and economic consequences were the lockdowns. Because the cost of this measure didn't seem to justify the scope and the benefits of it, scientific attempts were made to investigate such restrictions. A series of working studies were published between October 2021 and May 2022 by Johns Hopkins Institute for Applied Economics, Global Health, and the Study of Business Enterprise. The authors were scholars Steve H. Hanke, founder and co-director of the latter, Jonas Herby, special advisor at the Political Studies in Copenhagen, and Las Jonung, Professor of economics at Lung University, Sweden.[139] The final updated study, published in May 2022, addresses the accumulated scientific criticism in the Appendix, and focuses on the relation between the lockdowns applied during the pandemic and mortality:

> Starting from a lockdown with a stringency of 0 (no lockdown) and increasing stringency from there, a stricter lockdown increases mortality. But, at stringency 62.4, a stricter lockdown reduces mortality at the margin. However, the total effect is still an increase in mortality for stringency values below

---

[139] Jonas Herby, Lars Jonung, and Steve H. Hanke, "A Literature Review and Meta-Analysis of the Effects of Lockdowns Covid-19 Mortality-II," *Studies in Applied Economics,* No 210, May 20, 2022, i.

124. And because stringency values are capped at 100, there are no such lockdowns that decrease mortality overall.[140]

This systematic, peer-reviewed, cross-sectional, ranging across jurisdictions study by Johns Hopkins Institute covers countries world-wide, and separately European countries, the US, and OECD countries.[141] The scholars included a statement that their conclusions are in line with other reviews: "Overall, we conclude that stricter lockdowns are not an effective way of reducing mortality rates during a pandemic, at least not during the first wave of the COVID-19 pandemic. Our results are in line with the World Health Organization Writing Group (2006), Allen (2021), Iezadi et al (2021), Mendez-Brito et al (2021), and Herby (2021a)."[142] Scholars' final conclusive paragraphs read:

> Finally, allow us to broaden our perspective after presenting our meta-analysis that focuses on the following question: "What does the evidence tell us about the effects of lockdowns on mortality?" We provide a firm answer to this question: Our study finds that lockdowns had little to no effect in reducing COVID-19 mortality.
>
> The use of lockdowns is a unique feature of the COVID-19 pandemic. Lockdowns have not been used to such a large extent during any of the pandemics of the past century. However, lockdowns during the initial phase of the COVID-19 pandemic have had devastating effects. They have contributed to reducing economic activity, raising unemployment, reducing schooling, causing political unrest, contributing to domestic violence, loss of life quality, and the undermining of liberal democracy. These costs to society must be compared to the benefits of lockdowns, which our meta-analysis has shown are little to none.
>
> Such a standard benefit-cost calculation leads to a strong conclusion: until future research based on credible empirical evidence can prove that lockdowns have large and significant

---

[140] Ibid., 21
[141] Ibid., 24.
[142] Ibid., 61-62.

> reductions in mortality, lockdowns should be rejected out of hand as a pandemic policy instrument. [143]

Undoubtedly, the pandemic was used to advance the long-strategized agenda of the World Economic Forum's leaders. The WEF's founder Claus Schwab explains in his 2020 book *The Great Reset* the need of new kind of capitalism – stakeholder capitalism, which combines the power of private corporations with the power of the state. The author emphasizes that he has promoted this idea for 50 years. Schwab's definition suspiciously coincides with Benito Mussolini's definition of fascism, "Fascism should be more accurately called 'corporatism'" because it represents the fusion of corporations with the state. Both powers are excessive and therefore, problematic even without combining them; when merged, they inevitably lead to a dictatorship. The process, already seen during the pandemic, when governments overreached and shut down the global economy, implemented vaccine and mask mandates upon the advice of digital and pharmaceutical corporations and to their advantage, demonstrates abuse of power and totalitarianism.

The same process of combining private big tech companies with an all-powerful government is described by Schwab as the only solution to the pandemic. Since the ideology called "the great reset" is promoted by the most powerful institutions in the world such as the WEF (World Economic Forum), IMF (International Monetary Fund), WHO (World Health Organization), and backed by the wealthiest individuals in the world such as Gates, Bezos, Musk, among others, it could become reality, if this trend continues. In May 2022, during the annual WEF meeting in Davos, Switzerland, 146 panels had the title "Stakeholder Dialog, implying that the transition to stakeholder capitalism is in fast motion."[144]

The simulation in October 2019, sponsored by the WEF, Johns Hopkins, and Bill Gates, shows that the concerted efforts to set up a new economic, social, and political system has been in progress for some time. More importantly, judging by the uniform response to Covid globally, it demonstrates that the plan aims to severely infringe the rights of the mass populations in the world, regardless of whether it is called stakeholder capitalism or the great reset. The total control of the population, based on new technology and media-inflicted fear, easily leads to temporary measures that remain in place for decades and

---

[143] Ibid., 82-83.
[144] https://climatechampions.unfccc.int/davos-2022-what-to-expect-from-this-meeting-like-no-other/

turn into permanent authoritarianism. Full dependency of the global mass population on a handful of stakeholder capitalists is no different than fascist or communist dictatorships, feudal serfdom and slavery from the past. The circle would be closed and the phrase, "You will own nothing and will be happy" advertised in a video clip during the 2020 WEF conference could be fulfilled.[145] If we do not deter this process, the mission of creating a techno-feudal society where the majority is poor and dependent on a few technical lords would be accomplished. In every case described in the chapter, the unified actions of the ruling class lead to consolidation of power, infringing the rights of the general population, and deceiving it into believing that this is for its own improvement and safety.

---

[145] Schwab's speech at the 50th annual virtual conference of the WEF in Davos, titled "The Great Reset," June, 2020.

Chapter Four

The Role of Academia in Supporting the Status Quo: From Walter Lippmann and Edward Bernays to Barak Obama and Sheryl Sandberg, the Propaganda Wheel is Always Well-Greased.

> *It is important to distinguish between the kind of censorship that the English literary intelligentsia voluntary impose upon themselves, and the censorship that can sometimes be enforced by pressure groups.*
>
> ~George Orwell

Historically, American Higher Education was established as an elitist institution and has maintained this status since its inception. However, it allowed a few variations that enabled a more democratic and popular approach throughout its elitism and exclusion. Examples include the reconstruction of the 1870s, which introduced land grant legislation to fund higher education, the GI Bill of 1944, which provided free college education for veterans, and the Higher Education Act of 1965, which made available scholarships and grants for low-income students. However, this popular but insufficient help dried out during the neoliberal policies of the 1980s, and over the last forty years, higher education has gradually become unaffordable for middle- and working-class families. The solution has been to lend funds to students indiscriminately. Graduates have then become indentured and forced to participate in a system that does not benefit them.

Historian Sam Haselby and economist Matt Stoller explain in an article in *The Chronicle of Higher Education* from May 2021 that the increasing gulf between the rich and the poor in America now extends to the academic institutions as well. According to the authors, since the pandemic began more than half a million jobs disappeared from American universities, while the richest top 20 universities increased the value of their endowments with over $311 billion.[146] Furthermore, the authors emphasize the role of the academic elites in the ongoing crisis and their self-serving response to it as they receive bailouts from the public:

> Power in the U.S. flows through the gates of the Ivy League and a very small tier of other top universities. These institutions set and sanction the boundaries of knowledge, including what kinds of political and social views are welcomed in prestige cultural spaces.[147]

Therefore, a small minority of intelligentsia empowered by their rich institutions, sets the discourse of ideas, and either promotes or shuts down certain concepts. They can do this because of their political, economic and ideological power. For example, after the 2008 financial crisis, the richest universities asked President Obama to devote $40 to $45 billion to compensate them for their losses.[148] More recently, in 2020, the top 25 richest universities including Harvard, Yale, Columbia, Princeton and MIT, received more than $800 million in Coronavirus bailouts.[149] Moreover, higher education might seem disconnected from the financial crises of 2008 and 2020, but there is a relation that has been obscured through purposeful distractions by the media and academia. Upon close investigation of the financial crisis in 2008, and the ensued housing crisis in 2009, it appears that the collapse of the market was designed and executed by highly educated experts who had Ivy League

---

[146] Sam Haselby and Matt Stoller, "It's Time to Break Up the Ivy League Cartel," *Chronicle of Higher Education,* May 28, 2021.

[147] Ibid.

[148] Howard Wolinsky, "The Crash Reaches Universities. The Global Financial Crisis Threatens the University Funding in the USA and Europe." *EMBO Reports,* March, 2009 10 (3): 209-211.

[149] Adam Andrzejewski, "America's Colleges and Universities Awarded $12.5 Billion in Coronavirus Bailout – Who Can Get It and How Much," *Forbes,* May 5, 2020.

credentials and held the most powerful positions in the government and financial institutions.

For example, as discussed in the previous chapter, Alan Greenspan, a Columbia alumnus, was the architect of the long process of de-regulation of the financial sector that led to the repealing of the Glass-Steagall Act in 1999. Another dignitary, Laurance Summers, former President of Harvard and Treasury Secretary, director of the National Economic Council during the 2008 crisis also was a proponent of de-regulations. Paulson, former Treasury Secretary; Bernanke, Treasury Secretary in 2008; and Geithner, Treasury Secretary in 2009, were the architects of the bailouts of the largest banks who were responsible for the crisis.[150] From Greenspan to Summers to Paulson to Bernanke to Geithner to recent officials like Mnuchin and Yellen, every consecutive Treasury secretary had highly prestigious school credentials and embraced neoliberal policies of deregulations.[151] Similarly, from Clinton to Bush to Obama to Trump to Biden every consecutive president staffed their cabinets with Wall Street members, most notably, from Goldman Sacks.[152] The invisible connection becomes obvious when we explore the revolving door between Washington and Wall Street personified by the Ivy League's elites who transition back and forth from government positions to working for financial institutions.[153] Both the initiators of the reckless policies that led to the global financial collapse in 2008 and the designers of their bailouts were Ivy League graduates and wielded high power in the government as well as in the financial sector.

---

[150] $700B Troubled Asset Relief Program (TARP) were allocated to JP Morgan Chase, Goldman Sacks, Citigroup, Bank of America, American Express, US Bank, and Wells Fargo among others.

[151] They were graduates from: Summers - Harvard, Paulson – Harvard; Bernanke - Harvard; Geithner - Johns Hopkins. The trend continues with 2016-2020 Treasury Secretary Steven Mnuchin – Yale; Treasury Secretary Janet Yellen 2021 – current - Yale.

[152] Summers, Paulson and Robert Mnuchin (Steven Mnuchin's father) held high positions and partnership at Goldman Sacks prior to their appointments as Treasury Secretaries respectively by Clinton, Bush, and Trump. Geithner, appointed by Obama was President of the Federal Reserve Bank of NY prior to serving as Treasury Secretary. Yellen, appointed by Biden, received $7.2M in speech fees since 2019 from large banks and corporations including Goldman Sachs, Bank of America, and Citigroup.

[153] Paulson was a CEO and partner of Goldman Sachs from 1974-1988; Summers received $2,7M speech fees from Goldman Sachs, JP Morgan Chase, and Citigroup among others; Bernanke was a senior adviser at Citadel hedge fund Group; Geithner converted Goldman Sachs and Citigroup from traditional investment banks to bank holding companies to ensure their access to funding after the 2008 financial collapse.

According to scholar Noam Chomsky, education and especially higher education imposes the business model in universities, which is harmful because it measures success in extremely narrow, commercial terms.[154] Furthermore, Chomsky elaborates on the crippling effect of the corporatization of higher education on young people who are trained to be obedient cogs in the profit-making machine instead of being enlightened and free to aspire to improve the existing social system.[155] More importantly, Chomsky examines the elitist view of higher education among leading intellectuals such as 20th century icons Walter Lippmann and Edward Bernays. Lippmann invented the term "manufacturing consent" as a necessary tool for propagandizing the population into militant supporters of consumerism and wars. Lippmann's seminal book *Public Opinion: How People Decide; the Role of News, Propaganda, and Manufactured Consent in Modern Democracy and Political Elections*, contends that democracy is obsolete in the age of superfast communications. According to Lipmann, people are not capable of evaluating social and political events and need to be swayed in their beliefs by simplified stereotypes when reporting the news and through carefully selected propaganda, often against their own interests. Back in the 20th century Lippmann was using freely the term "propaganda" as it didn't have the negative connotation that it has now. The book was first published in 1922 and become a classical text of political science and media studies, which is quietly followed today. Lippmann displayed a condescending attitude towards regular people reduced to "bewildered herd" who must be governed by a "specialized class" of elite intellectuals like him.

The term "manufacturing consent" has been popularized later by Edward Herman and Chomsky's 1988 book about corporate media as a tool of propaganda for the ruling class, *Manufacturing Consent: The Political Economy of the Mass Media*.[156] According to Chomsky, government by propaganda is the equivalent of governing by education – those who control education control propaganda.[157] In *Requiem for the American Dream*, Chomsky reflects on another elite intellectual, Eduard Bernays, who concurs with the concept of propagandizing the masses, but calls it "engineering consent." [158] Bernays

---

[154] Samantha Schuyler, "Noam Chomsky on Higher Education," *Generation Progress*, November 13, 2013.

[155] Ibid.

[156] Edward S. Herman and Noam Chomsky, *Manufacturing Consent: The Political Economy of the Mass Media*, New York: Pantheon Books, 1988.

[157] Ibid., 133.

[158] Noam Chomsky, *Requiem for the American Dream*, New York: Seven Stories Press, 2017, 128.

founded the department of People Relations in 1928. He is notorious with his successful advertisement campaign that persuaded women to smoke. Bernays succeeded by flooding the TV, newspapers and magazines with glamorous images of Hollywood actresses smoking. His mission of adding women of all ages to the tobacco market was accomplished; as well as selling bacon as "hearty, wholesome" breakfast because he was working for George Washington Hills American Tobacco Company and Beechnut Packing company.[159]

According to Mark Crispin Miller, who wrote the introduction to Bernays' *Propaganda* in 2005, Bernays' audience wasn't the public, it was the corporations that paid him for his craft as a propagandist: "That propaganda easily seduces even those whom it most horrifies is a paradox that Bernays grasped completely; and it is one that we must try at last to understand, if we want to change the world that Edward Bernays, among others, made for us."[160] After all, as his contemporary, Lippmann, Bernays believed that the country should be run by the "intelligent minority" and public opinion should be governed by brilliant but invisible men. He summarized his view, "It is they [intelligentsia] who pull the wires which control the public mind, who harness old social forces and contrive the ways to bind and guide the world."[161]

The fascination with superiority of the privileged intellectuals and their role in undermining democracy is quite persistent throughout history. Chomsky traces this theory back to Madison and the philosophers from the Enlightenment who designed the US Constitution and the political branches in a way to protect the "minority of the opulent against the majority" who have the power of numbers on their side, and could potentially take away from the elites their property if they are not protected by laws.[162] Contrary to this elitist view is the democratic opinion of John Dewey, Howard Zinn, Chomsky, and other American social philosophers who maintain that workers should be educated universally and education should be available to all regardless of social class, race, or gender.

One of the democratic measures advocated by egalitarian philosophers that was implemented in higher education after WWII is the massive federal funding allocated to the universities including the GI Bill. This is significant

---

[159] Edward Bernays, *Propaganda*, "Introduction" by Mark Crispin Miller," Brooklyn: Ig Publishing, 2005, 24-25.
[160] Ibid, 30.
[161] Ibid., 17.
[162] Chomsky, *Requiem*, 2.

because it brought many low-income students to higher education from social groups that might never have attended college otherwise. Moreover, elite higher education in the US progressed into mass education as a result of social movements in the 1960s leading to further inclusion of women and minorities. Access to education raised the consciousness of the working class and inspired their indignation of the dehumanization of their social stratus.

Unfortunately, this progress suffered a backlash from both political parties – the Powell Memorandum (1971), representing the conservatives, and The Trilateral Commission (1975) on behalf of the liberal internationalists.[163] The latter's problem was too much democracy and participation, contrary to the desired "passive, apathetic masses." Both ends of the political spectrum preached the same theory of the "danger of democracy," and how this infringed the "rights" of the business class and large corporations. The conclusion was that the institutions responsible for manufacturing consent: universities, churches, the media, and elite intellectuals, were not doing their job appropriately and were not indoctrinating enough their students and audiences.[164]

The result of such concerted campaigns has been that public funds for state universities were greatly diminished over the past four decades, a purposeful decision given the goal of the indoctrination of the youth. Instead, funding comes from the corporate sector, which also takes advantage of academic efforts in science and privatizes the gains from the collective work of many scholars. At the same time, corporate funds lead to short-term profits and great secrecy in research. More importantly, producing graduates saddled with student loan debt is an operative way to control them and keep them obedient. Furthermore, the corporatization of universities harms higher education by forging "effectiveness" methods of commodifying science, students, and classrooms and shifting the cause of their business to the public. The danger of adhering to such a principle is that power and subordination are subject to profits above all. When applied to universities, this principle effectively corrupts higher education.

The corporatization of higher education reached its maximum in the last decades with the shrinking of tenured positions and the massive use of contingent faculty for the sole purpose of increasing profits. The enormous prices of college tuition also deepen the problem of freeing the minds

---

[163] Ibid., 26-27.
[164] Ibid., 26.

and attitudes of students. Instead of implementing democratic measures in academia, the dominating methods of indoctrination and censorship both reflect and reinforce corporate tyranny. Thus, the elitist philosophy of intellectuals such as Lippmann and Bernays guided successfully academia in enforcing policies of excluding the masses from important decisions about their lives. With the rise of technology, however, a more sophisticated way of leading the "bewildered herd" was required. In the age of information, it was impossible to promote publicly such patronizing views; therefore, the elites needed intellectual leaders that pretended to favor democracy. More importantly, they needed the leaders to look more like they belonged to the masses.

One such intellectual rose on the horizon in the early 21 century seemingly from humble beginnings. Barack Obama, a Columbia undergrad and Harvard Law School alumnus, became the 44th President of the US, the first black president in its history. He was famous with his charm and eloquence, and always delivered the right rhetoric. Obama's presidential campaign in 2008 was unprecedented and obviously successful. It was unprecedented because Obama won an award from the advertising industry for the best marketing campaign of 2008.[165] In his chapter "Selling Candidates" from *The Requiem for the American Dream,* Chomsky writes about Obama's election: "It wasn't reported here, but if you go to the national business press, executives were euphoric. They said, 'We've been selling candidates, marketing candidates like toothpaste since Reagan, and this is the greatest achievement we have.'"[166] According to Chomsky, in his presidential campaign Obama didn't really promise anything, just illusions like "hope and change." Chomsky revealed Obama as a product of the commercial success of the advertisement industry who represents the financial sector and sells presidents as toothpaste to the public. The entire process of campaigning explains the illusion of choice in politics and its role as a spectacle.

Obama was sold to the public as the first black president, but in reality, he did little for his race. In fact, he did more damage to black people with choosing Biden as his vice president – the designer of the Crime Bill of 1994. During Obama's last year of presidency there were 1, 526, 800 prisoners,

---

[165] Ibid., 129.

[166] Ibid. See Mathew Creamer, "Obama Wins!...Ad Age's Marketer of the Year," *Advertising Age,* October 17, 2008, 136.

more black than white among the male population.[167] The other racist policy implemented by the first black president was the escalation of wars. Obama continued the two invasions of Iraq and Afghanistan inherited by G.W. Bush, and added seven new countries that he bombed with drones: Yemen, Libya, Syria, Sudan, Somalia, Pakistan, and continued the support of the genocide against Palestine population in Gaza by Israel.[168] Historically, the US imperialist aggressions was aimed at black and brown populations in the Middle East, Southeast Asia, and Africa.

Another anti-democratic measure Obama executed was the consecutive bailing of the banks in 2009, and his continued work for Wall Street, big oil and big pharma. His controversial health care bill did nothing for regular people as there were 30 million Americans remaining without insurance, and the ones who qualified, paid high prices for poor services. For example, a person who paid the minimum $200 per month, practically could not use the insurance because the deductible amount was $7-8,000. Paradoxically, Obama was reelected in 2012 despite his malignant policies. This happened only because of the media's love affair with Obama as they couldn't get enough of their favorite president, and his smooth rhetoric. Obama always said the right words while doing the opposite behind the scenes. For example, in his victory speech in 2008, Obama started with:

> If there is anyone out there who still doubts that America is a place where all things are possible, who still wonders if the dream of our founders is alive in our time, who still questions the power of our democracy, tonight is your answer.[169]

As the first black president, he was supposed to epitomize the fulfilment of the American Dream. Many, including reverend Jesse Jackson, wept the night Obama was elected. Such victory is even more deceiving as it epitomizes the victory of the advertisement industry selecting the best person for Wall

---

[167] E. Ann Carson and Elizabeth Anderson, "Prisoners of 2015," *US Department of Justice, Bureau of Justice Statistics,* December 16, 2016. The black prisoners were 523,000; the white prisoners were 499,400.

[168] Willian Arkin, military analyst for NBC, "Resignation Letter" Jan 4, 2019.

[169] CQ Transcript Wire, Nov. 4, 2008." Sen. Barack Obama's Acceptance Speech in Chicago," *The Washington Post,* Nov. 5, 2008.

Street under the guise of "people's choice." Further in his speech, the charming president-elect continued to promise without intent of delivering:

> To our future as Americans: This is our time, to put our people back to work and open doors of opportunity for our kids; to restore prosperity and promote the cause of peace; to reclaim the American dream and reaffirm that fundamental truth, that, out of many, we are one; that while we breathe, we hope.[170]

During Obama's presidency the economy was so bad, that it provoked the famous movement titled "Occupy Wall Street," where the main motto was, "We are the 99 percent."

The media notoriously did not cover the movement for the first week, and finally, after the police arrested 700 protesters and used violence, the media started to demean and undermine the movement with derogative coverage. Amy Goodman, investigative journalist and author, wrote about the movement in her book *The Silenced Majority:*

> If 2,000 Tea Party activists descended on Wall Street, you would probably have an equal number of reporters there covering them. Yet 2,000 people did occupy Wall Street on Saturday. They weren't carrying the banner of the Tea Party, the Gadsden flag with its coiled snake and the threat "Don't Tread on Me." Yet their message was clear: "We are the 99 percent that will no longer tolerate the greed and corruption of the 1 percent." They were there, mostly young, protesting the virtually unregulated speculation on Wall Street that caused the global financial meltdown.[171]

The movement, which started in Sept. 2011, in the Zuccotti Park in NYC, lasted for two months, and ended when the occupants of the park were evicted violently by the police with rubber bullets and pepper spray, and their possessions were destroyed including books and laptops. However, the movement spread quickly to 113 cities in the US, and more than 80 cities

---

[170] Ibid.

[171] Amy Goodman and David Moynihan, *The Silenced Majority: Stories of Uprising, Occupations, Resistance and Hope,* Chicago: Haymarket Books, 2012, 214.

around the world. The police blocked coverage of the events of evictions by arresting journalists. Goodman, who was on the ground in Zuccotti Park, describes the eviction:

> Hundreds of riot police have already surrounded the area. As they ripped down the tents, city sanitation workers threw the protesters' belongings into dump trucks. Beyond the barricades, back in the heart of the park, 200 to 300 people locked arms, refusing to cede the space they had occupied for almost two months. They have been handcuffed and arrested, one by one.
> …The police had almost succeeded in enforcing complete media blackout of the destruction.[172]

Because of the media blackout, Obama was protected from the public. Many people to this day are unaware of the Occupy Wall Street movement, or think it was a minuscule event. In reality, the protest continued after the evictions all over the world intermediately and in different forms. For example, in March 2012, in NYC and other places people celebrated 6 months of Occupy Wall Street. Later, the movement gave rise to a host of protests such as Bernie Sanders's movement against inequality, Black Lives Matter against racism and police brutality, environmental movements and so on. However, uninformed citizens believed in Obama, because they only listened to what he said, and the media never reported his anti-democratic policies. For example, Obama said in 2015:

> It's the idea held by generations of citizens, who believed that America is a constant work of progress, who believed that loving this country requires more than singing its praises or avoiding uncomfortable truths. It requires the occasional disruption, the willingness to speak out for what is right, to shake up the status quo. That's America.[173]

Yet, when thousands of young people who believed Obama's words and tried to do exactly what he said, the police sent by his administration cracked

---

[172] Ibid., 224.
[173] The White House, *Office of the Press Secretary*, "Remarks by the President at the 50th Anniversary at the Selma to Montgomery Marches," March 7, 2015.

their heads, sprayed them in the face with pepper spray, and arrested them. The propaganda, recommended by Lippmann almost a century ago, still worked quite well. The media and higher education pounded in people's heads every day, from cradle to grave that they live in a democracy, and succeeded most of the time with some occasional flops.

Cornell West, African-American professor and dissident, was one of the most outspoken critics of the first black American president. He defined the phenomenon of Obama's selection by the elites as tokenism and repeatedly said that putting "black faces in high places" is meaningless if they only represent the interests of the elites. West understood the role Obama played in deceiving Americans that we live in a post-racial society because the president is African American. The commercial success of persona such as Obama was assured by Wall Street elites, who chose and sponsored Obama's candidacy. Obama had the perfect credentials, personality, and the will to serve the ruling class.

As WikiLeaks revealed in an email sent to the president-elect in 2008, Obama's cabinet was almost verbatim dictated by Citigroup. The memorandum, sent on October 6, 2008, signed by Citigroup CEO Michael Froman, was titled "Lists," and addressed to John Podesta, Hilary Clinton's campaign chair, a month before he was named chairman of Obama transition team.[174] According to the list, the proposed names were: Robert Gates, a Bush holdover, who later became Secretary of Defense; Eric Holder, who became Attorney General; Janet Napolitano, later appointed Secretary of Homeland Security; Rahm Emanuel, designated White House Chief of Staff; Susan Rice, appointed United Nations Ambassador; Arne Duncan, who became Secretary of Education; Kathleen Sebelius, appointed Secretary of Health and Human Services; Peter Orszag, appointed Head of the Office of Management and Budget; Eric Shinseki, appointed Secretary of Veterans Affairs; and Melody Barnes, who became Chief of the Domestic Policy Council.[175] These people, named in the leaked email, were selected by Wall Street based on their loyalty to the financial sector.

Thus, the chosen "black face in a high place" fulfilled his role as a token black president while the media were silent about it. Inversely, the mainstream media attacked WikiLeaks, an international non-profit organization that publishes leaked news provided by anonymous whistleblowers, and blamed

---

[174] Tom Eley, "Citigroup Chose Obama's Cabinet, WikiLeaks Document Reveals," October 15, 2016. https://www.wsws.org/en/articles/2016/10/15/wiki-o15.html
[175] Ibid.

them for their party's loss of the elections. The establishment media then became the greatest promoter of censorship and launched a smear campaign against Julian Assange, the founder of WikiLeaks, who is still in prison for exposing the truth about powerful governments' corruption.

Another scandal during Obama's two terms was whistleblower Edward Snowden's leaked information in 2013 about the illegal mass surveillance in the US. Former FBI, and NSA contractor, Snowden waited until Obama's second term in 2012 because he believed the president would act accordingly and stop the anti-constitutional spying on citizens in the US and the world. After Obama was informed by Congress and did nothing, Snowden leaked the information to the *Guardian* and the *New York Times*. The surveillance still continues to this day, and Snowden is in exile in Russia wanted for charges under the Espionage Act. Obama prosecuted more whistleblowers under the Espionage Act than all previous presidents combined including Thomas Drake, Bradley Manning, John Kiriakou, Jeffrey Sterling, Stephen Kim, and Shamai Leibowitz.

The damage that Obama has done to democracy was more than enough for people who didn't buy the media propaganda and followed his politics. For some who listen to the mainstream media, Obama remains the best president. Either way, with the help of the media favorite protege, Obama, the alliance between the media and the government become the most solid pillar of the status quo and the worst enemy of independent journalism. After his two terms as president, Obama become a major shareholder in Netflix, one of the biggest entertainment streaming services, and is currently a multi-millionaire, demonstrating the revolving door between the government and the media.

Another star created by the media is Sheryl Sandberg, a COO of Meta (formerly Facebook), and currently a billionaire. Sandberg became popular and prominent feminist leader after publishing her non-fiction book, *Lean In: Women, Work, and the Will to Lead* (2013).[176] Sandberg is a business woman with an impressive career with her first job as a research assistant at the World Bank during her undergraduate studies, later as Chief of Staff at the Treasury Department, CEO at Google, and finally COO at Facebook. Sandberg's career is in both government and technology, and she demonstrates perfectly well the revolving door between Silicon Valley and Washington D.C.

As revealed by Edward Snowden, tech companies such as Google,

---

[176] Sheryl Sandberg, *Lean In: Women, Work, and the Will to Lead*, New York: Alfred Knopf, 2013.

Facebook, and Microsoft, worked in closed cooperation with the government from their inception.[177] Sandberg's message to lean in has been amplified by mainstream media and sells thousands of books, despite the fact that she represents fewer than 1 percent of women in technology. With the help of the mainstream media, the book turned into a movement titled "Lean In," and Sandberg was ordained as a "feminist leader" with the concerted approval of the most powerful institutions. Sandberg's idea of Leaning In benefits big corporations as it provides them with cheap labor of women motivated to succeed just like Sandberg, if they only try harder. It hurts the perspective of women and minorities who represent the opposite of wealthy, powerful, and dominant people in new media, because the idea suggests that we live in a meritocracy where individual efforts are deciding factors and there are no institutional obstacles and oppression.

Sandberg's pro-corporate message is antithetical to the intersectional feminist concept of equality, anti-capitalism, anti-monopoly, and anti-exploitation of women and people of color. For this reason, Sandberg's ideas have been criticized by a number of feminist scholars, most notably, Susan Faludi, the late bell hooks, journalist Zoe Williams from *The Guardian,* and so on. Sandberg's persona and book represent the opposite views of those of the genuine feminist movement. For example, feminism supports independent investigative journalists, instead of mainstream media and their imperialistic views, which always promote wars. Despite Sandberg's support for the corporations and their exploitation of women and minorities, she still has multiple complaints as she presents herself as feminist. Ironically, Sandberg proves that even a white female billionaire who is married to a supportive husband, cannot avoid discrimination, sexism, and being mistreated from time to time.

In Sandberg's sanitized version of her life, she is treated respectfully most of the time by her male superiors such as Treasury Secretary Larry Summers, his predecessor Robert Rubin, senators and state officials among others. However, she describes a few of instances where this is not the case. Predictably, her criticism is contained to a couple of diseased powerful men: one senator and her boss at McKensie when she was very young. Inversely, Sandberg describes Summers, who became notorious with his sexist remarks about women's innate intellectual differences with men, as a generous mentor and progressive figure, whose mission at the World Bank is "to reduce global

---

[177] Edward Snowden, *Permanent Record,* New York: Metropolitan Books, 2019, 194.

poverty."[178] Sandberg might not have known at the time that the goal of the bank is to impose predatory landing on poorer countries at high interest in order to effectively run them politically.[179] However, there is a memo leaked to the press, in which Summers suggests that toxic waste should be dumped in developing countries in Africa, because" underpopulated countries are under polluted."[180]

Additionally, in response to the public controversy where Summers, then President of Harvard, made derogatory remarks about women, Sandberg defended Summer's overt male chauvinism and published a statement praising him for helping and supporting women.[181] Sandberg's loyalty proves that class and elite solidarity is above gender equality. The scandal about Summers's public statement undermining women's aptitude in math was not just rhetorical; it was entrenched in Summers' university policies. During his term as President at Harvard, the number of women offered tenure fell from 36 percent to 13 percent, and his last year only 4 of the 32 tenure positions were offered to women.[182] The same poor diversity policy was demonstrated by Summers's mentee Sheryl Sandberg. In 2018, she was still the only female chief executive officer at Meta, and hired only 22 percent female engineers, 1 percent black engineers, and 4 percent Hispanic engineers during her 10 years as COO.[183] Sandberg purports to be advocating for women while she refuses to use her powerful position, wealth, and influence to achieve fifty percent participation of women in technology, and to meet her own recommendation.[184]

One serious critic of Sandberg's ideology is Susan Faludi, a prominent feminist scholar, who is cited in Sandberg's book.[185] In her article, "Facebook Feminism, Like It or Not," Faludi depicts her inquiry to interview Sandberg

---

[178] Ibid., 55.

[179] Larry Elliot, "Greece's Bailout Is Finally at an End – But It Has Been a Failure," *The Guardian*, Aug. 19, 2018.

[180] Hearing before the Committee of Finance, United States Senate, First Session of the Nomination of Larry Summers to be under Secretary of the Treasury for International Affairs, March 18, 1993.

[181] Sheryl Sandberg, "Larry Summers' True Record on Women," *Huffington Post*, December 8, 2008.

[182] Suzanne Goldenberg, "Why Women Are Poor at Science, by Harvard President," *The Guardian*, Jan.18, 2005.

[183] Maxine Williams, "Facebook 2018 Diversity Report: Reflecting on Our Journey," July 12, 2018.

[184] Sandberg, *Lean In*, 50.

[185] Sandberg, *Lean In*, 142.

and how the company declined several times.[186] Instead, Facebook's administration offered her a conversation "off the record," which Faludi declined because she knew she could not publish such answers. Finally, Faludi sent another request for an interview with Sandberg accompanied by four questions in advance and received a standard reply from Facebook PR Department, which Faludi described as "vague and generic," with "a quote for your use."[187] It would be reasonable to presume that a movement like *Lean In*, in favor of women's equality, would be interested in a conversation with a famous feminist such as Faludi. To Faludi's disappointment, it was denied repeatedly and never took place despite their seemingly common goals of emancipating women in the work force.

Faludi's first question discussed the fact that *Lean In* purports to be a movement and revolution, yet it never calls for confronting the institutions that oppress women and minorities, and the corporations that exploit them. For example, the website's motto for the *Lean In* movement states: "We help women achieve their ambitions and work to create an equal world." The essence of this controversy is that Sandberg cannot support simultaneously the female precariat and the corporations that discriminate against them. More specifically, over 200 corporations signed in as "platform partners" of *Lean In*, including some of the largest American companies such as Chevron, General Electric, Procter & Gamble, Comcast, Bank of America, Citibank, Coca-Cola, Pepsico, AT&T, Verizon, Ford, GM, Pfizer, Merck & Co., Costco, Wal-Mart, Google, and Facebook.[188] The vast support by the biggest corporations of Sandberg's movement raises the question whether the corporations benefit from Sandberg's message to Lean In, given their eagerness to promote the movement. In contrast, Faludi supports female social groups that are excluded from Sandberg's movement or her message – the majority of American women and minorities. As Faludi articulates:

---

[186] Susan Faludi, "Facebook Feminism, Like It or Not," *The Baffler*, No. 23, August 2013.

[187] The letter stated: "Unfortunately, an interview will not be possible." They provided her a quote to use: "Lean In is a global community committed to encouraging and supporting women leaning in to their ambitions. We're incredibly grateful to our community and the individuals, and institutions, who have already made progress changing the conversation on gender. But we know there is so much more to do before we live in an equal world. That's why we're not just encouraging, but supporting, everyone and every company that wants to lean in. It's time to change the world, not just the conversation." Ibid.

[188] Faludi, *The Baffler*, 2013.

A star like Sheryl Sandberg, whose feminism seems a capstone of female ascendancy. Never mind that the "fastest-growing" future occupations for women—home health aide, child care worker, customer service representative, office clerk, food service worker—are among the lowest paid, most with few to no benefits and little possibility for "advancement." Progress has stalled for many ordinary women—or gone into reverse.[189]

Another critic of Sandberg's message, feminist scholar bell hooks, questions the lack of mentioning of both class and race in Sandberg's book. In her review of the book, hooks writes: "Race is certainly an invisible category in Sandberg's corporate fantasy world."[190] Furthermore, hooks defines Sandberg's rhetorical fight for equality as "faux feminism" because the author manages to be silent on important issues such as class, race, sexual orientation, and so on. For example, on the topic of money, according to hooks, Sandberg only uses the word once in the book.[191] Other terms that are never used are heterosexual patriarchy and white domination. With class, race, and sexuality taken out of the equation, there is only an empty shell of feminism left. hooks cautions us to "Remember that the women on the show are puppets and white men behind the scenes are pulling the strings."[192]

In their critique of the book both Faludi and hooks refer to Kate Losse's 2012 memoir *The Boy Kings,* depicting a very different picture of Facebook. The fact that Losse repeatedly addresses the issues of class, race, and sexuality in Facebook is juxtaposed to Sandberg's omission of the obvious sexism and class inequality in her sanitized version of the reality in Facebook. bell hooks finishes her article with a reference to her critique titled "Dig Deep" pointing to the need for a profound analysis of Sandberg's leadership, so "we can truly unpack and understand why she has been chosen and lifted up in the neoliberal market place." hooks raises a very interesting point about the selection of Sandberg to be the face of feminism. The question requires a broader analysis and will be discussed further in Chapter Six.

In conclusion, the sophisticated propaganda crafted in the early 20th century by intellectuals such as Lippmann and Bernays, is still in place a

---

[189] Ibid.
[190] Bell hooks, "Dig Deep: Beyond Lean In," *The Feminist Wire,* Oct 28, 2013.
[191] Ibid.
[192] Ibid.

hundred years later. Perfected by selected tokens such as Obama and Sandberg, who seemingly represent people of color and women, propaganda plays an important role in spreading the myth of democracy, equality, and meritocracy in the US. Obama and Sandberg convincingly sell the illusion that women and minorities can make it in this country, if they work hard enough, get the right education, and have the motivation of these two individual leaders. Even though it may be true that Obama and Sandberg had worked much harder and demonstrated more qualities than their white male counterparts, their success had nothing to do with such traits. On the contrary, their success was entirely contingent on their obedience, conformity, and loyalty to the ruling class.

Chapter Five

Academic Dissidents: The Glaring Absence of Noam Chomsky, Cornell West, and Chris Hedges from the Mainstream Media

> *In this country intellectual cowardice is the worst enemy a writer or a journalist has to face, and that fact does not seem to me to have had the discussion it deserves.*
>
> ~George Orwell, 1945

The elitist views in academia since its inception, discussed in the previous chapter still persist in the 21st century. As is the case with the elitist mainstream media who are stenographers for the ruling class, prominent academics continue to support the patronizing, self-serving views propagandized by Lippmann and Bernays a century ago. The intellectuals who want to prosper, quickly understand that there are certain beliefs that will propel them to the top, and others that will lead to their demise. George Orwell encountered this phenomenon and explained it perfectly well in his unpublished preface of his 1945 *Animal Farm:*

> It is important to distinguish between the kind of censorship that the English literary intelligentsia voluntary impose upon themselves, and the censorship that can

sometimes be enforced by pressure groups. Notoriously, certain topics cannot be discussed because of "vested interests."[193]

Orwell's preface was published only twice: the first time in 1972 in the *Times Literary Supplement,* and the second time in the Penguin's 2000 edition of the book; however, not as an introduction but as Appendix. It is still not published in his millions of copies of the *Animal Farm.* According to *Rare Book Monthly,* by 2016, Orwell's *Animal Farm* and *1984* sold 40 million copies.[194] The reason for censoring Orwell's preface is his thorough explanation of how the Western democratic countries are not much different than the Russian dictatorship, just more subtle by means of self-restraining from topics and opinions that are not approved by the ruling elites in academia and the press. Even though *Animal Farm* was written about Russia and published in England in 1945, it is still relevant and could be applied to 2022 US. We have here the identical mentality of self-censorship among scholars, journalists and writers. The few who dare to break the unwritten rules suffer financial losses, unemployment, demotion, ruined reputation, and in the case of Julian Assange, imprisonment. As a result, dissidents such as the late historian Howard Zinn, scholar Noam Chomsky, professor Cornell West, and journalist Chris Hedges, among others are not welcomed on college campuses or mainstream media despite their enormous popularity.

One example of the subtle censorship through blackout is the late historian and activist, Howard Zinn. He wrote *A People's History of the United States* (1980), an account of American history from the perspective of Native Americans, African Americans, women, and other oppressed social groups. Chronological events including the first European expeditions to America in the 15th century to modern actions are described through the lenses of the majority of the people whose views are usually not represented in history books. Such absence of traditional white male conqueror's perspective, which dominates historiography, was perceived as offensive by some scholars. Zinn's version of history triggered official attempts to ban the book in some states such as Indiana in 2013, by governor Mitch Daniels, and Arkansas in 2017, by Representative Kim Hendren. Notoriously, President Trump promised to ban Zinn's book from schools if reelected in his speech at the National Archive

---

[193] George Orwell, "The Freedom of the Press," *The Times Literary Supplement,* Sept. 15, 1972.

[194] Susan Halas, "Orwell Values Soar as Dystopia Closes In," *Rare Book Monthly,* Nov., 2016.

Museum in D.C. in 2020. Despite the opposition, the book was republished multiple times in 1990, 1995, 1998, 1999, 2003, and posthumously in 2015, after Zinn's passing in 2010.

According to his own words, Zinn was trying to shine a light to an alternative set of heroes who did more for the people than the celebrated personalities in the US history such as Columbus, Theodore Roosevelt, and so on. Instead, argued Zinn, there is a plethora of heroes such as Mark Twain who was famous not only with his Tom Sayer and Huckleberry Finn characters, but also as a Vice President of the Anti-Imperialist League and a critic of President Roosevelt for his warmongering policies. Similarly, Hellen Keller, who was widely known as a successful entrepreneur, was less known as socialist who refused to cross a picket line in a theatre featuring her own play in New York in 1957. In the Introduction to the 2015 edition of Zinn's *A People's History of the United States*, Anthony Arnove wrote:

> Howard Zinn fundamentally changed the way millions of people think about history with *A People's History of the United States*…The book grew out of his awareness of the importance of social movements throughout US history, some of which he played an active role in during the 1960s and the 1970s and beyond, namely, the Civil Rights Movement, mass mobilization to end the Vietnam War, as well as other anti-war movements, and the many movements for higher wages and workers' rights and the rights of women, Latinos, Native Americans, gays and lesbians, and others. He was also quick to acknowledge the many people who informed his view of history: Woody Guthrie, whose songs about working people in the 1930s and 1940s opened up chapters of US history to him that his formal education had kept hidden; Philip S. Foner; Herbert Aptheker; Richard Hofstadter; Elizabeth Martinez; and other writers, editors, librarians, historians who unearthed what he calls the "past's fugitive moments of compassion rather than…its solid centuries of warfare."[195]

Many of these individuals listed by Zinn as influences, were unorthodox

---

[195] Anthony Arnove, "Introduction to the 35th Anniversary Edition of *A Peoples' History of the United States,* New York: Harper Perennial Modern Classics, 2015, xiii.

and are missing from the standard history textbooks, despite their significant scholarship. Upon investigation, I learned that Philip S. Foner was a US labor historian, and a Marxist thinker, who wrote more than 100 books. Foner's emphasis on the US labor, the participation of blacks, women, and other groups neglected by mainstream historians is expressed in books such as: *Mark Twain: Social Critic* (1958), *The Black Panthers Speak* (1970), *The Great Labor Uprising of 1877* (1977), *Women and the American Labor* (1979), *Organized Labor and the Black Worker 1619-1981* (1981), and *US Labor and the Vietnam War* (1989). Foner was one of the 26 employees fired from their teaching and staff positions at City College of New York for their political views during the McCarthy era. Foner is best remembered for his 10 volume *History of the Labor Movement*, and *The Life and Writings of Frederick Douglas*, a biography of the abolitionist black leader.

Herbert Aptheker was also a Marxist historian and political activist who wrote over 50 books. Aptheker specialized in black history and wrote most notably, *American Negro Slave Revolts* (1936), A 7 volume *Documentary History of the Negro People* (1975), and *On Race and Democracy* (1950) among others. Like Foner, Aptheker was blacklisted in the 1950s for his political views and thus, barred from academia for most of his life. The common thread between these two influences is their focus on race and racism in American history at a time when this wasn't politically expedient. Even more dangerous was their interest in Marxism as an egalitarian ideology and their critical view of capitalism during the McCarthy's red scare.

Another influence mentioned by Zinn, Richard Hofstadter, was more established liberal historian during his late career; however, his early works, *Social Darwinism in American Thought* (1944), *The American Political Tradition* (1948), are radically different from his liberal consensus history, emphasized by his modern biographers. Richard Hofstadter's early works including essays on prominent historic icons such as Jefferson, Lincoln, FDR, and so on, were far more critical about the limits of American democracy and described by him as "the important and unfamiliar."[196] Moreover, Hofstadter explains his departure from his brief membership of the Communist party as an expression of his opposition to dogmatic measures, "I hate capitalism and everything that goes with it. But I also hate the simpering dogmatic religious-minded Janissaries that make up the CP." This statemen denounces the forced duality of choices by ideologues who insist that a person should commit to

---

[196] Draft Introduction to The *American Political Tradition*, RHP, Box 3.

either communism or capitalism. It is perfectly normal to reject both in favor of a third alternative and refuse to choose "the lesser evil."

Other influences to Zinn include Elizabeth Martinez, American activist, feminist, educator, and author of *500 Years of Chicana Women's History* (2008), *500 Years of Chicana History in Pictures* (1976), and *The Youngest Revolution; A Personal Report on Cuba* (1969), among others. Not surprisingly, singer Woody Guthrie was listed first among Zinn's influences as he played an important role in Zinn's formative years with his 1930s and 1940s songs about workers' uprisings. In modern American culture, Guthrie is known mainly for his catchy song "This Land is Your Land," popularized during the presidential elections in 2002. However, it is widely unknown to the public that two of Guthrie's verses of the popular song were omitted from the lyrics. The "lost" verses read:

> As I went walking I saw a sign there
> And on the sign it said "No trespassing."
> But on the other side it didn't say nothing,
> That side was made for you and me…
>
> In the squares of the city, in the shadow of a steeple,
> By the relief office, I'd seen my people.
> As they stood there hungry, I stood there asking,
> Is this land made for you and me?

Many American children grew up singing Guthrie's song without hearing the "lost" verses as they were conveniently scrubbed from the official version of the song. Similarly, Richard Hofstadter, discussed earlier as influential, was presented in a new Library of America collection of his work, edited and introduced by historian Sean Wilentz in 2020, as a champion of the liberal consensus by leaving out many of his earlier works. For example, Hofstadter's most critical works, *Social Darwinism of American Thought* (1944) and *The American Political Tradition* (1948), were omitted from the collection.[197] Not surprisingly, the deceiving effect of such misrepresentations are perfectly aligned with the dominant official narrative and the sanitization of certain authors by censoring their inconvenient work.

It is easy to understand how Zinn has been influenced by such historians

---

[197] Jeet Heer, "At Liberalism's Crossroads," *The Nation*, Oct. 6, 2020, Issue October 19/26.

and activists. They were all searching for the truth and criticizing the lack of democracy and social justice in the US as they encounter or observe it. They were unorthodox writers and were not willing to tow the official line of purported freedom and democracy. Zinn had similar urge to look for the truth, and when he found historians describing the reality in the same way regular people saw it, he was encouraged to do the same. Zinn's life and work were dedicated to searching for truth and social justice. His popularity exposes the scarcity of historians with integrity. One of the reviewers of Zinn's book, Eric Foner, a historian, wrote in the acclaim section of the *People's History*: "Zinn's public learned about ordinary Americans' struggles for justice, equality, and power. I have long been struck by how many excellent students of history first had their passion for the past sparked by reading Howard Zinn."[198] A more recent book by David Detmer, titled *Zinnophobia: The Battle over History in Education, Politics, and Scholarship*, was published in 2018.[199] The book offers an extensive defense of Zinn's work against his many critics, and a detailed response to twenty-five of Zinn's opponents, many of whom are (were) prominent historians. I believe that Detmer's work is well over due because the criticism of Zinn's work is politically motivated and could be revealed as such.

In the case of Chomsky, who was a close friend of Zinn, he became an outsider because of his condemnation of the imperialistic foreign policy of the US, and his criticism of the political two-party system. Based on a Princeton's study, Chomsky enunciates that only the top 10-20 percent of affluent citizens participate in decision making through policies, whereas regular people have little or no influence.[200] Similarly, Chomsky explains that American corporatocracy distorts higher education through a process of socialization that makes faculty and media members internalize the doctrines they inculcate. Moreover, in Chomsky's view, intellectuals in general abandon their moral duty for fear of losing their prestige and funding. Chomsky's exceptional productivity as a renown linguist and political dissident amounts

---

[198] Eric Foner, "Acclaim for Howard Zinn and A People's History of the United States," edition of *A People's History of the United States*, 3rd edition Oxford: Routledge, 2015.

[199] David Detmer, *Zinophobia: The Battle over History in Education, Politics, and Scholarship*. London: Zero Books, September 28, 2018.

[200] Martin Gilens and Benjamin I. Page, "Testing Theories of American Politics: Elites, Interest Groups and Average Citizens," *American Political Science Association,* Vol 12 No 3, Sept 2014.
https://scholar.princeton.edu/sites/default/files/mgilens/files/gilens_and_page_2014_-testing_theories_of_american_politics.doc.pdf

to publishing more than a hundred and fifty books and approximately two hundred speeches a year. Chomsky's dissident work influenced several generations. For example, his *Manufacturing Consent,* discussed earlier, impacted the way people perceived western media. Chomsky's five mass media filters became iconoclastic and were transformed later into a five-minute animation, produced and voiced over by Amy Goodman.[201] Because in the film the narrator concludes that Chomsky's theory "blasted apart the notion that media acts as a check on political power" the animation was only disseminated abroad; more specifically, on *Al Jazeera* in 2017."[202]

According to Chomsky's biographer, Wolfgang Sperlich, despite his abundant publishing on social and political issues, universities' departments devoted to history and political science rarely include Chomsky's work in their undergraduate syllabi. Sperlich explains that because Chomsky was vilified by corporate interests, despite his overwhelming recognition abroad, he became a pariah in the US media and academia in the 1980s. For example, Chomsky was voted "the world's leading public intellectual" by the 2005 Global Intellectual Poll; and ranks number eight among the top ten philosophers and thinkers most cited in the world among Marx, Lenin, Shakespeare, Aristotle, the Bible, Plato, Freud, Hegel and Cicero.[203]

Furthermore, 23 years ago, David Daley brought public's attention to the fact of the scholar's obliteration from mainstream media in an article from 1999 titled, "Chomsky's Glaring Absence." The author illuminates the fact that although Chomsky is often featured on TV on BBC, Europe and Canada, he is ostensibly absent from the US national TV because of his criticism of US foreign policy, social justice, and western democracy in general. Regarding academia, Chomsky believes that universities are not independent institutions because they rely on private wealth, corporate investments and government grants which are closely entangled. Not surprisingly, in academia Chomsky is conveniently received exclusively as a linguist and ignored as a renown political dissident.

In 2022, Chomsky infuriated the liberal warmongering media again with his adamant condemnation of the NATO/US aggressive involvement in the Russia – Ukraine conflict. Chomsky promptly addresses the past of the two countries and elaborates on the broken promises made by NATO

---

[201] https://www.youtube.com/watch?v=34LGPIXvU5M
[202] Ibid., 0:55.
[203] "Chomsky is Citation Champ," *MIT News on Campus and around the World,* April 15, 1992. https://news.mit.edu/1992/citation-0415

and US State Secretary James Baker to Gorbachev in 1990. Chomsky rightly condemns Putin's invasion as well; however, his position always has been that there is not much that can be done to stop other governments but every citizen's duty is to insert pressure on his/her own government. He enunciates that the US and NATO are fighting a proxy war with Russia in Ukraine so "we don't have to fight them here," citing the Senate Majority Leader Chuck Schumer. Also, Chomsky condemns the cruel disregard for regular citizens by both global powers, the US and Russia, willing to fight "to the last Ukrainian" in this unnecessary war.

Inversely, Chomsky fails to have the same critical position of his government in relation to the Covid response and the draconian measures including vaccine mandates that violate bodily autonomy and informed consent for an experimental medicine. Ironically, the scholar who was always skeptical about government intentions and actions that jeopardize human rights, was inconsistent with his democratic views in the case of the pandemic response.[204] In an interview that became viral, Chomsky states that citizens who refuse the vaccine should be kept in isolation from society even if that meant their starvation.[205] On this particular subject Chomsky abandoned his unyielding skepticism toward authorities and their legitimacy. Of course, according to his own words, no one should be admired or worshipped, just their ideas, precisely because humans are flawed.

Predictably, the conformist intellectual class accepted the totalitarian mandates and dismissed everyone who didn't as anti-scientific. British investigative journalist Ian Davis explains this phenomenon in his analysis of the policies towards a new technocratic totalitarianism as the ruling class takes advantage of the pandemic.[206] Davis interprets the private-public relationship advertised by the WEF and Schwab and the fusion of a new component, "civil society" and compares the complacence to the "new normal" with the communitarianism where social pressure is absolute:

> An individual suffering from groupthink possesses unquestioned certainty, intolerance for any opposing views and an inability to engage in logical discourse. Their

---

[204] Oliver Browning, "Noam Chomsky Calls for Unvaccinated to Be 'Isolated' from Society in Resurfaced Clip," *Independent,* Nov. 2021.

[205] https://www.youtube.com/watch?v=7RPt7hRfr8I

[206] Ian Davis, "The New Normal & the Civil Society Deception," *Unlimited Hangout,* http://i-this-together-com

critical thinking skills are impaired, because to question the community is to question their own identity.

Those who do not share the ordained group ethos, or those who question the evidence base underpinning the group certainty, are not part of the community. They are "other."[207]

Nevertheless, in Chomsky's analysis of the handling of the pandemic, he is unambiguous about the one-sided class war launched on American workers and the middle class, and the government welfare for the rich. In an interview discussing his 2021 book *Consequences of Capitalism,* the scholar notes that Moderna and other pharmaceutical companies made enormous profit using state sponsored research and federal subsidies for the vaccines while privatizing the gains.[208] He confirms the enormous upward transfer of wealth from regular people to the top one percent that amounts to over $50T for the last four decades.[209] Similarly, on the most recent topic of Russian invasion of Ukraine, Chomsky remains a staunch opponent of imperialistic aggression on both sides – Putin and NATO/US lead military intervention in the local conflict between Russia and its former republic Ukraine. Chomsky calls for complete ban of nuclear weapons globally, in order to prevent annihilation of human life on earth. He also recommends peaceful negotiations establishing an immediate cease of fire for the sake of the Ukrainian people.

Another iconoclastic scholar and public intellectual, Cornel West, who is a prominent American philosopher, political activist, social critic, and actor, is absent from the mainstream media apart from derogatory campaigns and misrepresentations. In 2021, Professor Cornel West was denied tenure by Harvard University, which demonstrates the censorship and discrimination against the scholar as a punishment for his political views. West has been an outspoken critic of Israeli politics of aggression and apartheid against Palestinians, a subtle taboo in academia. In addition, West is openly critical of President Obama and now President Biden for their massive incarceration of African Americans, foreign military intervention, and bailouts of Wall Street. After West threatened to resign, massive protests erupted among students

---

[207] Ibid.
[208] F. Tammy Kim, "Consequences of Capitalism," Lannan Foundation & *Haymarket Books*, Oct. 13, 2021.
https://podcast.lannan.org/2021/10/18/consequences-of-capitalism-13-oct-2021-video/
[209] Ibid.

and independent media, including a publicized letter signed by 150 doctoral students, professors and affiliates of Harvard. As a result, the administration offered West a chair position and a monetary promotion. West, who had previously held tenured positions at Harvard, Yale, and Princeton, declined the offer and explained that it was made only after the public protests.

Such an act of discrimination against West is not without a precedent. Back in 2001, when Laurance Summers was President of Harvard, and West was a tenured professor, Summers engaged in a disrespectful scrutiny of West's work. According to West, Summers "questioned his scholarship, asked to monitor his research and requested West's scores records to check for grade inflation." In an interview with ABC News in 2021, West emphasizes that his resignation from Harvard reflects his principles and explains that he puts intellectual freedom above lucrative positions awarded for complacence.

More importantly, West gave examples of multiple acts of discrimination that went unnoticed and noted that his resignation is in solidarity of other scholars who are subjected to discrimination but did not have his massive public support. In his letter of resignation, West introduces the letter with strong words, "I try to tell the unvarnished truth about the decadence in our market-driven universities! Let us bear witness against this spiritual rot!" In the letter, West calls out faculty members who conform to injustice because they fear losing their privileges and describes them as "talented yet deferential." Hours after publishing his letter on Twitter on June 12, 2021, West accumulated almost one hundred thousand likes and more than 20 thousand retweets. The public's robust reaction to this ostensible injustice led to Harvard's Dean's partial surrender and suggests that positive change in academia depends on massive public pressure and involvement.

As an activist, West supported Occupy Wall Street movement and was arrested in October 2011 during a protest against the NYPD stop and frisk policy. West supports People for the Ethical Treatment of Animals (PETA) and speaks against the cruelty towards animals in factory farms. In 2014, West co-initiated the Stop Mass Incarceration Network, a project of the Revolutionary Communist Party USA. West participated in the counter-protest at the Unite the Right Rally in Charleville, VA, in 2017, where the rally ended up with the violent death of a counter-protestor killed by a vehicle-ramming attack, and more than 49 injured.

Although West supported Barack Obama's presidential candidacy, he later retracted his support and criticized him for his conformist executive performance. More specifically, West renounced Obama's Nobel Peace Prize in 2009, and stated in a 2011 interview that "Obama is a black mascot of Wall Street oligarchs and a black Muppet of corporate plutocrats. And now he became head of the American killing machine and is proud of it."[210] West also characterized Obama as "Rockefeller Republican in blackface."[211] Because of his criticism, West became a pariah to the "liberal" mainstream media who shunned him for his objective definitions of Democratic leaders such as Obama, Clinton, and Biden, among other neoliberal politicians and democratic in name only.

West also created a weekly podcast, *The Tight Rope* with Tricia Rose from July 2020 to September 2021. During its short performance, the show featured Noam Chomsky, Michael Moore, Jane Fonda, Roxane Gay, Nicole Hana Jones, Killer Mike, Alexandria Ocasio Cortez, and Antony Fauci, among others until it was closed for financial difficulties.[212] In their last show, West and Rose reflect on the intensive events that happened during their tumultuous year, and the hostile opposition that West provoked in the establishment media. The two intellectuals shared bitter-sweet memories remembering the deep conversations with their guests and the level of openness West inspired in them, which made the podcast well worth and fulfilling.[213] Rose emphasized West's commitment to the cause of defending the rights of the black and poor population when it was detrimental to his career and elaborated on the effect such sincere bravery has on the lives of so many marginalized black individuals.

According to West, the corruption of the middle black class through its incorporating into to the mainstream politics hurts enormously the lower strata of their fellow citizens. Rose noted that the elevation of such members of the middle class transforms them into defenders of the system, which rewarded them for their betrayal.[214] The focus of the show has been on the "the ratcheted of the earth," which West remembered in relation to his introduction to the 60th edition of Franz Fanon's 1961 *The Ratcheted of the Earth,* where Fanon explains how colonialization dehumanizes certain members of society.

---

[210] Matt Schneider, "Wild Shoutfest between Al Sharpton and Cornel West on Obama and Race," *Mediate*, April 11, 2011. www.mediate.com

[211] Andrew Kirell, "Cornel West: Obama a "Republican in Blackface," 'Black MSNBC Hosts are Selling Their Souls,' *Mediate*, Nov. 12, 2012.

[212] Cornel West and Tricia Rose, "Tight Rope Final Episode: Reflecting on a Year of Love, Wisdom, and Fortitude," September 9, 2021. https://www.youtube.com/watch?v=clFVKr-rtxs

[213] Ibid, 07:16.

[214] Ibid, 29:20.

West noted that the question becomes how we make sure that we don't become indifferent to the oppressed. He enunciates that one main point of his introduction was "the massive neglect and pervasive betrayal of poor and working people by their own elites, be it national, gender, what have you."[215] The show ends with a call for empathy, sensitivity, and compassion towards "the ratcheted of the earth" and recommends that we always keep in mind the bigger picture, where there is something greater than ourselves.

In 2016 and 2020, West supported democratic socialist presidential candidate Bernie Sanders, and campaigned for him along with Chris Hedges. Noam Chomsky also fully supported Sanders' candidacy and defined it as a unique success despite the opposition of the billionaire's class. West collaborated with Hedges on his educational project in the NJ prisons and visited famous political prisoners such as Mumia Abu-Jamal, serving life in sentence for an alleged murder.[216] West has written 20 books, and has edited 13 books including *Race Matters* (1993), *Jews and Blacks: A Dialogue on Race, Religion, and Culture in America* (1995), *The Future of the Race* (1996), *The Rich and the Rest of Us: A Poverty Manifesto* (2012).

In 2011, West participated in a "Poverty Tour" with Tavis Smiley, his co-host on the *Public Radio International* Program *Smiley & West.*, which West co-hosted with Tavis from 2010 through 2013. On Cornel West website, there are relevant quotes that define the dissident scholar, cordially called by many "Brother West." For example, his multifaceted personality is described by aspects of his service to society supported by quotes. Examples include "servant" depicted with, "You can't lead the people if you don't love the people; "scholar" –" Deep education requires habitual vision of greatness;" "activist" – "Justice is what love looks like in public;" "lover of music" – "I'm a blessed man in the life of the mind. I'm a jazz man in the world of ideas."[217] Cornel West continuously stands up for the impoverished, down-trodden Americans of all races. He is an unyielding, staunch fighter for justice in America and an inspiration for all dissidents and peaceful supporters of human rights and the constitution of the US.

Perhaps the most outstanding is the case of Chris Hedges, an investigative journalist, author, minister, commentator, and political activist. Hedges was a war correspondent in Central America, the Middle East, Eastern Europe,

---

[215] Ibid, 32:10.
[216] Kathlyn Gay, *American Dissidents: AN Encyclopedia pf Activists, Subversives, and Prisoners of Conscience,* Sept., 2018.
[217] www.cornelwest.com

and the New York Times Middle East and Balkan Bureau Chief. Hedges won a Pulitzer Prize for Explanatory Reporting in 2002, when he worked for the *New York Times*. Three years later, Hedges was fired for his opposition to the Iraq War after 15 years of reporting for the newspaper. Hedges was a columnist at news outlet *Truthdig* for 14 years until its closing in 2020. When the publisher of *Truthdig* decided to fire the Editor-in-Chief Robert Scheer, and refused to address some labor violations, Hedges organized the staff to go on a strike and as a result they were all fired.[218]

As a writer, Hedges was a finalist for the National Book Critics Circle Award for Nonfiction for his book *War is a Force that Gives Us Meaning* (2002). A quotation from the book served as an opening title citation for the Academy Award-winning 2009 film *Hurt Locker*: "The rush of battle is often a potent and lethal addiction, for war is a drug."[219] Some of Hedges' books include *American Fascists: The Christian Right and the War on America* (2007), *I Don't Believe in Atheists* (2008), *Death of the Liberal Class* (2010*), Days of Destruction, Days of Revolt* (2012), *America: Farewell Tour* (2018), and his newest book *Our Class: Trauma and Transformation* (2021). Hedges taught at Columbia University, NYU, Princeton University, and the University of Toronto.

In 2005, Hedges became a senior fellow at Type Media Center and in 2006, he was awarded a Lannan Literary Fellowship for nonfiction. Through a program offered by Princeton University and later Rutgers University, Hedges has been teaching writing classes in prisons in New Jersey for a decade. Hedges became a fierce critic of mass incarceration in the US and his experience as an educator inspired his latest 2021 book. In collaboration with his students from prison, in 2013, Hedges co-created a play titled *Caged,* which premiered on May 3, 2018, in Passage Theatre in Trenton, NJ.[220] Hedges often works with his colleague, Cornel West, whom he calls "magnificent" and James Cone, father of Black Liberation Theology, either in prison or otherwise. Hedges took West to visit Mumia Abu-Jamal, the black journalist and activist, accused of murdering a policeman and sentenced to death in 1982. In 2001, his sentence was overturned by a Federal court and Jamal became "the world's best-known death-row inmate," according to the *NYT*. During the visit, Cornel West put

---

[218] Chris Hedges, "The Chris Hedges Report," *Scheer Post,* March 17, 2022. https://scheerpost.com/2022/03/17/the-chris-hedges-report/
[219] Chris Hedges, *Academic Dictionaries and Encyclopedias*
[220] John Timpane, "'Caged': How 28 Inmates' Tales of Prison and Poverty Became New Jersey's Must-See Play," *The Inquirer,* May 2, 2018.

his arms on Jamal's shoulders and told him that he has Frederic Douglas in him; Jamal cried in response.[221]

Hedges' latest Emmy-Award nominated show *On Contact,* featured since 2016 by RT America, was abruptly de-platformed in 2022 as a reaction to the Russia-Ukraine conflict, which started in Feb., 2022. Multiple American programs, hosted by American creators including Chris Hedges, Jesse Ventura, and Lee Camp among others, found themselves without jobs. It is worth noting that none of these authors commented or covered Russian news; both hosts and their guests were discussing exclusively American events. Such journalists and politicians were given platforms in Russia Today's TV because they were dissidents and as such had no access to American TV. The action of banning American television shows could not be justified with the Russian invasion of Ukraine because they were not engaged in Russian politics. Chris Hedges explains in multiple interviews that the rare occasions when he commented on Russia, he was critical of its politics. Specifically, Hedges condemned Putin's invasion of Ukraine when it happened. However, he also criticized the American invasions of Iraq, Afghanistan, Libya, Syria, Somalia, Sudan, and the military help for Yemen, Gaza, and Pakistan. Hedges contrasted the reprimand he received from the *New York Times* for his criticism of the Iraq war to RT America, who made no comment on Hedges condemnation of the Russian invasion of Ukraine.[222]

According to Hedges' own description of his writing,

> I write for those like myself, grounded in the world of ideas, uncomfortable with the easy cant that infects public discourse, searching for the right questions, able to cope with complexity, nuance, and ambiguity, distrustful of dominant narratives, willing to do the hard labor of trying to understand how those in other cultures and societies see us. Outsiders. Searchers. Not easily labeled.[223]

Hedges filed a lawsuit against President Obama in 2012 for violating the constitution by signing the National Defense Authorization Act (NDAA), which allowed indefinite detention without *habeas corpus* (the right to due process within hours/days of detention). He was later joined by other

---

[221] Chris Hedges, *The Sanctuary for Independent Media.*
[222] *Academic Dictionaries and Encyclopedias.*
[223] Ibid.

activists including Noam Chomsky and Journalist Daniel Ellsberg, famous with publishing The Pentagon Papers in 1971. Initially, Hedges won the suit as Judge Katherine B. Forrest of the Southern District of New York ruled that the section of NDAA violated *habeas corpus* and therefore, was unconstitutional. However, Obama appealed the motion, and the Court of Appeals overturned the decision in 2013, suspending one of the most ancient human rights – *habeas corpus* from 1166, that precedes even the Magna Carta of 1215. Hedges petitioned the US Supreme Court to hear the case, but the Court denied hearing in 2014. In addition, Hedges was a plaintiff in another lawsuit against the government for illegal mass surveillance, Foreign Intelligence Surveillance Act (FISA) Amendment Act of 2008, in *Clapper v. Amnesty International US.*

Hedges actively participated in Occupy Wall Street Movement of 2011. He wrote and edited *The Occupy Wall Street Journal,* which chronicled the events. For the first issue of the journal, Hedges' article was described as "a call to arms" by the *NYT.* Hedges appeared on *CBC News* in October 2011 to discuss his support for the protest. Because host Kevin O'Leary's attitude was dismissive and pejorative, Hedges announced that this would be his last time on the program. CBC's ombudsman found later O'Leary's remarks in violation of the public broadcaster's standards.[224] In November 2011, Hedges was arrested along with other protestors while performing "people's hearing" on the activities of Goldman Sachs and blocking the entrance of their headquarters. As an activist, Hedges supports sustainable energy and preservation of the planet from climate change. In 2014, he joined a panel discussion before People's Climate March, and briefly considered running as a Green Party member in 2020.

Consequently, Hedges' absence from the mainstream media remains the same since the 2011 CBC News interview. However, Hedges' presence is strong otherwise as he appears frequently on alternative media programs and in NJ prisons where he teaches his aspiring students. According to the summary of Hedges' new book, *Our Class: Trauma and Transformation in an American Prison,* the book "gives a human face and a voice to those our society too often demonizes and abandons. It exposes the terrible crucible and injustice of America's penal system and the struggle by those trapped within its embrace to live lives of dignity, meaning, and purpose." In his two decades of

---

[224] Cassandra Szklarsky, "Kevin O'Leary 'Number' Remark Violated Journalistic Standards: CBC Ombudsman," *The Huffington Post Canada,* October 14, 2011.

teaching inmates and condemning American justice system, Hedges tirelessly fought to educate the public about the private prison industry that destroys human lives for profit, in lockstep with the corrupt machine of institutional and judicial double standard.

Thus, the scholars and journalists who dissent from the orthodox doctrine proselyted by the mainstream media and academia are left out of the official platforms. They are made invisible to the public and suffer complete blackout of the news. The late anti-war activists such as Eugene Debs and Howard Zinn are not glorified in recent history literature like figures with much less achievements but more conformist attitudes. Academics such as Noam Chomsky, Cornel West and Chris Hedges with prolific publications and popularity are omitted from textbooks and college syllabi. Despite their high credentials and unquestioned success, these representatives of the people are ostracized by the powerful elites. Nevertheless, dissident scholars and journalists find various ways to deliver their messages. They have been successful so far in reaching out to the public and gaining its trust with consistent integrity and stamina against hard blows. With flexibility and determination, dissidents change their forums when censored or banned. Their continuous presence out of the mainstream media and their growing popularity is proof of their rising influence and that they have the unyielding support of the masses.

Chapter Six

The Infiltration and Co-option of Genuine Movements: Neutralizing Opposition through Corruption and Violence from the Black Panthers and the NOW to #BLM and #MeToo

We're not a racist organization, because we understand that racism is an excuse used for capitalism, and we know that racism is just – it's a byproduct of capitalism.

-Fred Hampton

Throughout history grassroots movements against the ruling class rise from time to time and demand human rights or improvement of life conditions, most notably, the human rights movements in the 1960s, which spread throughout the world. The 1960s wave started on college campuses in Europe, US, Canada, and Latin America, and gradually involved workers' unions, political parties, and organizations for racial equality, women's emancipation, disability, and gay rights. In the US, the most massive movements were against racial discrimination and women's rights led by groups such as the Black Panther Party (BPP) for self-defense, founded in 1966, the Nation of Islam, founded in the 1930s, the National Organization for Women (NOW), founded in 1966, and the National Women's Political Caucus (NWPC), founded in 1971, among others.[225] Although all social movements were informed by human rights, the BPP was distinguished by class warfare against exploitation and imperialism, which placed the party on the FBI black list as the most dangerous enemy of the US government.[226] However, the BPP ended in 1982, and despite the attempt to reinstate it in 1998 as the New Black Panther Party, the new political organization was reduced to a shadow of its previous power and a caricatures of its principles.

A traceable pattern of neutralizing genuine movements has been established as a result of the party's serious threat to the ruling class, more specifically, the FBI special Counter Intelligence Program titled COINTELPRO. The program, which used agent provocateurs, sabotage, misinformation, and lethal force, targeted many progressive movements such as anti-war oppositions and union strikes among others.[227] However, BPP was the secret services' main priority in their subversive activities such as bribes, blackmail, recruitment, or jailing members and ultimately assassination of oppositional leaders. Among the government's prominent secret operations were the assassinations of Martin Luther King, Malcolm X, and Fred Hampton; imprisoning Angela Davis and Huey Newton; recruiting William O'Neil and exiling Huey P. Newton to Cuba.

The Black Panther Party was founded by Huey P. Newton and Bobby Seale in 1966 as a self-defense organization against police brutality and harassment of black people. The BPP members were patrolling black neighborhoods with legal weapons exercising their second amendment rights and called for the arming of all African Americans, their exemption from the military daft, reparations, jobs, housing, education, justice, and peace. Although legal, such actions and demands infuriated the police and the secret services and led to several clashes with law enforcement. The BPP called for cooperation with all oppressed social groups such as white poor workers, women, and other racial or religious minorities. Unlike other political organizations, namely the Universal Negro Improvement Association and the Nation of Islam, the BPP recognized that their issues are based on class rather than race, gender, or other factors. As a result, the party gained popularity and established chapters in 48

---

[225] Black Panther Party for self-defense (BPP), founded by Huey P. Newton and Bobbie Seal in October 1966.
NOW – found by Betty Friedan, Shirley Chisholm, Pauli Murray, and Muriel Fox in Jan 1966.

[226] *Encyclopedia Britannica,* June 29, 2022.

[227] Ibid.

states. Moreover, the BPP grew into an international organization with support groups in Japan, China, France, England, Germany, Sweden, Mozambique, South Africa, Zimbabwe, Uruguay, and elsewhere.[228] More importantly, the BPP launched over 35 Survival Programs that provided community help including education, tuberculosis testing, legal aid, transportation assistance, ambulance service, free shoes and free meals distribution. The most popular initiative was the Free Breakfast for Children Program of 1969.

Despite the party's obvious positive charitable actions, the FBI and its director Edgar Hoover declared the group a communist organization and an enemy of the government. Hoover pledged to destroy the party by 1969 and dedicated his special program COINTELPRO to completing the task. As always, the media ignored the scandalous unconstitutional spying on US citizens because of their political views and the existence of the FBI program COINTELPRO remained unknown for decades until recent declassification of documents. Although the exposure of the illegal activities of the secret services happened in 1968, the focus of the media was on Watergate scandal during that year and the COINTELPRO revelation was only mentioned by the media as a footnote. Despite the fact that the program's consequences were far more important to the public than the exposure of Nixon's White House spying of Congress members, the elitist affair was made by the media a daily spectacle at home and abroad.

The FBI campaign against the BPP reached its culmination in December 1969 with a five-hour police shoot-out at the Southern California headquarters of the BPP. Parallel with the militarized shooting in CA, the Illinois state police launched a raid and cold-bloodedly murdered Chicago Black Panther chairman Fred Hampton in the middle of the night in his bed with his pregnant wife next to him. The story and life of the 21 years old Fred Hampton was featured in the 2020 film *Judas and the Black Messiah*. As the title suggests, Judas was William O'Neal, a member of the BBP who was recruited as an informant by the FBI to spy on Fred Hampton. O'Neal provided the police with a detailed blueprint of Hampton's apartment prior to the raid, as well as allegedly drugged Hampton the same night. O'Neal committed suicide after receiving a small amount from the FBI that resembled closely the biblical 30 silver coins earned by Judas, thus the title of the film. O'Neal used the money to fulfill his dream of opening a private gas station and later committed suicide.

---

[228] Ibid.

According to the *Encyclopedia Britannica,* "the measures employed by the FBI were so extreme that, years later when they were revealed, the director of the agency publicly apologized for 'wrongful uses of power.'"[229] Hampton's family received a settlement payment of $1.85 million; however, none of the officers involved in the assassination were convicted of a crime. The case of Fred Hampton was successfully obscured for many decades until the new Black Lives Matter movement shed a light on some anti-racial events from the past and led to the feature movie that popularized Hampton's important role in the US history. The omission of a leader such as Hampton from national history is necessary to the ruling class because his principle of unification of the oppressed undermines the rule "divide and conquer."

Fred Hampton was a unique political activist because he advocated for uniting all marginalized groups regardless of their race, nationality, or gender, and is famous for his call for a "rainbow coalition." The broad alliance of the Panthers with other groups such as Puerto Rican Young Lords Association, the Poor White Young Patriots Organization, and the Blackstone Rangers street gang provided essential aid to multiple communities including free health clinic and food. This is the core of Hampton's danger to the government secret services whose goal is to protect the status quo and remain in power. Similarly, Martin Luther King's legacy was white-washed to exclude his call for unification of all economically exploited groups of society under the banner of social justice and anti-war voices. King's speeches that address class war and imperialism are not taught in schools but instead his legacy is reduced to his speech "I have a dream." As revealed by unclassified FBI documents, King was spied on and blackmailed by Hoover's FBI, which notoriously offered King to commit a suicide as an alternative to his exposure as having extramarital affairs. When threats to ruining his reputation failed and King refused to cooperate, he was murdered while planning a national occupation of Washington, D.C in 1968, titled the Poor People's Campaign.

Other methods of neutralizing progressive movements besides the discussed assassinations and imprisonment include wracking of the careers of political activists, intimidation, and bribery. Such is the case of Angela Davis, a scholar who became popular after her successful self-defense in court. Davis was a vocal supporter of the BPP, anti-racial activist, feminist and author. In 1970, she became involved in a notorious case of a hostage situation led by the BPP in an attempt to free three African American prisoners accused of

---

[229] Ibid.

murdering a guard. Ultimately, after going underground and entering the FBI's ten Most Wanted Fugitives list, and after over a year in prison, Davis was acquitted of all charges in 1972. There has been a strong social movement in her defense led by John Lennon, Yoko Ono, and help from the United Presbyterian Church, a dairy farmer, a businessman, and a defense attorney, who paid her bail and court fees. During the same time, because of her political views, she was denied a renewal of her appointment as a lecturer in philosophy at the University of California, LA, with the active help of then Governor Ronald Reagan. Davis remains a controversial figure as she supports the Boycott, Divestment, and Sanctions (BDS) campaign for boycotting Israel for their human rights abuse of Palestinians. As discussed in Chapter Five, academia is complicit in sanctioning scholars who do not hold orthodox political views. Davis's Fred Shuttlesworth Human Rights Award granted by the Birmingham Civil Rights Institute (BCRI) was rescinded in 2019 with the justification of "not meeting all the criteria." More specifically, Birmingham Mayor Randal Woodfin and other members criticized Davis for her active support of Palestinian rights.

Inversely, feminist organizations such as the National Organization for Women (NOW) or the National Women's Political Caucus were moderate institutions that worked within the political system and did not pose a threat to the status quo. For this and other reasons, such organizations still exist and are praised occasionally by the media as powerful and progressive precisely because of their ineffectiveness. They stand for cosmetic changes instead of fundamental reforms and occasionally install female leaders who support patriarchy. For example, feminist icon and founder of the National Women's Political Caucus Gloria Steinem was recruited by the CIA in the 1960s, revealed in an interview with the *NYT* in 1967.[230] According to the interview, the Independent Research Service foundation as well as the National Student Association were funded by the CIA.[231] Steinem noted that she worked full time for the Independent Research Service from 1958 to 1962, and added, "The CIA's big mistake was not supplanting itself with private funds fast enough."[232] Perhaps Steinem's image as a feminist icon and her influence as a writer prompted the agency to recruit her. Most importantly, Steinem was an anti-war activist and opposed the Vietnam war. The important

---

[230] Johnny Cirucci, "CIA Subsidized Festival Trips: Hundreds of Students Were Sent to World Gatherings," *The New York Times,* Feb. 21, 1967.
[231] Ibid.
[232] Ibid.

logical deduction from the events of the 1960s is that the neutralization of progressive movements such as the anti-racial and gender emancipation uprisings was achieved through subversive methods that effectively eliminated them. Some of the government methods include infiltrating the organizations, blackmailing their leaders and eventually assassinating them when everything else fails. The trend continues in modern times, as evident in the movements of the 21st century such as Black Lives Matter and #MeToo.

Black Lives Matter movement began in 2013 as a response to the acquittal of George Zimmerman for shooting dead a 17-year-old unarmed African American, Travon Martin. Protests with hashtag #BlackLivesMatter erupted all over the country in 2015, when more police executions resulting in the deaths of unarmed black citizens were revealed. Some of the high-profile victims killed by the police are Michael Brown (18) in Ferguson, MO; Eric Gardner (43) in NYC, NY; Tamir Rice (12) in Cleveland, OH; and Laquan McDonald (17) in Chicago, MI, among the thousands of black people murdered every year. Trevon Martin was a teenager who was going home in Sanford, FL, when an armed neighborhood watch volunteer started following him, called 911, and continued to chase Martin against the advice of the police operator. After getting in an argument with Martin, Zimmerman shot dead the teenager. The other cases resemble Trevon Martin's fatal shooting – Michael Brown was stopped by the police for jaywalking in a quiet street in Ferguson, and after the officer chased him down the street and open fire at him, Brown stopped, raised his hands, and turned around, then was shot dead. Of the 12 bullets shot, 6 were fatal, all of them from the front. Eric Gardner was confronted by NYPD officers for celling cigarettes without permit and was choked to death in a prohibited chokehold amidst his repeated pleads that he cannot breathe. In the case of the 12-year-old African American Tamir Rice, the boy was playing with a toy gun in a Cleveland Park when two officers, responding to a 911 call, shot him from their vehicle 30 yards away, seconds after arriving at the scene. In the case of Laquan McDonald, he was shot dead with 16 bullets after he was stopped while walking away from the police car in the streets of Chicago.

With the exception of the last case, none of the police officers were charged by the courts for their slaughter of innocent black children, teenagers, and adults. The reason these cases are even known to the public is that bystanders took videos of the murders, or in the case of McDonald, the judge ordered the police to turn in the dashboard camera video record after 13 months of protests in Chicago and around the country. During the protests accompanying all the public executions of black people by the police, some of the last words of the victims became slogans of the Black Lives Matter movement. Some examples include "Hands Up! Don't Shoot!" associated with Michael Brown, "Can't Breathe!" repeated 11 times by Eric Gardner while held in a chokehold by an officer who was never indicted by the Richmond Grand Jury or any other legal procedure.

According to the *Statista*, a German company that covers statistics for 170 industries and over 160 countries, between 2017 and 2020, the US police have murdered 3986 people, an average of 996.5 per year.[233] The number of murdered people has been increasing every year, reaching 1,004 in 2020.[234] In comparison, in the UK during a period of 15 years between 2004/5 and 2018/19 there were 40 people killed by the police, averaging 2.6 per year.[235] The cases of mass murder by the police are very common in the US judicial system and have been happening for decades without media coverage or public awareness. The reason this discussion is happening now is the digital technology, which allows bystanders to take videos of the acts of police brutality. Thanks to the iPhones' cameras, these cases become high-profile sensations on social media that sparked massive protests. After years of covering up and coordinated false police testimony with the cooperation of the judicial system, now video records released by witnesses become public and are seen by millions around the world. As a result, the courts are compelled to indict crimes previously denied routinely by the police during investigations.

The culmination of the public outrage came during the pandemic lockdowns in 2020 when another black man, George Floyd, was executed cold-bloodedly by a police officer in Minneapolis, MN. Allegedly, Floyd's crime was trying to use a counterfeit bill of $20. The policeman murdered him slowly by placing his knee on Floyd neck for nine minutes until the man took his last breath. The video record taken by a bystander shook the world – it was clear that the officer knew he was been video-taped and still publicly lynched the man in the midst of his pleads for mercy and the outrage of the crowd around him.[236] Regardless of the lies and justifications of the police, initially supported by the mainstream media, the recorded murder went viral

---

[233] https://www.statista.com/statistics/585152/people-shot-to-death-by-us-police-by-race/
[234] Ibid.
[235] https://www.statista.com/statistics/319246/police-fatal-shootings-england-wales/
[236] Although the names of the officers are public record, I do not popularize their names on purpose because my emphasis is on holding responsible the system and the institutions not individuals.

on social media and people were appalled. Protests erupted for months and Black Lives Matter movement was revived and became widely popular. For the first time, white and black people in all 50 US states and all over the world protested together in defense of black lives. In some states and towns with predominantly white population, people were out in the streets in huge numbers protesting in solidarity with black people. George Floyd became a symbol for all brutalized people of color who suffer racial discrimination and the epitome of people's struggle for justice. The slogan "No Justice, No Peace" was commonly heard during the series of protests in 2,000 cities and towns in the US, and in over 60 countries around the world.[237] According to polls, in the summer of 2020 between 15 million and 26 million people had participated in demonstrations making the protests the largest in US history.[238]

At the movement's apogee, the process of coopting and neutralizing began. Giant corporations such as Amazon, Walmart, Google, and Meta, quickly adopted the language of the protesters and started an op-ed commercial campaign that performed lip service to Black Lives Matter movement. The companies posted emblems and symbols on their walls, and plastered their headquarters with signs in support of BLM. These actions were prompted not only by fear of the masses, who for the first time in many years realized that they are many and have the power, but also by the goal of corrupting the movement. Politicians pretending to be on the left were equally fast to announce their support for the movement. Democrats in Congress worn Ghana's kente garb while kneeling in the most ritualistic display of ignorance and hypocrisy. The use of Africans and African culture as props to deflect criticism from their uselessness to African Americans is very common in politics. Because Republicans were against the BLM movement, by making it partisan, the politicians severely eroded it. Coopting a massive movement by a party that doesn't represent it, defies the rule that police brutality should be beyond political party struggles. The Republicans denounced the movement, and selectively showed random acts of violence or looting to justify their opposition. In contrast, the Democrats flaunted their fake support of the movement, hoping to be elected again. The Democrats also assumed that people will not remember that the movement started in the beginning of

---

[237] Richard Luscombe, and Vivian Ho, "George Floyd Protests Enter Third Week as Push for Change Sweeps America," *The Guardian,* June 7, 2020.

[238] Larry Buchanan, Quoting Bui and Jugal Patel, "Black Lives Matter May Be the Largest Movement in US History," *The New York Times,* July 3, 2020.

Obama's second term and that multiple murders of black teens and children happened during the first black president who literary did nothing to prevent it. While his party held super majority in Congress, and they dominated in all three branches of the government, Obama did nothing to stop police brutality.

Additionally, for the first time, white innocent people experienced massive police brutality as the cops crack their heads and drew blood with buttons and rubber bullets. Similarly to the Occupy Wall Street, the law enforcement's response to the peaceful protests in 2020 was brutalizing and arresting demonstrators, proving that the main function of the police is to protect the ruling class. According to ABC News, there were 14,000 arrests in 49 cities in the US during the first month of Floyd's death.[239] During this time, BLM became immensely popular at home and abroad, averaging millions of demonstrators and social media activists sending nearly 48M tweets by June of 2020.[240] However, the movement has been compromised since large corporations including Amazon, Walmart, Google, Meta, and Netflix, started coopting it in order to divert real changes and replace them with superficial rhetoric and slogans.[241] To this day, the movement is systematically corrupted by BLM-themed corporate advertisement, and reports about abuse of donation money in the realm of millions started surfacing the media.

The last movement analyzed in this chapter is #MeToo, which confronts sexual harassment, sexual abuse, and rape culture by publicizing and condemning such acts. It was initiated in 2006 by Tarana Burke, a black woman from Alabama, with the intent of exposing such misconduct and supporting the survivors with empathy and solidarity. More importantly, the movement's goal was to empower survivors of sexual assault by demonstrating their vast numbers and providing support for them. In her speech in 2007 titled "Me Too," Burke publicly discussed the issue of sexual harassment, something not very common during this time.[242] Burke's initiative was repeated more than a decade later in 2017, and popularized by actress Alyssa

---

[239] Emily Olson, "Antifa, Boogaloo Boys, White Nationalists: Which Extremists Showed Up to the US Black Lives Matter Protests?" *ABC News*, Australian Broadcasting Corporation, June 27, 2020.

[240] Anderson, Monica, Skye Toor, Lee Raine, Aaron Smith, *Pew Research Center*, July 11, 2018. "2. An analysis of #BlackLivesMatter and other Twitter hashtags related to political or social issues". Pew Research Center: Internet, Science & Tech.

[241] Megan Ming Frances, "The Price of Civil Rights: Black Lives, White Funding, and Movement Capture," *Law and Society*, Jan. 29, 2019.

[242] Laurie Penny, "We Are Not Done Here," *Longreads*, Jan 2018.

Milano who invited all women who had experienced sexual harassment to answer her hashtag on Twitter with a simple phrase "Me too." Milano had over 30,000 responses in the first 12 hours including high profile Hollywood actresses, unknown workers, and housewives.[243] CNN reported next day that in 24 hours, 4.7 million people used the phrase "Me too" on Facebook in a total of 12 million posts.[244] Apparently, it took digital technology and someone famous such as actress Milano with 3.4 million followers on Twitter to transform Burke's initiative into a massive movement. Such popularity illustrates the depth and the scope of the abuse and demonstrates that the waves of victims reached their turning point and are determined to rise from obscurity.

The initial impact of the movement was promising. Tarana Burke proposed valuable changes for safety in work places and schools. For example, processing all untested rape kits, examining local school policies, improving the vetting of teachers, and updating sexual harassment policies. Burke also called for all professionals who work with children to be fingerprinted and subjected to background check before being hired. Similarly, Milano suggested in 2017 that changing protocols would protect victims of harassment from retaliation when filing complaints. She supported legislation that makes it difficult for publicly trading companies to hide cover-up payments and prohibits signing non-disclosure agreement with employees. Other suggestions include the idea promoted by gender analyst Anna North that sexual harassment should be addressed as a labor issue due to the economic disadvantages of reporting such behavior. In addition, North proposed addressing power imbalances by raising the tipped minimum wage and providing protection such as "panic buttons" that could be used by victims of assault on the job.

However, very few of these practical suggestions were transformed into legislations. For example, after five years of debates, Congress finally passed in Feb 2022 ME TOO Congress Act proposed in 2017 by Jackie Speier. The bill prohibits any settlement to be paid by federal tax funds and requires Representatives and Senators to pay for their harassment settlements. Furthermore, 19 states have enacted more than 200 new sexual harassment protective bills. Another result of the movement was the very public class-action lawsuit against Hollywood producer Harvey Weinstein who was found

---

[243] "Alyssa Milano's #MeToo Tweet on Sexual Harassment Gets Thousands of Replies," *Sky News,* Oct 17, 2017.

[244] Lisa Raspers France, "#MeToo: Social Media Flooded with Personal Stories of Assault," *CNN,* October 16, 2017.

guilty of systemic rape. The lawsuit started when actress Rose McGowan made public her accusation, followed by more than 300 women. The extensive media coverage led to many more accusations of high-profile men in powerful positions in all fields and professions, and became a global trend known as "the Weinstein effect." According to the *NYT*, 201 prominent men lost their jobs as a result of public allegations of sexual harassment.[245] In addition to Hollywood, #MeToo movement impacted the music and entertainment industry, science, academia, politics, and cable news media.

However, despite the initial domino effect of the anti-harassment movement, it backlashed soon and powerful corporations and political organizations started the corruption, cooption and suppression of the leaders of the movement. As in the case of BLM, the first step in the process of neutralization was to make the movement highly partisan. For example, the leadership presented by Milano consisted of active supporters of the Democratic party, and gradually became an arm of the party in the course of coopting it. This resulted in prosecuting only men with ties to the opposite Republican party. Such policies were evident in the procedure of evaluating Justice Brett Cavanaugh's nomination for the Supreme Court in 2018. During the hearings, Cavanaugh was accused of sexual harassment by a college associate, Christine B. Ford. The mainstream left media unanimously supported the accusations and reported it incessantly; whereas the conservative media defended him uncritically. In contrast, when prominent Democrats were accused of sexual harassment, #MeToo took the side of the abusers and mercilessly smeared the victims.

In 2019, former Senate aid Tara Reade accused candidate President Joe Biden of sexual harassment during her time in the Senate. To get legal help, Reade reached out to Time's Up, established with the purpose of helping survivors of sexual assault by raising funds for PR and subsidize legal assistance to #MeToo victims. Reade was denied support because Biden was a federal candidate and assisting a case against him could jeopardize the organization's nonprofit status. In addition, *Vice News Time* reported in 2021, that "The leaders of Time's Up had sacrificed sexual misconduct survivors, and their allies, in favor of preserving their proximity to power."[246] The magazine show-

---

[245] Audrey Carlsen, Maya Salam, Claire Cain Miller, Denise Lu, Ash Ngu, Jugal K Patel, and Zach Wichter, "#MeToo Brought Down 201 Powerful Men: Nearly Half of Their Replacement Are Women," *The NYT*, Oct. 23, 2018.

[246] Carter Sherman, "How Time's Up Failed Sexual Survivors and Cozied Up to Power," *Vice News,* Sept. 1, 2021.

cased stifled allegations against Governor Andrew Cuomo of NY.[247] Inversely, the organization was very active during Cavanaugh's scandal and didn't have scruples to support a victim against a federal appointee. Furthermore, the public relations firm that works on behalf of Times Up Legal Defense Fund had a managing director Anita Dunn, who is now senior adviser to President Biden, demonstrating once again the revolving door of power. Reade exposes the hypocrisy of #MeToo and the smear campaign against her after her revelations in her 2021 book *Left Out: When the Truth Doesn't Fit In.*

According to the *CUT*, at least seven other women accused Biden of inappropriate sexual behavior.[248] In contrast, *Time* magazine, *Forbes*, *Politico*, *Washington Post*, and the *NYT*, used their platforms to discredit Reade and to undermine her accusations. Headlines such as "'Manipulative, Deceitful, User': Tara Reade Left a Trail of Aggrieved Acquaintances" imply that Reade had alternative motives and fraudulent character without serious evidence.[249] The couple interviewed in the article were former landlords that complained about Reade's financial struggle with the rent and being late in payments – hardly serious evidence for such strong accusations. In September 2020, the *NYT* published an article, titled "Examining Tara Reade's Sexual Assault Allegation against Joe Biden," which focuses only on the side of the accused and sites a slew of witnesses in Biden's favor against Reade's point of view.[250]

In her book, Reade explains the synchronized campaign against her including cooperation between the movement's leadership and the media. When she asked for help the Time's Up Legal Fund, which pledged to support the #MeToo survivors with funds and bona fide lawyers, she was turned down. Similarly, when she contacted several media outlets, they didn't return her calls. Only after some independent digital media journalists such as Kate Helper and Megyn Kelley interviewed Reade and published their conversations on social media, Reade was subjected to a series of biased, demeaning phone interviews as the mainstream media continued to ignore her story. Reade reveals what happened between her and Biden in the interviews with the former, as well in her 2021 book. Reade's book was forwarded by actress Rose

---

[247] Ibid.

[248] Amanda Arnold and Claire Lampen, "All the Women Who Have Spoken Out Against Joe Biden," *Mass Central Media, Facebook*, April 12, 2020.

[249] Natasha Korecki, "'Manipulative, Deceitful, User': Tara Reade Left a Trail of Aggrieved Acquaintances," *Politico*, May 15, 2020.

[250] Kate Conger and Rachel Shorey, "Examining the Allegation against Joe Biden," *NYT*, Oct 28, 2020.

McGowan who fully supported Reade and revealed her similar experience of smear campaigns orchestrated by Harvey Weinstein. According to McGowan,

> By speaking up on behalf of Tara, I have been blackballed by so many including *The New York Times,* whom I helped win a Pulitzer Prize. Fake news isn't only what's written, it's what's purposely omitted. When it comes to observing the cabal of liberal media titans working against Tara, the only word that comes to mind is sad. I used to believe they were the good guys, just as I used to believe the Democrats were. After one call from Hilary Clinton's spokesman to NBC News executives, an expose of my own rapist was shut down. I know who is colliding with whom, and why. By witnessing the vitriol aimed at Tara by all too many on the left, it has cemented for me the fact that they can be just as foul as the worst of those on the Right. The delusion millions of Democrats seem to have, is that by being "liberal," they are exempt from being bad humans. What a long con this two-party system has run on the American public. What a long con people have run on themselves.[251]

McGowan refers to her ordeal with the media, and secret services after she publicly accused Weinstein in sexual assault in 1997. Investigative reporter Ronald Farrow describes the process in his 2019 book *Catch and Kill: Lies, Spies, and a Conspiracy to Protect Predators*[252] published in consecutive series in the *New Yorker*. In an interview with *The Guardian,* McGowan explains that she called the *NYT* and blew the whistle on Weinstein, for which the newspaper received a Pulitzer Prize mentioned in the Forward of Reade's book.[253] The story of Tara Reade is the epitome of the corruption of the #MeeToo Movement. It has been coopted by the Democratic Party machine, effectively managed by Hilary Clinton. During the Presidency of her husband Bill Clinton, she was notorious with her smear campaigns against the victims of Bill Clinton's harassment, for which he was impeached. Back in the 1990s,

---

[251] Tara Reade, *Left Out: When the Truth Doesn't Fit In,* Los Angeles: TV Guestpert Publishing, 2021, xi.
[252] Ronan Farrow, *Catch and Kill,* Boston: Little, Brown, and Co, Oct 15, 2019.
[253] Evan Real, "Rose McGowan Rips NYTimes, Claims She was the First to Speak Out in #MeToo Movement," *The Guardian,* July 1, 2019.

Hilary had to eliminate many women who filed complaints against her husband including Monica Lewinsky, Juanita Broaddrick, Lesley Millwee, Paula Jones, and Kathleen Willey, among others. The same procedure was used in these cases: scrutinizing the lives of the accusers and trying to discredit their characters, careers, and testimonies.

After turning Reade down, Alysa Milano, a celebrity champion of #MeToo, made a statement: "The allegations against Joe Biden concern me, deeply. He is a man I know, respect, and admire, and who I can't picture doing any of the things of which he is accused."[254] The apparent controversy of double standard was revealed by Milano who plead that all women should be trusted, and later backtracked her previous statements. Conservative magazine *National Review* published an article reflecting this hypocrisy, titled "Alysa Milano Ties Herself Up in Knots."[255] In the article, the author contrasts the stand Milano took in 2018 against conservative Justice Kavanaugh regarding allegations against him, when she supported the victim on the grounds that we should "believe all women," to her current stand in favor of Biden.[256] The author points out that the change of heart Milano and the organization had, is necessary to weaponize the movement and use women's allegations when it is politically expedient.

Similarly, Tara Reade concludes in her book, "What I learned is that #BelieveAllWomen is a hashtag that did not include me because I accused a Democrat."[257] Reade was not alone in her rejection by the Time's Up Legal Defense Fund. Several other women, interviewed by *Vice News* shared their experience of receiving lackluster or no response from the Foundation. Some of the cases include involvement in government agency run by a Democrat, excuses about statute of limitation, and list of attorneys not authorized for the specific state of the survivors, or not calling back the victims. Although the focus of this chapter is on the Democratic party because of their ties to BLM and #MeToo movements, it is worth noting that the Republican Party uses identical tactics and partisanship, always defending their accused leaders and pointing only to the crimes across the aisle. This is why both parties are elitist and useless when it comes to working in the interest of regular people. Unfortunately, the propaganda machine of the mainstream media works

---

[254] Alysa Milano, "Living in the Gray as a Woman," *Deadline,* April 29, 2020.
[255] Alexandra DeSanctis, "Alysa Milano Ties Herself in a Knot," *National Review,* April 30, 2020.
[256] Ibid.
[257] Reade, 15.

tirelessly to brainwash the population in hating each other and constantly pitting supporters of either party against each other. The media and the ruling class know perfectly well that if both camps unite, they comprise 99 percent of the country and thus, will bring the end of the elites.

This is a serious enough reason to produce the hard work of diminishing movements such as BLM, #MeToo, and previously the Civil Rights Movements of the 1960s. Nothing fundamentally had changed since then – the demands for economic, political, and social equality is the same, the struggle against wars, racial and gender discrimination is the same, and the four estates of power still work together against most regular people. The executives in the White House, the legislators in Congress, the Judicial system, and the mainstream media still work in unison as they did in the 1960s. Despite what they want you to believe, very little progress has been made in the last decades besides the rhetoric. To the contrary, we even have regressed since the 1960s, because the inequality gap approaches that of the 1930s, the time of the Great Depression. The only difference is in the decline of the press, or the fourth estate, whose job is to keep in check the powerful. While back in the 1930s, the few corporate magnates were called "robber barons" and caricatures of their grotesque images were widely spread in the mainstream media, now the fourth estate glorifies their personalities. Moreover, false stories about the origins of the billionaires' wealth are diligently told on their platforms, claiming that they started "from scratch" in their own garages. Consistently, the "self-made" billionaires are worshipped by the media, and routinely asked for advice on topics that are out of their expertise such medicine, agriculture, and politics.

Wealthy people like Amazon's Jeff Bezos, Microsoft's Bill Gates, Tesla's Elon Musk, and Meta's Mark Zuckerberg among others are touted as experts on every topic by virtue of being the top richest people in the world. For example, Gates, Musk, and Zuckerberg are college drop-outs, and Bezos have an engineering degree conferred to him, not earned, yet they are revered as geniuses. The companies they own would have been complete failures both from financial and humane perspectives, if it was not for government subsidies, mostly Pentagon contracts. In addition, complete monopoly and lack of competition, merciless exploitation of workers, outsourcing production and services in third-world countries prevent their corporations from bankrupting. As discussed in more detail in Chapter Three, Amazon and Tesla have multi-million annual contracts with the Pentagon, which make these companies effectively working for the military industrial complex. Furthermore, they are reworded by the government for spying on its citizens through technology and internet devices, which makes them contractors for the secret services. They focus their spying algorithms on progressive movements such as the ones we discussed in this chapter, and submit the results to the government. This is the subversive way of eliminating the movements' leaders if they refuse to be compromised.

Billionaires such as Bill Gates operate similarly blurring the lines between the government and private business. Gates investments in pharmaceutical companies, the World Health Organization, and global media, wields him unique power with more influence on policies than governments. More specifically, Gates' investments in vaccines and computer software reveal his role in the global pandemic measures when he profited not only from the medicine, but from the lockdowns because of the imposed massive use of his digital programs and products. However, his focus shifted to the pharmaceutical industry, influencing media, and buying farm land; therefore, Gates disassociated himself from Microsoft in the beginning of the pandemic, in March 2020, when he left his seat as board director. Similarly, Jeff Bezos stepped down as CEO of Amazon in July 2021 after more than a year of massive protests of Amazon workers all over the US and abroad. Workers protested the poor working conditions, poverty wages and unsafe practices during the pandemic. Perhaps demonstrators' setting up a guillotine outside Bezos' mansion in Seattle influenced his decision to resign and avoid such negative attention.[258] Mark Zuckerberg, the owner of the largest global social network Facebook, has similar ties with the government and is rewarded for selling private information of his billions of users. Zuckerberg had to change the name of his company to Meta because it became extremely notorious with its abusive and addictive content, censorship, and advertisements targeting children.

A powerful demonstration of the effect of private corporations spying on their customers on behalf of the government was continuously revealed by journalist Julian Assange through Wiki Leaks since 2008. Assange is a somber example of the fate reserved for those who publicize government misdeeds. Assange was spied on for years until he was finally arrested under the Espionage Act. It has been revealed in 2021 by Yahoo News, that the CIA plotted to assassinate Assange in 2017, but opted out because it was

---

[258] Aaron Holmes, "Protesters Set Up a Guillotine Outside Bezos' Mansion and Demanded Higher Wages for Amazon Workers after the CEO's Net worth Surpassed $200 Billion," *Business Insider*, Aug. 27, 2020.

too dangerous to execute the operation in a crowded city like London where he resided.[259] After CIA Director Mike Pompeo publicly declared Assange as "non-state hostile intelligence service," later in his capacity of Secretary of State, he and other government executives plotted to murder him.[260] More recently, in 2022, US lawyers, journalists, and doctors filed a lawsuit against the CIA and Mike Pompeo for violating their constitutional rights while visiting Assange at the Ecuadorian Embassy in London.[261] The lawsuit claims that over 100 US visitors to the Embassy were required to surrender their electronic devices before they were allowed to see Assange, and their legal representatives report that there is strong circumstantial evidence that staff working for the security company Undercover Global S.L. copied their electronic information on behalf of the CIA.[262]

The common mechanism of changing corporate names or companies' leaders resigning is used by giant corporations with ruined reputations. As a result of massive public pushback, companies switch names and continue quietly their illegal activities. For example, Monsanto, which is well-known for using toxic products that cause cancer, and for imposing genetically modified seeds (GMOs) on global markets, was gradually banned in Europe, China, India, and Canada. As a result, Monsanto recently changed its name to Baer when merged with the pharmaceutical company. The banning of Monsanto happened because of popular movements in these countries against the use of GMOs. When similar movements against Monsanto increased in the USA and threatened to result in Monsanto's ban, the company merged with Baer. They will continue the same unpopular practices stealthily, under a new name, to avoid protests and lawsuits. Monsanto, Meta, and perhaps soon Amazon presume that it will take a while before a new movement gains a momentum, and if it happens, the "new" company will use the government, the secret services, and the media to crush it, and the process will have to start all over again.

---

[259] Zack Dorfman, Sean D. Naylor, and Michael Isikoff, "Kidnapping, Assassination, and London shoot-out: Inside the CIA Secret War against Wiki Leaks," *Yahoo News*, Sept 26, 2021.
[260] Ibid.
[261] Kanishka Singh, "CIA Sued Over Alleged Spying on Lawyers, Journalists Wo Met Assange," *Reuters*, August 15, 2022.
[262] Ibid.

Chapter Seven

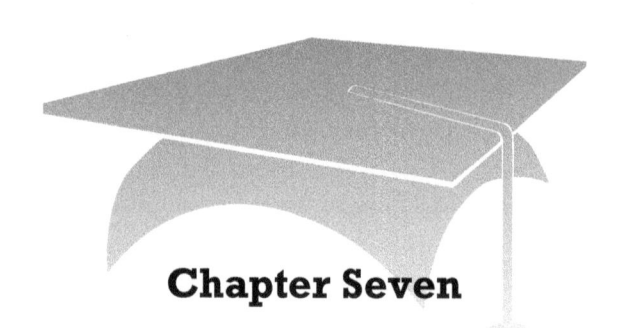

The Climate Change Disaster: From the Oil Industry Sabotage to the New Green Deal Profiteers, No One Has the Wellbeing of Species in Mind

And you are not going to be able to just switch to battery operated vehicles or wind for your electricity. And just having this conversation around why that's not possible in the next ten years is critically important to the work we do.
~Keith McCoy, Senior Exxon Mobil Lobbyist

In January 2021, *Channel 4 News* released a video that went viral, where a senior Exxon Mobil lobbyist reveals how the oil giant announces publicly its support for carbon taxes while making sure that it would never happen. Greenpeace Unearthed, a UK located environmental organization, posing as a hiring agent in a job interview, reveals Exxon Mobil's lobbying strategies. Keith McCoy, the senior lobbyist for Exxon Mobil, believing that the interviewers were hunting for talent, shares with the activists the names of Congressmen bought by his company, and brags about their aggressive promotion of legislations against science that will destroy the environment.[263] McCoy details the company's strategy for stifling the debate about harming

---

[263] Alex Thomson, "Exxon Mobil Lobbyist Reveals Company's Involvement with 'Forever Chemicals,'" *Channel 4 News*, July 1, 2021.

the environment through Exxon Mobil's production including manufacturing PFAS (Per-and Polyfluoroalkyl Substances) known as "forever chemicals." Once released, the PFAS cannot be cleaned; therefore, poison the water and the soil, which lead to cancer, hormone disruption and weakened immunity.[264] In the covertly recorded conversation, McCoy claimed:

> We manufacture PFAS, the chemical. We use it in our firefighting equipment. So, we have pushed our associations to be out front on that…You know all these people have been working on this issue and then you have a member of Congress that has a bill who has been pushing and pushing for this bill. Then all of a sudden you know; they start talking about how this is an Exxon Mobil chemical and Exxon Mobil is poisoning our waterways; the debate is pretty much over.[265]

Similarly, McCoy's response to the concern over plastic pollution was not only that his company sees the plastics as huge growing business but as "the future." He explains that the strategy is to condition people to think that it is not possible to change everything instantly, and it is a long process, among other reasons for objections and the longer this discussion continues the better for Exxon. In McCoy's own words "And just having this conversation around why that's not possible in the next ten years is critically important to the work we do."[266] McCoy underlines how prolong discussions about measures benefit Exxon, while actions are harmful for the company's profit, especially government regulations. In McCoy's opinion, "Once there starts to be government intervention you lose control. You lose control over your business. You lose control over the narrative. You just lose control."[267] The official response from the Exxon's CEO Darren Woods to this video was to issue a statement claiming that McCoy does not represent the company and their views on the environment.[268] Mr. Woods replaced the former CEO, Rex Tillerson, after his appointment as Secretary of State for Trump's cabinet in 2016. Tillerson worked for Exxon since 1975, and he is invested in the

---

[264] Ibid.
[265] Ibid.
[266] Ibid.
[267] Ibid.
[268] Ibid.

company's profit, which makes him unfit for the position of Secretary of State because of an obvious conflict of interest.

For decades, the strategy for Exxon and other oil and gas companies has been to deny and disseminate doubt about the findings of science on climate change. *The Guardian* reported last year that an increasing number of lawsuits against petroleum companies are being filed on the grounds of purposeful deceit and cover up the growing threat to life caused by their products.[269] According to the outlet, after centuries of wielding extraordinary economic and political power, the giant industry finally faces consequences for driving the greatest climate crisis in the history of humans. The wave of lawsuits filed by cities and states across the US accuse the industry of being responsible for the destruction of crops and homes by mega-rains, loss of fish in warming waters, coastal cities' loss of property because of the rising sea, and wildfires among others. The most powerful claim is that the industry "severely aggravated the environmental crisis with a decades-long campaign of lies and deceit to suppress warnings from their own scientists about the impact of fossil fuels on the climate and dupe American public."[270]

According to the documents, as early as 1958, oil company Shell's executive Charles Jones presented a paper to the American Petroleum Institute (API) warning about the increased carbon emissions from car exhaust.[271] Other research through the 1960s led to the White House advisory committee to express concern about measurable changes in climate by 2000.[272] The largest oil company in the US, Exxon Mobil, concluded in their own research year after year that the danger is so serious that in 1978 their science adviser, James Black warned that there is "a window of five to ten years before the need for hard decisions regarding changes in energy strategy might become critical."[273] Despite the hard data from the industry's own scientists, they chose to hide it from the public and the legislators.

Instead, the industry launched a massive campaign led by Exxon Mobil, Chevron, Shell, and BP against the unanimous scientific opinion. A leaked document dated April 3, 1998, titled "Global Science Communication: Action Plan," published by *The Guardian,* shows a nine-page plan to counter

---

[269] Chris McGreal, "Big Oil and Gas Kept Dirty Secret for Decades. Now They May Pay the Price," *The Guardian,* June 30, 2021.
[270] Ibid.
[271] Ibid.
[272] Ibid.
[273] Ibid.

the science on climate change and blatantly deceive the public.[274] Among the five points victory goals were: Making sure that average citizens "understand" [quotation marks in the original] uncertainties in climate science; Media "understands" [quotation marks in the original] uncertainties in climate science; Media coverage reflects the balance and validates the viewpoints that challenge the current "conventional wisdom;" Industry's senior leaders understand the uncertainties of climate science, which makes them stronger ambassadors for shaping climate policies in a certain way; Make the promoters of Kyoto Treaty appear out of touch with reality.

The major encompassing goal combining all five points, was to make climate change a non-issue, as defined under the title "Current Reality" of the document. The previous title was "Situation Analysis," and the following titles were "Strategies and Tactics," and "Measurements." The assigned budget for influencing the media was $600,000 plus paid advertising. Allocated for Global Climate Science Data Center was $5,000,000, and for the National Direct Outreach Program - $2,000,000. The Action Plan was addressed to "Global Climate Science Team," forwarded to Michelle Ross and Susan Moya, and the email signed by Joseph L. Walker, public relations representative for the American Petroleum Institute.[275] As stated in the document, the fossil fuel industry worked toward the goal of shifting public attention away from the imminent climate crisis. In addition, the industry used its massive profits to pour billions of dollars into political lobbying to block measures against pollution.

Moreover, the industry funded front organizations with neutral or scientific-sounding names who worked on its behalf. For example, one such front organization was the Global Climate Coalition (GCC) used by President George W. Bush to reject the Kyoto protocol, mentioned in the Action Plan.[276] Furthermore, *The Guardian* exposes the fact that Exxon Mobil alone has funded more than 40 groups to deny climate science including GCC, Partnership for Better Energy Future, Coalition for American Jobs, Alliance for Energy and Economic Growth, and Alliance for Climate Strategies. In 2019, Martin Hoffert, a New York University professor of physics and a consultant to Exxon Mobil on climate modeling in the 1980s, testified in a

---

[274] Joe Walker, "Global Science Communication: Action Plan," April 3, 1998. http://www.sourcewatch.org
[275] Ibid.
[276] Ibid.

Congressional hearing that "They deliberately created doubt when internal research confirmed how serious a threat it was."[277]

According to the same hearing, the timeline of Exxon's knowledge of the scientific consensus on the climate change leads back to 1977, when Exxon Scientist James Black told the company's top executives that fossil fuel usage was releasing enough carbon dioxide to change the planet's climate. In 1979, an internal memo of the company stated that the buildup of CO2 in the atmosphere "could bring about dramatic changes in the environment," and in a memo from 1981, Exxon executive Roger Cohen warned against understating the threat to our planet because rising the temperature could "produce catastrophic effects."

During the hearing, Chairman Jamie Raskin enunciated:

> When faced with the reality of the massive damage fossil fuels were likely to cause, Exxon could have chosen to present this truth to the American public, redirect its own research and resources, and lead the way to a global shift toward alternative energy sources. But this is not the path Exxon chose. Instead, it sold off its renewable energy companies. Like Shell and Mobil, it launched an extensive and sinister campaign of climate denial, undermining the work and warnings of its own scientists.
>
> To make matters worse, big oil companies fortified their own infrastructure against climate change, factoring in the anticipated rise in temperature and sea levels when deciding how and where to build their own infrastructure.
>
> This revealing course of conduct simply gives the game away. They used their knowledge of climate change to protect their future profits, while preventing the American people from acting together to protect our collective future. They used their knowledge of climate change for purposes of corporate planning, but publicly denied the reality of climate change for purposes of national planning.[278]

---

[277] *House Hearing, 116 Congress,* "Examining the Oil Industry's Efforts to Suppress the Truth about Climate Change," Hearing before the Subcommittee on Civil Rights and Civil Liberties of the Committee on Oversight and Reform, Oct 23, 2019.

[278] Ibid.

However, two-year research conducted by the Energy and Environmental Reporting Project published in 2015 by the Columbia Journalism School in cooperation with *The Loss Angeles Times* and *The Guardian,* raises the question: Why the mainstream media and Congress waited for so many years to take this information seriously and to publicize it appropriately? According to the investigation led by Susanne Rust,

> Our reporting shows the company has been aware of climate change risks since the 1980s. Company officials were concerned enough about these risks to incorporate engineering safeguards against rising seas and thawing permafrost into the design of pipelines, near-shore facilities and offshore rigs as far back as the 1990s. As the nation is now likely to back out the Paris Climate Accord, the battleground will likely shift to shareholders of companies such as Exxon Mobil, who are demanding accountability, transparency and action.[279]

In 1988, NASA scientist James Hansen, director of Goddard Institute for Space Studies, testified before the Senate's Committee on Energy and Natural Resources, warning that climate change is already large enough to cause extreme weather events, and with 99 percent certainty is caused by human activity. The alarm was significant enough to make headlines in the media and to prompt the founding of the International Panel on Climate Change (IPCC) the same year, which collected and studied massive data on the patterns of global climate with the participation of 195 countries. The same organization released an alarming report in November 2018, stating that we only have 12 years to change the global warming effects; after which the process would be irreversible.[280] The last IPCC report released in Jan 2022, confirms the findings of the previous and counts only eight years for climate crisis measures.

Ironically, the Paris Climate Accord from 2017 did not call for sufficient actions and according to some scholars, was weak. In Dec 2017, the agreement was signed by 190 countries, although some of them withdrew later including the US. The goal of the summit was to keep the average global temperature

---

[279] Ibid.
[280] http://www.ipcc.ch/2018/10/08/summary-for-policymakers-of-ipcc-special-report-on-global-warming-of-1-5c-approved-by-governments-ipcc

increase below 2 degree C, and to achieve net zero carbon emissions by 2050. Alarmingly, there is no legal obligation for the countries who signed the agreement. If we compare the three existing climate agreements so far, the Kyoto Protocol from 1997 was more binding than the Paris Accord from 2017. The first global effort to contain climate change happened under the banner of The Rio Earth Summit in 1992 with the participation of 197 countries. They only requested that 40 developed countries work to reduce their carbon emissions. However, there was no legal binding for them if they did not follow the measures. The next international meeting happened in 1997 in Japan and produced the Kyoto Protocol, which aimed at 5 percent reduction of the fossil fuel emissions. Similarly to the previous one, the measures were volunteer, and took eight years for 193 countries to ratify the agreement in 2005. The US did not join, and countries becoming industrialized like China and India, were absent. The second part of the Kyoto protocol included legal obligations for the countries that signed it and it was ratified by only 29 countries.

The most recent IPCC report from 2022 and was approved by 195 countries line by line.[281] The conclusion is unequivocal that the climate change is caused by human activity and the results are catastrophic. Compounded extreme events that were rare in the past will become more frequent and with longer durability. Right now, extreme events occur nearly five times more often than historically; however, if the temperature increases with 1.5 degrees C, the frequency will be nine times more often. If the temperature rises with 2 degrees C, the frequency will occur fourteen times more often. This means that catastrophic events such as wildfires, rain floods, drought, hurricanes, and cyclones will happen fourteen times more often than now.

Despite the ample information, the reaction to climate crisis has been inadequate, especially in the US. For example, after the 2018 IPCC report there has been an initiative for developing a Green New Deal presented by Senator Ed Markey and junior congresswoman Alexandria Ocasio Cortes (AOC). In March 2019, not a single senator voted for the Deal, including Markey, or 57 voted against it and 43 voted "present." The justification for this act was the high cost of the Deal, $51T or $93T over the next decade.[282] Compare this amount to the $20B subsidy to the oil industry that the US taxpayers provide every year, contributing to their own demise.[283] Or compare

---

[281] http://www.ipccch/report/sixth-assessment-report-working-group-ii
[282] *Senate Committee on Natural Resources*, August 10, 2021
[283] Janet Redman, "Report: Trump's 'Energy Dominance Plans Rely on Billions on Fossil Fuel Subsidies," *Oil Change International*, October 3, 2017.

this all-encompassing solution to the ever-increasing military annual budget, now $780B in the range of decades, and especially the unaccounted or missing $21T reported in the first auditing the Pentagon's budget. Similarly, the bailout of Wall Street during the crash in 2020, triggered by the Covid pandemic, in a single month from March 9 to April 7, 2020, the government poured a record $6.6T to the financial market by buying directly corporate bond and stocks.[284] The priorities of the government are clear, and its legislative brunch – the Congress, quietly bails out Wall Street and supports year after year the inflated budget and subsidies for the military industrial complex, the greatest consumer of fossil fuel and the greatest polluter on earth.

However, despite the government's criminal passivity, a number of new environmental movements rose spontaneously comprised of mostly young people including the Sunrise Movement from 2017 and Extinction Rebellion from 2018. The new generation realizes that there is no future for them unless radical changes to the western economy are done, and that people of all countries are affected by climate change and should work together to this end. All groups support the Green New Deal, and work actively to implement it. In the fall of 2018, 200 Sunrise movement youth occupied the Office of House Minority Leader Nancy Pelosi, demanding a Green New deal. This protest was followed by a January 2019 letter to Congress from a wide range of more than 600 progressive organizations including Greenpeace, Friends of the Earth, 350.org, Sunrise Movement, Rainforest Action Network, the Indigenous Environmental Network, and Amazon Watch, who requested social justice.[285] According to Aviva Chomsky's "Brief History of the Green New Deal," the signatories were small organizations, whereas large groups like Sierra Club, the Natural Resources Defense Council, and the Environmental Defense Fund were absent from the petition.[286]

Sunrise Movement, founded in 2017, was self-defined on their website as "A youth movement to stop climate change and create millions of good jobs in the process. We are building an army of young people to make climate change an urgent priority across America, end the corrupting influence of fossil fuel executives on our politics, and elect leaders who stand up for the health and

---

[284] Heather Long, "The Federal reserve Has Pumped $2.3T into the US Economy. It's Just Getting Started," *The Washington Post,* April 29, 2020. https://www.washingtonpost.com/business/2020/04/29/federal-reserve-has-pumped-23-trillion-into-us-economy-its-just-getting-started/

[285] Aviva Chomsky, "A Brief History of the Green New Deal (So Far), *Lit Hub,* April 25, 2022.

[286] Ibid.

wellbeing of the people."[287] According to the Sunrise Movement page, their short history starts with "a lot of energy drinks and a little help for Sierra Club."[288] According to E&E report, Sunrise used a $30,000 grant and free office space provided by Sierra Club and Wesleyan University Green Fund.[289] This small detail reveals the connection with a mainstream environmental group and begs the question why would such club help youth organizers launch a movement. Since Sierra Club did not participate in the 2019 petition, the organization is in favor of keeping the status quo, perhaps its intention is to establish a front group like Sunrise to secure controlled opposition.

Posted in Sunrise Movement's website, there is a video where a young leader urges people to participate in support of the Green New Deal and points out to other grassroots movements in the past, which successfully led to the New Deal of 1930s, and the Civil Rights Act of 1960s. While this is true and the victory of such legislations were based on massive movements, the Sunrise leader suspiciously maintains her partisan approach and discusses the failure of one party without critical statements about the other. The video is from 2022 when the supported by Sunrise Democrat Party is fully in charge of the House, the Senate, and the White House. No questions are asked about what is holding up the passing of the Green New Deal. In fact, in 2021, the Bill was reintroduced by congresspeople Markey and Cortez, only to be replaced with a far weaker version of Biden's Plan for a Clean Energy Revolution and Environmental Justice.[290] For example, the Green New deal aimed to achieve net-zero greenhouse gas emissions and 100 percent clean, renewable energy by 2030, whereas Biden's plan aimed to achieve the same by 2050; while the GND could cost between $51T and $93T, Biden's bill would cost between $1.7 and $5T.[291] In comparison, the ratio between renewable and petroleum, gas, and coal energy in 2020 was 12:79 percent, and the remaining 9 percent was produced by nuclear energy.[292]

To understand better the dynamics of the cooption of this youth movement by the establishment, we need to investigate both parties lobbying

---

[287] www.sunrisemovement.org

[288] Mark Mathews, Nick Bowlin, and Benjamin Hulac, "Inside the Sunrise Movement (It didn't Happen by Accident)" *E &E News,* Feb. 19, 2019.

[289] Ibid.

[290] Jeff Koss, "Senate Rejects Green New Deal as Marathon Voting Begins," E&E News, August 10, 2021.

[291] Deborah D'Souza, Sierra Murry, and Kristen Rohrs Schmitt, "The Green New Deal Explained," *Investopedia,* May 28, 2022.

[292] Ibid.

process, and the money they receive from the oil industry. According to *Open Secrets*, a non-profit organization that follows money in politics, in 2022 the top recipient of oil and gas money was Joe Manchin, Democrat with the amount of $730,620.[293] Kyrsten Sinema, also Democrat, received $227,285. Two more Democrats received close to $200,000, and the rest were Republicans whose amounts varied from $385,272 to $148,801. It is clear that the leading recipient, Joe Manchin, received almost twice as much money as the next person, Republican Kevin McCarthy with $385,272. This explains why Manchin and Sinema had so much weight in their party and single-handedly gutted the Green New Deal and voted for the severely reduced budget for environment changes proposed by Biden. More importantly, it explains why the GND cannot be passed when the supposedly environmental-friendly Democrats oversee both Congress and the White House.

In 2020, the two top recipients of oil money among the presidential candidates were Donald Trump with $3,834,354 and Joe Biden with $1,628,7023.[294] Although Biden received less than half the amount Trump did, he was second to number one Trump, and the top two recipients from the oil industry for 2020 ended up the two nominees for the two major parties. This fact demonstrates that the industry leaves nothing to chance and always lobbies both parties. From environmental perspective, the death of life on the planet is imminent regardless of which party is in charge: in one case the death is going to be sudden and quick, in the other it would be slower and perhaps more painful. Even the IPCC report released during the Trump administration in 2018 recommended drastic solutions and rejected incremental changes due to the urgency of the climate crisis, suggesting that there are only 12 years for action before the process is irreversible.

According to a 2015 Stanford and Berkeley study, the US all-purpose energy systems could be replaced 80-85 percent with renewable wind, water, and solar by 2030, and 100 percent by 2050.[295] The study shows that the process of conversion would provide 3.9M new construction jobs and 2M

---

[293] *Open Secrets: Following the Money in Politics*, "2022 Top Recipients," accessed on July 10, 2022. https://www.opensecrets.org/industries/recips.php?ind=E01&cycle=2020&recipdetail=P&mem=N&sortorder=U

[294] Ibid.

[295] Mark Z. Jacobsen, Mark A. Delucchi, Guillaume Bazouin, Zack A.F. Bauer, Christa C. Heavey, Emma Fisher, Sean B. Morris, Diniana J.Y. Piekutowsky, Taylor A. Vencill, and Tim W. Yeskoo, "100% Clean and Renewable
Wind, Water, and Sunlight (WWS) All-sector Energy Roadmaps for the 50 United States," *Energy & Environmental Science*, 2015, No. 8, 2093. https://web.stanford.edu

operation jobs replacing the existing 3.9 M jobs in the conventional energy sector.[296] In addition, the energy conversion will eliminate $3.3T global cost per year in damage including destroyed houses, loss of property, health care and human displacement.[297] According to a newer study from 2019, climate change will cost the US $500B a year in economic loss by 2090.[298]

President Biden, initially opposed by Sunrise, was endorsed by the Sunrise Movement when the party nominated him after cheating the more progressive candidate, Bernie Sanders. Surprisingly, despite the open opposition to Biden from many of the 400 chapters of the movement, the co-founder of Sunrise, Varshini Prakash, joined Biden's Unity Task Force, enticed by Sanders' participation. Since Biden did not support the Green New Deal and openly promised that "Nothing will fundamentally change," by participating in Biden's taskforce, Sunrise leader is legitimizing candidate Biden and thus helping him to win the election. This extreme compromise effectively coopted the movement into the establishment. Biden worked actively against the Green New deal and instead of passing it, his administration greenlit two other bills – The American Rescue Plan and Bipartisan Infrastructure Law, both passed in 2021. The goal of the latter clearly contradicts the IPCC report that warns us to achieve net-zero carbon emission by 2030. Instead, the plan aims at 2050 for zero-net emissions and reducing the 2005 levels by 50 percent in 2030.[299] According to the White House report, abandoned sites of former oil, gas, and coal energy production called Superfund Sites, cause pollution of air and drinking water. The report estimates that about 10 million households and 400,000 schools and childcare centers lack access to safe drinking water, and will invest $55B to expand access to safe water.[300] In addition, 26 percent of black Americans and 29 percent of Hispanic Americans live within three miles of such sites, for which the bill will invest $21B.[301] In comparison, the

---

[296] Ibid.
[297] Ibid.
[298] Jeremy Martinich,, and Allison Crimmins, "Climate Damages and Adaptation Potential Across Sectors of the United States," *Nature Climate Change*, Vol. 9, April 2019, 394-404.
[299] "Fact Sheet: The Bipartisan Infrastructure Deal Boosts Clean Energy Jobs, Strengthens Resilience, and Advances Environmental Justice," *The White House Briefing Room*, Nov. 8, 2021.
[300] Ibid.
[301] Ibid.

initial proposal by Senator Sanders required $3.5T, later reduced to $2.2T and effectively killed by Senator Joe Manchin.[302]

The Sunrise Movement emphasizes the great importance of the Green New Deal, also known as the Resolution 109 on their website. However, the GND is nonbinding and therefore, does not have legislative power or legal impact. Yet, because it is an idea, or rather a blueprint for direction, it meets a notable resistance among the conservative politicians. The latest action on the Green New Deal, is that it was re-introduced in the House in April 2021, then referred to the Subcommittee on the Constitution, Civil Rights, and Civil Liberties in October 2021. As every other serious social issue, the political approach is to make it partisan and neutralize it by endless battles between the left and the right. In reality, both parties have no intention of supporting the bill and instead are invested in making the issue a spectacle – a gladiator's fight between the two elitist parties.

Sunrise Movement, whose official moto is "We Are the Climate Revolution," offers no radical actions aside from calls to volunteering to "phonebank for the Squad." According to the Sunrise Movement website, they endorse 13 Democrats, more specifically, members of the "Squad" including AOC, Rashida Tlaib, Ilhan Omar, Ayanna Presley, Jamaal Bowman, and Cori Bush among others. Sunrise activists never challenged these representatives or held them accountable for voting for the gutted environmental bill when their numbers were more than enough to counter the two most loud opponents of the Green New Deal from their party, Manchin and Sinema. No questions were asked why the thirteen "progressive" members did not withhold their votes to prevail in the process but obediently voted for the bill without any efforts to collectively oppose the weakened bill.

Sunrise website reveals their strategy under the banner "Our Theory of Change," which has three brunches: people power, political power, and people's alignment. The political power aims at accumulating "a critical mass of enthusiastically supportive public officials who will fight for our shared vision of a just future."[303] According to the record, there are thirteen politicians in the Democratic party who have Sunrise's endorsement. Since their supported party has the majority, voting for controversial issues such as the Green New Deal, only six progressives withholding their votes would have been enough to win. However, the 100 members of the Progressive Caucus

---

[302] John Feffer, "What Remains of the Green New Deal?" *Foreign Policy in Focus,* May 5, 2022.
[303] Ibid.

of the Democratic Party including the thirteen endorsed by Sunrise, weren't strong enough to counter Manchin and Sinema who killed the deal. Instead of criticizing their endorsed politicians, Sunrise website very much resembles an election campaign where the youth members work hard for electing more Democrats by phone banking, raising money, and so on.

By focusing so much on the electoral process and making the environmental movement a partisan issue, Sunrise succumbs to the elitist duopoly that rules the country and gives up its grassroots power. Furthermore, by uncritically endorsing candidates like Biden, Sunrise activists inadvertently support the establishment Democratic party and therefore, sabotage their own progressive goals. As the Bernie Sanders campaign and his movement "Our Revolution" ended up completely capitulating to corporate power, Sunrise' slogan "We Are the Climate Revolution" seems to be equally powerless to influence politicians to make significant changes. In the two years in office, Democratic party supported by Sunrise did only cosmetic changes while offering abundant rhetoric. More recently, in March 2022, Sunrise issued a memo, warning the Democratic leadership, that if they want to win their vote in the coming elections, they must run on a strong climate agenda.[304] However, history teaches us that there is a crucial difference between making pre-election promises and fulfilling them when in office.

Finally, the renewable energy sources need a closer look. Although they use clean energy such as wind, sun, and water, these sources require manufacturing of solar panels, wind mills, and turbines. The production of such equipment is not harmless – to the contrary – it requires minerals provided in unclean mines, e.g., solar panels are made through a process fueled by oil. In his 2019 film *Planet of the Humans,* Michael Moore reveals some ominous facts about the green energy sources and the subversive organizations behind them.[305] According to Michael Moore, "*Planet of the Humans* is a documentary that dares to say what no one else will – that we are losing the battle to stop climate change on planet earth because we are following leaders who have taken us down the wrong road – selling out the green movement to wealthy interests and corporate America."[306] Moore released the film on

---

[304] Lexi McMenamin, "Sunrise Issues a Memo to Democrats Calling for Green New Deal Commitments," *Teen Vogue,* March 17, 2022.

[305] Jeff Gibbs, dir., Michael Moore, producer, *Planet of the Humans,* Huron Mountain Films, July30, 2019.

[306] https://planetofthehumans.com

his You Tube Channel on the 50th Earth Day. In a week, it had more than 3.9 million views.[307]

The film starts with a TV announcement from 1958, warning that the release of fossil fuel emissions would eventually warm the planet to a point of melting the ice caps on the poles, which would drastically change the life on earth as we know it. Filmmaker Jeff Gibbs, who wrote, directed and narrated the documentary, states that we have known about the inevitable climate disaster for six decades. According to the documentary, during the Obama administration, $1T stimulus funds including $100B for renewable energy were released in stimulus programs. Billionaires such as Richard Brandon invested $3B in manufacturing clean energy, and Sierra Club received $50M from Mayor Bloomberg. Major banks such as Goldman Sachs were quick to jump in, requiring $395B a year. Bill McKibben founded his organization, 350.org, aiming at a limit of 350 carbon dioxide particles per a million air particles, in order to save the planet. Then, director Gibbs interviewed GM, which opened a new line for electric cars Chevy Volt in Lancing, MI, and found out that their cars are 95 percent charged by coal.[308] A local Lancing leader invited Gibbs to look at their football sized solar panels display, titled "Cedar Street Solar Array." However, when pressed for details, the official admitted that their panels have only eight percent efficiency, therefore it would take one year to produce the power to meet the needs of 10 families.[309]

Next, the documentary analyses wind power in McKibben's native state, Vermont. The wind turbines are made by fiberglass and weigh 800 lb. each; they can only function for about 20-21 years and afterwards they are not only useless but environmental hazard. Furthermore, sometimes the production of the turbines requires mountain top removal used for coal mines, therefore, it destroys the natural environment. Because the wind energy is intermittent, during idling hours the turbines leave more carbon footprint than oil and gas production. In addition, the company that installs wind turbines in Vermont, is the brunch of a Canadian firm that builds the pipelines for Key Stone and transports tar sand – a connection counterproductive to the idea of replacing fossil fuel energy.[310] Another source – ethanol plants, rely on giant fossil fuel consumer farms to produce corn, which is used in fermentation, and even more carbon emitting coal mines to produce ethanol. Thus, the big irony is

---

[307] Chris Lang, "Planet of the Humans (Part 1): Blood and Gore," *Redd,* April 29, 2020.
[308] Ibid, 0:11:55-0:14:32.
[309] Ibid., 0:14:44-0: 16:02.
[310] Ibid., 0:20:30.

that to produce clean energy, most plants use fossil fuel to replace the old energy with renewable.[311]

Ozzie Zehner, a visiting scholar at the University of California, Berkeley, who wrote the 2012 book *Green Illusions: The Dirty Secrets of Clean Energy and the Future of Environmentalism,* was a participant and producer of the film. Zehner explains the process of creating solar panels. The panels contain two major products – quartz and coal melted together at a temperature 1800 degrees F, emitting ample amounts of CO_2.[312] Furthermore, Zehner enunciates that for every coal plant retired, there are being replaced with two natural gas plants for the production of solar panels and wind mills, as is the case with Las Vegas, NE.[313] Zehner adds that the new bigger natural gas plant produces four times the CO_2 that the coal plant that it is replacing produced. Similar replacements happened in North Carolina and other places, celebrated by the media and the public as progress.

Similarly, Steven Running, ecologist from the University of Montana found out from his research that our finite resources cannot be sustained including drinking water, mentioning Colorado River, which was unable to reach the Pacific Ocean in recent years.[314] The issue of infinite growth of the population includes the steep increase of ten times more humans in two hundred years since the beginning of the industrial revolution. More specifically, the discovery of fossil fuel and its industrial universal use sped up the population explosion. Human consumption also exploded during the same time, which compounded the existing problem.[315] Scholars such as environmental sociologist Richard York from the University of Oregon studied the green energy sources and came to the conclusion that green energy is not replacing fossil fuel sources, just perpetuating them.[316] Nina Jablonski, anthropologist from Pennsylvania State University, asserts that studies show that none of the existing green energy sources so far is replacing any of the fossil fuel sources because their production requires the use of old energy.[317] Furthermore, Jablonski explains that the solution cannot be more technical advancement because each new step brings its own environmental disaster.

---

[311] Ibid., 0:22:06.
[312] Ibid., 0:26:34.
[313] Ibid., 0:26:42.
[314] Ibid., 0:46:47.
[315] Ibid., 0:49:09.
[316] Ibid., 0:22:55.
[317] Ibid., 0:23:20.

Furthermore, elements like polymers, silver, cobalt, graphite, steel, nickel, copper, concrete, lithium, tin, indium, lead, petroleum products among others, are all used to produce high-tech digital electronics, electrical cars, and renewable energy sources such as solar panels and wind turbines. Most of them produce 23 times more CO_2 than the traditional fossil fuels.[318] The conclusion reached gradually by the documentary is that the green energy production is not for saving the planet, but for saving our way of life. The problem of finite resources is exacerbated by the beliefs across the aisle – both liberals and conservatives invested in different illusions. For example, the conservatives are in denial of the climate disaster, whereas the progressives' solution is green technology, which does not replace the fossil fuel. Philosophically speaking, according to social psychologist Sheldon Solomon at Skidmore College, environmentalists including the authors – Gibbs and Moore, have their own religious belief that technology is going to save us. In fact, explains the psychologist, most contemporaries are driven by their desperation that prompts them to believe that technology is the solution because they cannot face their own mortality.[319]

Another illusion is the use of biomass, produced of living plants, which requires cutting down trees and burning them for electricity.[320] For example, in Vermont, a facility burns 400,000 tones green trees a year while also using natural gas in the process, or 30 quarts of wood per hour.[321] For this procedure the plant gets $11M grant subsidies from the government.[322] Because the biomass cannot produce the required temperature, it is necessary to use tire chips or other highly poisonous rubber or plastic debris. The notion of cutting entire forests for wood chips is so outrageous that became controversial among environmental groups. When interviewed by Gibbs, most activist leaders had ambiguous answers, whereas rank and file members were adamantly opposed to biomass and did not perceive it as clean and renewable source.

In contrast, leaders such as Bill McKibben, the founder of 350.org, was openly promoting burning biomass in his speeches at events. However, when confronted about the harm done from cutting down trees – our only natural protection against CO_2 emissions, he became unsure and evasive. Leaders of local chapters of Sierra Club were also uncertain – for example, a young leader

---

[318] Ibid., 0:41:05.
[319] Ibid., 0:50:05.
[320] Ibid., 0:55:41.
[321] Ibid., 0:54:23.
[322] Ibid., 0:57:32.

from Pennsylvania chapter of the Club, responded that she is not prepared to answer the question about biomass. Other Sierra Club leaders were in support of the use of biomass. The only environmentalist leader who was willing to reject the use of biomass was scholar Vandana Shiva, an environmental and human rights activist from India, whose honest opposition was refreshing to Gibbs.[323] The author mused whether the leaders are just misguided, ignorant, or corrupt.[324]

In the end, the authors raise the final question, as Gibbs expressed it, "the elephant in the room," or the question of profit. The reason the public is constantly fed the story of renewable energy, is the simple fact that billionaires, corporations, banks, and some activist groups are profiting from the new industry. Many activist leaders are invested in the green resources and receive handsome returns.[325] According to the author, capitalism's ever increased expansion needed a new more reputable industry of investment.

Michael Bloomberg, who is leading the campaign for clean energy titled "Beyond Coal," is working along with Sierra Club in this process of replacement fossil fuels with wind, solar, and natural gas. Natural gas is always included as if it were a clean source of energy. Since some solar panels' life endurance could vary from 10 years to 12-13 years, the business of replacement is long lasting and profitable. It builds a positive reputation and brings the opportunity of federal subsidies. It is no wonder some fossil fuel companies are actively participating in the renewable energy production, knowing that every renewable source requires oil, gas, or coal. For example, energy consuming corporations such as Tesla and Apple use massively ethanol, natural gas, graphite aluminum and other metals that emit more CO_2 than oil and coal. Even the Cox corporation has its own line of solar panels titled Solar Molex.[326]

Bloomberg publicly announced his $30M investment in his Beyond Coal campaign, and noted that his partners would match his investment.[327] One of the partners was Jeremy Grantham, an owner of timber companies eager to cut forests for fuel. On the tax return document of Sierra Club, the name of Grantham and his $3M donation was blacked out, which raises the question why would a person of his field donate to an environmental

---

[323] Ibid., 1:09:00.
[324] Ibid., 1:10:09.
[325] Ibid., 1:10:50.
[326] Ibid., 0:36:32.
[327] Ibid., 1:10:57.

organization.³²⁸ Similarly, billionaire Richard Brand invested his money in bio fuel for his jets and for commercial planes.³²⁹ Another billionaire, former CEO of Goldman Sachs David Blood, is a big supporter of turning trees into fuel and making money of it. He requested $40T to $50T from the government for his profitable destruction of forests, and activist Bill McKibben joined in the effort of persuading governments to do it.³³⁰ The idea of destroying living forests that are literary the planet's lungs for fuel is so absurd that requires a specific language to cover up its malevolence. Big airline corporations rushed in to buy this new oil, called "green oil." Both the producers and the consumers of this new fraudulent resource claim that there is no downside to using it. The authors dug deeper into the investors in this "green oil" and found out that there were mostly the largest polluting companies such as Coca Cola – the biggest producer of plastic on earth, Black Rock – the greatest global deforestation corporation, and some large banks.

Similarly, environmental organization Sierra Club partners with the largest polluters such as Chevron, Boeing, Exxon Mobil, Russian giant Gas Prom, and Viva – the world largest forest destroyer.³³¹ Another environmental champion, Vice President Al Gore, partnered with Sugar Cane Ethanol industry mogul David Blood to launch a company called Generation Investment Management. The problem is that David Blood, the former Goldman and Sachs CEO, is the greatest champion of deforestation of Amazon that causes pollution of the earth on epic scale. More importantly, Blood displaces the indigenous population whose homes are destroyed. In addition, Al Gore sold his TV network for $100M to Al Jazeera not understanding the irony of partnering with a country that bases its wealth on oil.³³²

The last irony is that the US Navy, one of the biggest polluters on earth, considers using animal fat, algae, grass, and sea weed, among other natural sources for fuel.³³³ According to the documentary, the Union of Concerned Scientists has become a Union of Concerned Salesmen, having taken millions of dollars not to protect the environment but to sell electric cars.³³⁴ When pressed in an interview about his sponsors, McKibben admitted that the

---

[328] Ibid., 1:11:51,
[329] Ibid., 1:12:53.
[330] Ibid, 1:15:06.
[331] Ibid., 1:17:51.
[332] Ibid., 1:26:05.
[333] Ibid., 1:22:53.
[334] Ibid., 1:23:48.

Rockefeller Foundation funds 350.org.[335] The most famous environmental organizations including Earth Day are funded by automobile producers, bulldozer companies, and banks. The founder of Earth Day, Denis Hayes, thanked his sponsors, Toyota, Citi Bank, and Caterpillar, during a concert to celebrate earth day.[336] Toward the end of the film, Gibbs concludes, "The takeover of capitalism of the natural environment is now complete." He continues that the merger between capitalism and environmentalism is also complete and muses whether it was always meant to be this way.[337]

Understandably, the documentary generated criticism and even was pulled out of You Tube for half a day, and then put back on. Apparently, the gatekeepers of Internet decided that direct censorship is counterproductive and resolved to the old, classic propaganda. Traditionally, Michael Moore attacks the conservative Republican party and usually has the uncritical support of the partisan left. However, this time he attacked the core idea of the Democrats and their leaders for green energy and saving the planet. Therefore, the universal problem that concerns the planet once again is transformed into a partisan struggle. The critics of the film argue about some technically outdated products shown in the documentary such as inefficient solar panels with 10 years lifetime and compare them to newer panels that last for 20-30 years.[338]

Nevertheless, there is no response to the argument against the method of production of the solar panels through melting quartz and coal. However, this is not the main point of the film. The critics have nothing to say about the connection between the fossil fuel industry and the new green companies, and the profit motifs including the funding and donations revealed in the film. It is worth noting that no critic defends the biomass and deforestation, which confirms the exposure of the compromised position on this issue by environmental groups such as 350.org and Sierra Club.

The second important point of the film is that searching for technological cure is the wrong path because it preserves a lifestyle of overproduction and overconsumption that is unsustainable on a finite planet. Technology can be useful, of course, but only when its purpose is free of the profit incentive. According to another film review, "With plenty examples to back up his

---

[335] Ibid., 1:25:01.
[336] Ibid., 1:28:36.
[337] Ibid., 1:24:42.
[338] Ben Wehman, "6 Reasons Why *Planet of the Humans* is a Disaster," *Films for Action,* April 29, 2020.

arguments, Gibbs posits that we are turning what was left of nature into profit."[339] The obvious conclusion is that politicians and business people fund environmental groups who represent their interests and work together to increase their profits. As discussed in earlier chapters, the mainstream media and academia are always there to serve the interest of the powerful. For decades, the media ignored the climate crisis and sporadically reported it as a minor issue. Since the Obama Administration made it profitable, everybody is on board, led by the media in the wrong direction.

In conclusion, the problem is not the technology, or the search for innovation, or any kind of progress in science. The problem is the existing social and political systems, which reward greed and unscrupulous pursuit of wealth, power, and control. If the social system was democratic, the motif for any enterprise would be the wellbeing of all humans. If the focus of the global governments was the preservation of a healthy and sustainable planet, the endless production and consumption would have been ruled out at the beginning of the industrial revolution. The simple slogan of the 19th century "Back to nature," revisited in the 1960s ecological movements, is currently revived in the 21st century.

During the recent pandemic of 2020, people gradually started to realize that the governments do not have their wellbeing in mind. Through the criminal response to the pandemic with a mixture of incompetence and totalitarian measures, the ruling elites demonstrated their lack of concern for the general population. As a result, people all over the world started to move away from their dependance on the exploitive system that does not support them. By building communities that are self-sufficient and sustainable, more and more people respond to the climate and social crises by removing themselves from the toxic grid that is annihilating them. Yet, many more are still captured by the intensive media propaganda and remain frozen in the artificial light of false information. As always, the cure is in the intelligent observation, research and thorough analysis of the world around us. The reporting of events should be met with a healthy dose of skepticism, in order to avoid the media's enticement into lazy consumption of readily available and omnipresent propaganda.

---

[339] Frederic and Mary Ann Brussat, "Film Review of *Planet of the Humans*," *Spirituality and Practice*, April 21, 2020.

Chapter Eight

The Dissident Indie Media: If They Can See Through Propaganda, We Can Too

Once safely captured, we are trained to consume the news the way sports fans do. We root for our team, and hate all the rest.

-Matt Taibbi

Being a dissident is not easy. Even in a political system where the consequences are mild, such as not being hirable in well-paying jobs, or constantly being discredited in your profession, these reasons are more than enough to deter you from being one. The extreme version of retaliation for non-conforming consists of life-threatening consequences such as being arrested, imprisoned, or murdered. This simple calculation explains why there are so few dissidents among both regular people and the professional class in academia, media, and recently, medical research. As Chomsky reiterated in different speeches and writings, the Western political systems reward obedience and punish any deviation from the strict line of conduct designed by the elites. The conditioning starts in kindergarten and continues through school, college, and graduate programs. It is universal and no one is exempt from it. Yong children, and later young people learn throughout their education what is acceptable to say, do, or believe. The ones who deviate from the conventional wisdom are ostracized socially, reprimanded through the grading system and continuously filtered out from privileges, prestigious schools, and lucrative careers. There are plenty financial incentives such as scholarships, grants, and fellowships for going in the right direction by choosing the right academic topics, the right theses, and the right doctrines. Students learn by experience to avoid controversial subjects and to tow the right ideological line. Throughout their experience, students often subconsciously make choices because of some hardship they have gone through, or witnessed their classmates being flaked for the wrong choices they made intellectually or professionally. One of the consequences is self-censorship, a practice widely used in western societies. George Orwell explains this phenomenon in his 1945 unpublished preface to the *Animal Farm,* titled "Freedom of the Press:"

> This kind of thing is not a good symptom. Obviously it is not desirable that a government department should have any power of censorship (except security censorship, which no one objects to in war time) over books which are not officially sponsored. But the chief danger to freedom of thought and speech at this moment is not the direct interference of the Ministry of Information or any official body. If publishers and editors exert themselves to keep certain topics out of print, it is not because they are frightened of prosecution but because they are frightened of public opinion. In this country intellectual cowardice is the worst enemy a writer or journalist has to face, and that fact does not seem to me to have had the discussion it deserves.[340]

This practice, described so well by Orwell back in the 1940s is not only well and alive in the 21st century; it is even more refined, sophisticated, and effectively obscured by the same lacking courage intellectuals, mentioned earlier. The fact that this 70-year-old preface is still only found on the internet, not attached to the book it meant to introduce, is proof that the text is still applicable to our modern reality. In fact, it presents such an accurate picture of the condition of western societies that the readers might assume it was written by a contemporary author. Consider Orwell's lines, "Anyone who challenges the prevailing orthodoxy finds himself silenced with surprising

---

[340] George Orwell, "The Freedom of the Press," *Orwell's Proposed Preface to Animal Farm,* 1945, first published in *The Times Literary Supplement,* Sept., 15, 1972.

effectiveness. A genuinely unfashionable opinion is almost never given a fair hearing, either in the popular press or in the highbrow periodicals.[341] This description applies to any "unfashionable" opinion in recent times such as anti-war voices, anti-censorship protesters, and especially anti-establishment stand on any medical issue during the pandemic. In recent years, the use of silencing methods escalated to direct censorship both from the government and the private owners of the media.

Furthermore, to maintain the illusion of scholarly freedom and intellectual integrity, mass media and academia allow rigorous debates within very narrow frames. Chomsky summarizes the illusion of free speech, "The smart way to keep people passive and obedient is strictly limit the spectrum of acceptable opinion, but allow very lively debate within that spectrum…"[342] For example, when discussing the question of US participation in any war, the debate is premised on the notion that this participation is inevitable, and the argument becomes whether to put troops on the ground or just bomb the country in question. The obvious option of not participating is never brought up, and the division of opinions is built on two or more details, whereas the fundamental premise remains untouchable. This is the case with every important philosophical, ideological, or intellectual issue in western cultures, and especially in the US. Chomsky shares an experience in his 1998 *The Common Good*, "…when you come back from the Third World to the West – the U.S. in particular – you are struck by the narrowing of thought and understanding, the limited nature of legitimate discussion, the separation of people from each other. It's startling how stifling it feels, since our opportunities are so vastly greater here."[343]

The issue of keeping people divided has been brought up frequently in this discourse. It is the building block of the successful oppression of the people in every oligarchy in the world. It is best described by Chomsky in the same book, "…the power of business propaganda in the U.S.…has succeeded, to an unusual extent, in breaking down the relations among people and their sense of support for one another."[344] Curiously, this principle of separation is implemented physically in the American lifestyle, lauded so much in literature, and celebrated by Hollywood. The principle started with the expansion of settlement to the wild west promoted by the government

---

[341] Ibid.
[342] Noam Chomsky, *The Common Good*, Odonian Press: *Open Library*, 1998, 43.
[343] Ibid., 154.
[344] Ibid., 140.

during the 19th century, when new settlers were rewarded with land and subsidies. Later, the glorified rugged individualism was promoted again in the 1950s by extolling the suburban lifestyle and popularizing the slogan "my home my castle." However, the hyped suburban life caused millions of housewives to be severely depressed for decades – a cause very profitable for the pharmaceutical industry and the rapidly developing field of psychotherapy in medicine.

The same strategy of division and manipulation applies to controlling the narratives and the beliefs of the masses. Thus, supporting the mainstream doctrines becomes defending their way of life, or their fundamental beliefs that their worldview is justified. Most people have the need to believe that the world is fair, and this is the reason why it is so much easier to believe the concepts spread by propaganda than to question them. In her article, "People who Defend Empire Narratives Are Really Just Defending Their Worldview from Destruction," counterculture writer Caitlin Johnstone explains perfectly well such a paradox:

> There is a great comic by *The Oatmeal,* which explains the psychological defense mechanisms human have in place to protect their worldview from information that could destabilize it. Because of our tendency to select for cognitive ease over cognitive challenge in order to conserve mental energy, we tend to be heavily biased against consciously helping new worldview-disrupting information get past those psychological defense mechanisms.
>
> And it doesn't get more worldview disrupting than questioning mainstream consensus reality. Because on the other side of that investigation is the realization that pretty much everything you've been trained to believe about your society, your nation, your government, and your world, is a lie.[345]

In the study, mentioned by the author, scientists examined human brain and found out that when presented with threatening information, the same centers of the brain get activated that react to physical threat in the amygdala, the area that processes emotional triggers. Furthermore, the study found that

---

[345] Caitlin Johnstone, "People Who Defend Empire Narratives Are Really Just Defending Their Worldview Form Destruction," June 1, 2022.

humans' core beliefs develop from childhood and are compounded by life experiences because they are inflexible, rigid, and sensitive to challenges.[346] Because of these obstacles in the way of new information, especially if it questions established concepts, people are willing to defend old and harmful ideas. It is easier to preserve such ideas than to suffer through a painful process that resembles death in a symbolic way. Johnstone's article puts in perspective a phenomenon that is often overlooked or dismissed as character shortcoming of the people who are literary fighting for their livelihood.

The article also clarifies the scientific view of the brain process that is in place when someone's core beliefs are challenged by using a metaphor of a house. The walls, the floor, and the roof are our social influences such as family, school, media, and other institutions. If a new concept doesn't fit in the house, it literary could break the house down. Therefore, people who fiercely battle new ideas are fighting for their homes of cards. Furthermore, Johnstone appeals to brave dissidents like her to remember how the same process was for them when they went through the pain of disillusioning from their own outdated beliefs. The detachment of anything from the past is always difficult. The process resembles birth and death at the same time. Fortunately, Johnstone comes with an optimistic idea that the way narratives are woven in order to make society, they could be undone. The way individuals are awakened from illusions, the society could be reborn if the narratives that hold it together are exposed and deconstructed. The author sees the important role of dissident messengers in the enlightening process that could bring the house of narratives down. She summarizes how the ruling mechanisms depend on the narratives that create these stubborn core beliefs in individuals and societies alike:

> And then, there are the oligarchs. The master manipulators. These corporate kings of the modern world have learned the secret that every ruler since the dawn of civilization has known: whoever controls the narratives that are believed by a society is the controller of that society. Identity, language, etiquette, social roles, opinions, ideology, religion, ethnicity, philosophy, agendas, rules, laws, money, economics, jobs, hierarchies, politics, government, all mental

---

[346] J. Kaplan, S Gimbel, S Harris, "Neural Correlates of Maintaining One's Political Beliefs in the Face of Counterevidence," *Scientific Report*, 6, No 39589, 2016.

constructs which only influence society to the extent that they are believed and subscribed to by a significant majority of the collective. If you have influence over the things that people believe about those mental constructs, you have influence over society. You rule it. The oligarchs manipulate the narratives of entire societies.[347]

In sum, the social narratives are so important that the ruling elites invest substantial amounts of their appropriated money in the media, education, and other institutions whose mission is to maintain the right narratives. Since these institutions are led by groups of highly educated professionals who comprise about 12 percent of the population, the task of the ruling elites is to attract this minority on their side to help them control the masses.[348] They do this through saving a special place for these representatives at the top of the hierarchy and offering them prestige, money, and privileges they cannot resist. For those who cannot be bought, there is a system of flak, which takes care of the dissidents and makes sure that they are powerless economically, politically and have no access to big platforms. In rare occasions when dissidents fall through the cracks and generate massive followers thus become influential, the system resorts to imprisoning or murdering them as it is the case of Julian Assange and political leaders such as Martin Luther King, Jr. With the help of the intelligentsia, these events are successfully buried and not discussed publicly. However, to stifle the dissidents who persist in their research and demand answers, there are plenty of think thanks sponsored by the elites that make sure the counterculture voices are suppressed, ridiculed, and called "conspiracy theorists."[349]

In recent times, many dissident voices come from the comedy sector. As was the case of late comedians such as Lenny Bruce and George Carlin among others, in the 21st century, we are fortunate to have comedians such as Jimmy Dore, Russel Brand, Lee Camp, Ron Placon, Sabby Sabs, Kelly Carlin, Katie Halper, Graham Elwood and many others. As is commonly agreed upon,

---

[347] Caitlin Johnstone, "Society Is Made of Narrative. Realizing This is Awakening from the Matrix," *Caitlin's Newsletter*, July 13, 2021.

[348] Richard Florida, *The Rise of the Creative Class: And How It's transforming Work, Leisure, and Everyday Life*, New York: Basic Books, 2002, 69.

[349] In was explained previously that the term "conspiracy theory" was coined by the CIA as a response to the growing suspicion among the public regarding the official versions of the assassinations of MLK, JFK, RFK, among others in the 1960s.

too often the truth is said in jest; therefore, in times of mass propaganda, the comedians are the only ones allowed to say the truth perhaps because presumedly, they are joking. As Jimmy Dore frequently reiterates, since the mainstream media will not do their job, it is up to him and his colleagues to deliver the news. In all seriousness, Dore and his fellow counterculture comedians report every filtered piece of news that didn't make it through the self-censored news media. Moreover, they interview other dissidents and whistleblowers that are not allowed on TV programs or websites. Examples include journalist Chris Hedges, whistleblowers Julian Assange, Chelsey Manning, Edward Snowden, and George Kiriakou, attorney Steven Donziger, and many other representatives of the banned opposition.

Late counterculture legend George Carlin, who has been a comedian for 50 years, is still relevant today as he was in the height of his career. According to some, he will never be out of style, because he challenges power, something the media are supposed to do; however, either fail or refuse to do. Ironically, it is delegated to comedians and independent reporters to tell us the truth. Carlin severely criticized consumerism constantly imposed through commercials, the state of education, money in politics, and most of all, the American Dream revered by both Americans and immigrants. According to Carlin's daughter, Kelly Carlin, her father appealed to audiences across age barriers, from 9 to 90 because he always had a fresh perspective on regular topics, provoking people to look at trivial things from a new angle.

A new 2022 documentary directed by Michael Bonfiglio and Judd Apatow, *George Carlin's American Dream*, presents Carlin's life and work. In an interview with comedian Jon Steward also featured in the film, Apatow discusses his film and why an icon such as Carlin is so significant. Steward ponders on the difficulty to be relevant in the field of comedy even for a brief moment, let alone during five decades and especially posthumously for 14 years.[350] The director notes that Carlin's daughter gave him permission to tell the truth in honor of her father who always told the truth.[351] Apatow explains his view that Carlin's relevance is based on exposing the truth about the corporate takeover of the country, which negatively affects the general public.[352] Steward underlines that when Carlin targets corruption, it resonates with people because they are always the victims regardless of where it happens.

---

[350] Jon Steward, interview, Jon and Judd Apatow on Why George Carlin Still Resonates, *The Problem with Jon Steward Podcast*, June, 2022, 16:03.
[351] Ibid.
[352] Ibid., 18:55.

Carlin's extreme criticism of typical cultural customs forces people to question the established narrative.

Some examples of challenging the narrative include Carlin's statement that the world we were granted is so beautiful; however, we decided to live in Malls, or that the world is a freak show and Americans have front row seats to watch it. Moreover, Carlin's opinion about education is still relevant today:

> But there is a reason, there is a reason, there is a reason for this, there is a reason education sucks and for the same reason it will never ever be fixed. It's never getting any better, don't look forward to it; be happy with what you've got; because the owners of this country don't want that. I am talking about the real owners now; the real owners, the big wealthy business interests that control things and make all the important decisions. Forget the politicians – the politicians are there to give you the idea that you have a freedom of choice. You don't. You have no choice. You have owners. They own you. They own everything. They own all the important land. They own and control the corporations. They've long since have bought and paid for the senate, the congress, the state houses, and the city halls. They've got the judges in their back pockets, and they own all the big media companies so they can control the news and all the information you get to hear. They got you by the balls. They spend billions of dollars every year lobbying… lobbying to get what they want. Well, we know what they want – they want more for themselves and less for everybody else. But I'll tell you what, they don't want – they don't want a population of citizens capable of critical thinking – they don't want well-informed, well-educated citizens capable of critical thinking. They are not interested in that. That's against their interest. It doesn't serve them. (2005)[353]

Further, Carlin underlines the idea that education is designed to produce obedient workers who are smart enough to operate the machines and to do the paperwork, but are not capable of figuring out the system that exploits

---

[353] Apatow, *Part II*, 1:35:02-1:39:38.

them. He emphasizes the fact that people with modest income continually elect wealthy officials who don't care about them. Towards the end of the monologue Carlin's throws his iconic phrase, "It's a big club and you ain't in it." In his short under five minutes rant, Carlin succeeds to reveal the entire corrupt system of exploitation and propaganda. The final conclusion is that the owners of this country count on people's oblivious state of remaining willfully ignorant because of the illusion called the American Dream. Because, Carlin remarks sarcastically, "You have to be asleep to believe it." The documentary is dedicated to this counterculture concept of the American Dream and thus, titled *George Carlin's American Dream*.

In the interview with Steward, Apatow reflects on the risk every creative person takes when they put their art, comedy, or creation out there for all to judge and how brutal critics can be, and compares the process to leaping off a cliff.[354] Then they both reminiscence on the extreme critique Carlin experienced during the 1980s when he literary became "the bud of the joke."[355] However, despite his brief periods of downfall, Carlin always somehow succeeded to climb back up. Moreover, Carlin is still trending on You Tube posthumously after 14 years, and his popularity exceeds any other comedian icon of his rank including Richard Pryor. According to Apatow, the reason for Carlin's phenomenon is that the comedian rose above the petty political jokes about the president who was in charge at the time, beyond the right and left dichotomy, and targeted real power, which appealed to both aisles of the political spectrum.[356]

Carlin was always ahead of his time – he was talking about the environment in the 1970s, he was anti-war all the way through the Vietnam War, and throughout the Iraq and Afghanistan wars. Carlin discussed our government not spending money on education and healthcare while heavily investing in bombing other countries in the height of the Iraq war. He was against police brutality long before the BLM movement.[357] Carlin discussed homelessness and understood why it cannot be eliminated – because there is no money to be made in solving this problem back in the 1990s, before homelessness became epidemic in the U.S.[358] For decades, Carlin defined education as

---

[354] Ibid., 30:37.
[355] Ibid., 30:41.
[356] Ibid.
[357] Judd Apatow and Michael Bonfiglio, dirs., *George Carlin's American Dream*, doc., May 2022, *Part Two*, 1:37:38.
[358] Ibid., 1:38:00.

an indoctrination camp for shaping obedient servants for the corporations. Unfortunately, this idea is yet to be comprehended by the general public.

In a different interview with MSNBC, Apatow defined Carlin as a thinker who likes to break things down, distrusts power and looks everywhere to find and take apart amusing, ironic and absurd things. According to Apatow, Carlin was "up in the Rushmore of Comedy."[359] Apatow commented on the darkness of Carlins' humor and how he was worried about issues that we only now take seriously, "It is pretty wild that people say, he is too dark; now you look at it and say, maybe he wasn't dark enough."[360] According to Kelly Carlin, the darkness came from the fact that the audience was not ready to hear the truth, let alone to accept it. The interview ended with the profound take away from the film that Carlin cared deeply about other people and his final words on his shows were always, "Take care of yourself. Take care of each other."[361] Another scene in the documentary revealed a less discussed side of Carlin – his idealism, when comedian Rosanne Barr tells Carlin that she thinks he is very spiritual, and he responded that, "If you scratch the surface of any cynic, there is a disappointed idealist underneath." He added that he likes to see himself as such.[362]

Inversely, the establishment including the MSNBC anchor Stephanie Ruhle, who conducted the interview, and others have to pretend that they don't understand the appeal of Carlin to vast audiences and mused about it. Thanks to the media information eclipse and propaganda, many Americans know Carlin solely as the comedian arrested at Summerfest in Milwaukee in 1972 for indecent performance in public while reciting the "Seven Words You Can Never Say on TV."[363] As a consequence, the Supreme Court banned the "seven words" in 1978; however, Carlin succeeded in exposing the hypocrisy of the culture and gained more popularity. Like other progressive dissidents whose images were distorted by the media and reduced to one non-threatening aspect of their personas, Carlin's name was attached to the seven obscene words because they were shown constantly on TV as a distraction from his more serious ideas.

---

[359] Stephanie Rohle, "George Carlin's Daughter Kelly and Judd Apatow on the Legacy of Comedian George Carlin," *MSNBC*, May 20, 2022.
[360] Ibid.
[361] Ibid.
[362] Apatow, *Part Two*,1: 29:24.
[363] Ironically, the case was used in future lawsuit of Pacifica Radio vs. FCC and the Supreme Court banned the "seven words" in 1978.

Hopefully, after the 2022 documentary, more people will learn the true rebellious side of Carlin who fought against the establishment all his life. When Carlin first became successful, he admitted that he hated to be part of the establishment because he was a rebel, "I was a victim of my own success and here is what I was missing: I was missing who I was…What I really was, was an outlaw, a rebel, who swam against the tide of what the establishment wants from us. That person has been suppressed."[364]

This paradoxical phenomenon expressed so clearly by Carlin explains the sharp turn his performance took when he abandoned the mainstream comedy and became a counterculture comedian. He took a big cut in pay in his transition from over $12,000 a week in Las Vegas to almost nothing in colleges and coffee shops in Greenwich Village.[365] Ironically, Apatow's counterproductive choice of stars for the documentary conflicts the purpose of Carlin's work. All comedians participating in the film were establishment performers, perhaps with the exception of Jon Steward. Understandably, they couldn't sympathize with the counterculture presented by Carlin. Although they showed sincere admiration for Carlin, they had to tip-toe around his fame and be careful not to say anything meaningful.

Like the news anchors from the establishment media, these mainstream comedians, whose success precludes real criticism of the status quo, had to pretend they didn't understand the real reason Carlin was popular then and is still trending now. Jon Steward and Bill Burr were the ones who slipped through the cracks of self-censorship their meaningful comments. For example, Burr made a profound statement that Carlin had several sharp turns of growth in his career – he went from conservative, mainstream comedian to counterculture, and from there to a more extreme rebellious level, and he emphasized how much courage it takes to do so. Because every time Carlin moved to the next level, he left behind a segment of his audience that was not ready to move forward with him. Burr concluded that Carlin was determined to tell his truth regardless of what the cost would be, as if he did not care whether his audience was three people or three thousand people.[366]

Besides these profound revelations, the rest of the comedians featured in the film reiterated praises within the narrow scope of permitted rhetoric. For example, Steven Colbert who comments about Carlin in the movie, started his career as the opposite of Carlin's – he was a counterculture comedian making

---

[364] Apatow, *Part One* 42:37.
[365] Ibid., 49:56-50:48.
[366] Ibid., *Part Two*, 32:13.

fun of real power in his show *The Colbert Report*. Later, when he became super popular because of his critique, Colbert turned his success into profit. Colbert changed his humor in a retrograde direction resolving to trivial petty partisan jokes pretending that he believes in the shallow, artificial division between left and right. Now he is a big star in the *Tonight Show* and unfortunately, an obedient stenographer to power interviewing rich and powerful individuals who became his milieu. All he had to say about Carlin, was how funny he was. Although true, this statement is depriving Carlin of his rebellious nature, to which he remained loyal. As Upton Sinclair famously said, "It is difficult to get a man to understand something when his salary depends upon his not understanding it."[367]

An interesting part of Carlin's work was his adroit use of language to convey his profound messages. Jon Steward, who interviewed Carlin, brought the theme of language in the conversation. Steward inquired about Carlin's fascination with language, which is apparent in his monologues and analyses.[368] Steward compared Carlin's craft of using language to the art of a musician. Carlin confirmed that he perceives language as music, and that he composes the rhythm and melody of his speech.[369] In addition to perfecting the sound of language, Carlin really had a talent of deconstructing speech and skillfully detecting the hypocrisy of the avalanche of messages disseminated on TV.

In his earlier performance, Carlin deconstructs the advertisement language, a type of humor that is easy to accept. Most people could relate to such examples because nearly every individual has a personal experience of being disappointed from unfulfilled promises by advertisers. Furthermore, he extends this deconstruction to the news, the slogans and the language used, which is deceptive and manipulative. He actually deconstructs the propaganda, and the purpose of education, which to these days eludes many people. Therefore, when Carlin tells the audience that the purpose of education is to produce obedient workers and passive consumers, who remain willfully ignorant to their reality, it is hard to digest such information. Nevertheless, such provocations meet a heartfelt approval increasingly more often because very few things had changed since Carlin's time and usually for the worse.

Undoubtedly, George Carlin is every modern dissident's hero precisely

---

[367] Upton Sinclair, *I, Candidate for Governor: And How I Got Licked,* U of CA Press, Dec. 16, 1994. (First published in 1934).
[368] 40 Years Comedy, *HBO*, 1997.
[369] Ibid.

because he was ahead of his time and his social critique is still relevant now. Carlin was concerned about reproductive rights long before the recent 2022 overturn of Roe vs. Wade. He was talking about dividing regular people and turning them against each other as he drew the line between the powerful and the powerless, instead of left and right.[370] Unlike every other comedian who plays for a certain team, Carlin was against the two-party duopoly for most of the 20th century all the way until his passing in 2008. He ranted about destroying nature, and the endless consumption and unhealthy lifestyle of the United States. Carlin was the first to clarify that the U.S. bombs predominantly brown people and always was a strong anti-war voice, a voice against police brutality and violence in general.[371] He condemned the virus mania and the dismissal of natural immunity way before it reached its grotesque proportions during the 2020 pandemic. Carlin defined himself as a rebel and his legacy is his rebellion against the corrupt and mindlessly self-destructive system. For these reasons, Carlin is constantly featured by counterculture comedians such as Jimmy Dore, Russel Brand, Lee Camp, and all the brave dissidents that risk their livelihood every day by reporting the censored news.[372]

From contemporary counterculture comedians, I analyze Jimmy Dore because he closely resembles the principles and warnings Carlin so generously left us. Dore clearly enunciates the rebellious nature of Carlin's work, and criticizes mainstream comedians who took the easy path of supporting power. Besides frequently citing Carlin, Dore invited his daughter, Kelly Carlin, to his show and interviewed her about her father long before Apatow made him fashionable with the mainstream media. After Carlin persistently trended online for years, HBO decided to make some profit from its former employee and commissioned the task to director Apatow. Prior to the debut of the film, Kelly Carlin was briefly on every establishment news outlet. However, Dore interviewed Kelly Carlin in 2015, because of his admiration for her father. The way Carlin followed Lenny Bruce's counterculture comedy, Dore followed Carlin's. As a result, Dore's show has been systematically suppressed by the You Tube algorithms, and harassed by the ersatz fact checkers. Such self-appointed fact-checkers usually are officially proven wrong after suspending Dore's show for a time. Expectedly, the censors never issued an apology or

---

[370] Apatow, Part Two, 1:38:34
[371] Ibid., 1:37:38.
[372] Russel Brand, "'It's a Big Club and You Ain't' in It – How the Game is Rigged," *Under the Skin,* June 30, 2021.

retracted their claims. As other dissidents, Dore is compelled to resort to *Rokfin, Substacks, Rumble, Spotify* and other uncensored (for now) platforms. Regardless of the suppression, Dore's platform generated over a million subscribers, and keeps growing.

As independent journalists, counterculture comedians, and many other creators did, Dore started his own platform, *The Jimmy Dore Show*, because by the second decade of this century, the mainstream media or the fourth estate was completely captured by the secret services and big business. There are no official platforms that are free from control by these institutions, which they are supposed to question.[373] Dissident journalists such as Hedges, Blumenthal, Webb, among others often expose the ties between mainstream official websites and government institutions. For example, Wikipedia, which is supposed to be a grassroots project, is completely controlled by the secret services and big business. As a result, the website regularly features misinformation, propaganda, and biased definitions. For example, in Dore's Wikipedia page, there are listed several "conspiracy theories" that Dore supposedly spreads, an error in reporting that he since retracted, and an unproved sexual harassment accusation by his former colleague without legal consequences.

Nowhere in Wikipedia are Dore's followers mentioned, even though the page has been visited more than five million times. Among great many people, frequent guests on Dore's show are Pulitzer Prize winning Glen Greenwald, Izzy Award winning journalist Aaron Mate, Pulitzer Prize winning Chris Hedges, Independent Feature Award winning journalist Max Blumenthal, presidential candidate Dr. Jill Stein, presidential candidate Marianne Williamson, Dr. Robert Malone, Dr. Robert Kennedy Jr., among others. However, the only person mentioned in Dore's profile among his guests, is a Boogaloo Boys member featured under the subtitle "Controversy."[374] According to Dore, he was inspired by George Carlin, Bill Hix, and Jerry Steinfeld. In an interview with *Trigonometry*, Dore shared that he is a populist and the establishment is afraid of commentators uniting people. More specifically, creators who explain to audiences that they have more in common with each other than they have with the ruling class of either party.[375]

Dore believes in free speech not in theory only but in practice because he understands that this concept is easy to defend when you agree with the

---

[373] Max Blumenthal, *Collision Tech Conference,* Toronto, July 16, 2022.
[374] https://en.wikipedia.org/wiki/Jimmy_Dore
[375] Konstantin Kisin, "Jimmy Dore: They Won't Let the Great Unwashed Have a Voice," *Trigonometry*, Feb., 2022.

person but the ultimate test is protecting the rights of people with whom you disagree. Dore has a track record of defending every person who is censored regardless of their beliefs because he acts on principal. The list of people he openly defended includes notorious figures such as Alex Jones, President Trump, as well as likeminded people such as Joe Rogan, Jackson Hinkle, Aaron Mate, Max Blumenthal, and Chris Hedges. All these people have been demonetized, suspended, or permanently banned from platforms such as You Tube, Twitter, Meta, Instagram, and other monopolists on the Internet. These platforms are aligned with the government and big business; therefore, they are protecting their own interests not the public. Dore understands well that dissidents are the most vulnerable targets and tries to communicate this to his audience. In an interview with counterculture activists Fiorella and Pasta from the *Convo Couch,* Fiorella explained that not only creators who contradict the mainstream narratives with large followers are targeted routinely, but even people with small followings who reveal the truth.[376] Dore always maintained the view that the answer to bad speech is more speech not censorship.

Furthermore, Dore is not afraid to comment on highly controversial topics such as money in politics, the two-party duopoly, the corruption of the mainstream media, the imperialistic wars, homelessness, and police brutality. More recent controversies that Dore brings up frequently are the Covid vaccines, the mandates during the pandemic, the biggest upward transfer of wealth during the pandemic, and the censorship that escalated to unprecedented levels in silencing oppositional voices. As we witness a newer controversy, the war in Ukraine, Dore investigates the events and questions the mainstream media narrative. The omnipresent propaganda dictates that Putin's "unprovoked" invasion of Ukraine causes all the ills in our society including high prices of gasoline, inflation, poverty, increased death rates, and so on. The dissident opinions regarding the war expressed by Noam Chomsky, historian John Mearsheimer, former general Scott Ritter, Chris Hedges, Aaron Mate, Max Blumenthal, Caitlin Johnstone, and Richard Medhurst among others, were flagged, demonetized, or simply purged from You Tube, Twitter, and other large public platforms. As Dore continues to invite or cite opponents to the war state line, he lately quoted Chomsky's eloquent comment on the war and censorship:

---

[376] Dore, "You Tube Host Silenced for Challenging U.S. Gov on Ukraine," *The Jimmy Dore Show,* July 14, 2022.

>
> Of course, it was provoked. Otherwise, they wouldn't refer to it all the time as an unprovoked. By now, censorship in the United States has reached such level beyond anything in my lifetime. Such a level that you are not permitted to read the Russian position…I have never seen a level of censorship like this.
>
> …Most of this is not obvious to western audiences simply because rational voices are not allowed to talk and because rationality is not permitted. This is a level of hysteria that I have never seen, even during the Second World War, which I am old enough to remember well.[377]

Undoubtedly, Chomsky witnessed the WWII propaganda, McCarthy's red scare, and the concentration camps in the U. S., yet he is astounded by the level of the current censorship. It is alarming that the 94-year dissident sees no comparison to the current totalitarian measures in his lifetime. As a guest of Dore's show, investigative reporter Isabella Fiorella who left the country and works for the RT now in Moscow, reminds Dore that RT America was banned in the U.S. and Europe in 2022, and notes that she is not censored by her program management and has now health insurance in addition to free speech.[378] Among other dissidents, Dore is not only a counterculture comedian but an activist for human rights.

For example, Dore attracted a lot of attention during his campaign "Force the Vote" launched in 2020, which promoted Medicare for all. To this end, Dore teamed up with NFL Chargers running back Justin Jackson and a number of public figures. The movement received massive support from regular people and independent media members such as Aaron Mate, Brianna Joy Gray, Caitlin Johnstone, Dr. Cornel West, Chris Hedges, Graham Elwood, Katie Halper, Krystal Ball, Kyle Kulinski, Marianne Williamson, Max Blumenthal, Nick Brana, Ron Placon, Ryan Knight, Susan Sarandon, and Stef Zamorano. Dore's idea was that there were enough progressive representatives in the House to force a vote on the floor and to stand up to establishment Democrats and make serious demands in exchange for their vote for Speaker Nancy Pelosi. Because the Democrats ran under the slogan "healthcare is a human right," the voters should hold them accountable and

---

[377] Ramzy Baroud, "Not a Justification but a Provocation: Chomsky on the Root Causes of the Russia Ukraine War," *Counterpunch*, June 28, 2022
[378] Dore, July 14, 2022.

press them to deliver their basic promise. The campaign's official statement included:

> We put the Squad and House progressives in office to stand up to Nancy Pelosi, establishment Democrats, and the insurance companies that fund them. This is a rare moment where Pelosi needs something form progressives. It could be years before we have another chance and millions of people do not have that long.
>
> This country needs Medicare for all now. A floor vote is the absolute least we must demand. We want a vote om the last full week of January, after Biden is inaugurated. The progressive movement has shown huge support to this campaign and we want to know: Will you stand up to Democratic Party leadership when we need it most?[379]

Even though the campaign did not succeed, it attracted much attention on Twitter, Meta, You Tube and other social networks and drew strong support from the public. More importantly, Dore succeeded in exposing the hypocrisy of the progressive Democrats. He demonstrated that even progressive politicians who don't receive money from the corporations are useless because they are afraid to confront powerful corrupt leaders who do. In this way, the campaign was an eye-opening experience to many regular people who were invested in supporting such representatives by volunteering their time and hard-earned money. Dore became so popular that people started to ask him to run for president in 2024. However, according to Dore, this is not his call and he realizes that as a comedian he can be plenty more useful because he is so good at exposing corruption and persuading people to make positive changes. In a way, Dore exceeded his hero, George Carlin, because he was doing comedy and activism at the same time. It is phenomenal how such comedians could cut through the lies, the propaganda, and the brainwashing, and see clearly what most people cannot or would not see.

In his interview with Carlin's daughter, comedian Kelly Carlin, Dore and she agreed that it is essential to be an outsider as a professional in order to hold people in power accountable. The same applies to independent media because if you are part of the power machine or aiming to be part of it, it is

---

[379] www.Forcethevote.org

impossible to challenge such power.[380] Contrary to the common belief, Kelly Carlin shared memories about her father's spirituality. She explained that because Carlin was always a seeker, it was inevitable that he would stumble upon some mysterious experience. She emphasized his search for meaning, his sense of wonder and awe toward the oneness of everything in the universe. Carlin experienced this connection during one of his acid trips, and realized that everything in the universe is linked. Carlin shared with Kelly that he felt he is in everything and everything is in him; therefore, he could not be afraid anymore. This profound conclusion contradicts the conviction that Carlin was an atheist. Kelly admitted that her father did not like the term atheist because it made him a part of a group. Included in Apatow's documentary is a stage monologue toward the end of his life, where he talks about "the big electron" referring to higher power.[381] Kelly clarified that the term big electron was coined by Carlin's brother Patrick, and George adopted it in their regular conversations.

Following the legacy of Carlin, Dore offers a deconstructive analysis of our society, which contradicts the official narrative; therefore, it is difficult to accept. It is no surprise that he is a controversial figure and a target of the establishment media. Last year, *The Daily Beast* published a hit piece on Dore, fraught with misinformation and slander.[382] However, Dore is ready to pay the price for telling the truth. He has been suppressed on You Tube by the algorithms, he has been warned, suspended and demonetized. He keeps provoking power and jokes that at least he is not in jail like Julian Assange. Perhaps the road he has chosen will become mainstream; perhaps he would cave and collapse under pressure. For now, he is doing an excellent reporting of the news; therefore, replacing the news anchors who would not do their job.

Ultimately, as Jimmy Dore and other comedians continue to carry on the legacy of George Carlin who never gave up, the world would be more informed, and a better place. As Carlin always urged people to take care of each other, Dore never gets tired of reiterating how his neighbor is not his enemy, the ruling class is, and that we have a lot more in common with each other regardless of our race, nationality, religion, and politics than we have with the elites. Although it is a straightforward concept, as Caitlin Johnstone warned us, it is painful to feel that way – the way Carlin felt – a disillusioned idealist. It is not a coincidence that dissidents are always a minority because

---

[380] "Kelly Carlin on *Growing Up with George,* Interview with Jimmy Dore, *TYT,* 2016.
[381] Apatow, Part Two, 1:43:33.
[382] "Hilarious Hit Piece on Jimmy Dore by Democratic Rag," *The Jimmy Dore Show,* 2021.

telling the truth is never easy. Facing the reality is also difficult but to listen to the counterculture reporting is relatively easier than standing up for the unorthodox with all its consequences. The least we can do to honor iconoclasts such as Carlin among other counterculture comedians, Assange and his fellow whistleblowers, and Chomsky among other dissident scholars, is to listen to them and try to understand the dynamics of power in order to transform them into more just and egalitarian structures.

Chapter Nine

Never Trust Politicians, Mainstream Journalists and Academics: They Are the Ruling Class

> *The Media is only one facet of the deeper problem in America. That problem is money in politics. Our officials serve money and not the people.*
>
> *-Jimmy Dore*

I discussed the regulatory capture of the mainstream media, the academia, and the co-opting and infiltrating grassroots movements in previous chapters. However, a recent lesson from the last two elections, 2016 and 2020, teaches us not to trust politicians even if they refuse to take corporate money. The core problem with such politicians is that they only take money from grassroots supporters, which makes them trustworthy, and then they betray their followers. In 2016, a new phenomenon occurred in American politics. For roughly two centuries, the winner of the elections could be predicted by the money they spend in the race – the success was always proportional to the amount of money invested. But this time it was different.

An unknown older senator from Vermont, Bernie Sanders, who did not take money from corporations rose to prominence and appeared to be winning inequivalently. For forty years the senator condemned the same injustices – greedy corporations were exploiting workers, healthcare was a human right, economic inequality has grown to an unsustainable level, and media were controlled by their investors – the pharmaceutical, oil, and military industries. People believed Sanders because he always conveyed the same messages not just when he ran for elections. His supporters found old videos of younger Sanders reiterating the exact same criticism 40 years ago. Finally, there was a politician who was not corrupt, did not take money from billionaires and corporations, and didn't change his standing on any important issue. Most importantly, he did not belong to any of the two major parties – he was Independent. Sanders was drawing huge crowds and was unstoppable.

The catch was, he ran as Democrat, not Independent. The proverbial wisdom dictated that you cannot run as a third party, you would not have enough votes to be taken seriously, and everyone who voted for a third party was wasting their vote. The pundits, the media, and scholars preached this mantra since the 1940s when a third-party candidate, Henry Wallace, was destroyed. Completely ignoring the fact that Lincoln ran as a third party and founded the Republican Party, defeating the Whigs in 1850s, propaganda machine reiterates the same mantra every election. It is much easier to control two parties with corrupt leaders than multi-parties with multiple leaders. The mantra was invented and maintained for the convience of the ruling class – the real owners who wanted to deal with as few politicians as possible. After all, they had to buy the media, the academia, and the judges, they did not want to spend too much time bribing politicians who were there just to give people the illusion that they have a choice. Thus, Sanders started in the wrong path from the beginning, as he agreed to run as Democrat. Next blunder was when he almost won the primary and the Democratic National Convention (DNC) outright cheated him and nominated Hilary Clinton, their beloved former Secretary of State. The Democratic leadership was not sure that they can trust a senator who does not take money from corporations. Sanders not only quietly accepted the shenanigans of the DNC but he even endorsed Clinton and campaigned for her. People were appalled of the actions of the Democratic party and because Hilary Clinton was widely unpopular, most of the electorate opted for the Republican candidate – Donald Trump.

When analyzing the elections of 2016, people usually overlook the fact that Trump ran almost verbatim on the same platform as Bernie Sanders – he criticized the media, the corrupt Democratic Party, the endless wars and NAFTA's outsourcing jobs abroad. He even went after his party's candidates and exposed their corruption too. The only difference was, Trump didn't mean any of his rhetoric. He was a showman, and knew how to win an audience. Even after winning the elections, he continued to gaslight his people and said the right things while making backdoor deals with the people he criticized. Of course, Obama, Clinton, and other officials did the exact same thing – they had public opinion and private opinion, usually the opposite.[383]

Then in 2020, when Sanders ran again, and the DNC executed the same operation – they cheated him from the nomination and chose Biden instead. Again, they went for the well-known senator who had a long record of accepting money from the main business industries of oil, pharma, military, financial, and digital sectors. Similarly, the DNC had a long history of cheating progressives while pretending to be the liberal party. Back in 1944, they defeated Vice President Henry Wallace whose progressive role in the F.D. Roosevelt administration was significant before and during WWII. In 1944, the Democratic party nominated Harry Truman – a candidate who had only two percent of the votes, instead of Wallace, who had 65 percent of the popular votes for his nomination for Vice President.[384] Thanks to such shenanigans, Wallace was not re-elected and was succeeded by Harry Truman. DNC nominated Truman because he was a politician who pursued aggressive military policies by establishing the Truman Doctrine, NATO, and is notorious for unprecedented use of the atomic bomb in densely populated cities, Hiroshima and Nagasaki. In contrast, Wallace promoted ending the cold war with Russia, and domestic policies benefitting Americans such as universal healthcare.[385]

After being cheated a second time by the DNC, Sanders repeated his humble response and actively helped Biden to win the elections. If anything, Sanders knows American history. He knew the fate of Wallace and did not want to end up like him. After his defeat by the DNC, Wallace was fired by Truman in 1946 from his position as Secretary of Commerce for delivering a speech, in which he promoted peace with the Soviet Union. He then established the Progressive Party; however, was accused of being Communist and fell into political obscurity in the 1950s. A more recent example Sanders didn't want to follow, was the 2000 presidential candidate, Ralf Nader, who ran independently with the Green Party. However, Nader not only lost the elections, he was physically obstructed from participating in the debates, even

---

[383] Ben Wolfgang, "Hilary Clinton says She Has Both a Public and a Private Position on Wall Street: Wiki Leks," *The Washington Times*, October 8, 2016.

[384] Zain Raza, "Noam Chomsky and Peter Kuznick – The Untold History of the United States," *AcTVism*, Feb. 5, 2019, 1:11:28.

[385] Chris Hedges, "Bernie Sanders' Phantom Movement," *Tikkun*, Feb. 14, 2016.

though he qualified for such activity by the number of the votes he earned. Moreover, he was forever accused of being the reason Al Gore lost to Bush and hated for this, thanks to the lies and manipulations of the media and the establishment. Like Wallace before him, Nader fell into political obscurity regardless of his enormous activity as a lawyer, politician, scholar, and activist.

Chris Hedges, who was a speech writer for Nader, explains the phenomenon of Sanders:

> Bernie Sanders, who has attracted numerous young, white, college-educated supporters in his bid for the presidency, says he is creating a movement and promises a political revolution. This rhetoric is an updated version of the "change" promised by the 2008 campaign of Barak Obama and by Jesse Jackson's earlier National Rainbow Coalition. Such Democratic electoral campaigns, at best, raise political consciousness. But they do not become movements or engender revolutions.[386]

Hedges understands the mechanism of artificial division in two-party duopoly that serves the same business interests. He explains the uselessness of both parties to regular people under the guise of opposing each other, "The Democrats, like the Republicans, have no interest in genuine reform. They are wedded to corporate power. They are about appearance, not substance."[387] As other iconoclasts note when evaluating the two-party system in the U.S., representatives of genuine left are missing here, and there is a discrepancy in labeling political views with the rest of the world. According to Hedges, "In Europe, America's Democratic Party would be a far-right party. The Republican Party would be extremist. There is no Liberal – much less left or progressive – organized political class in the United States."[388] Hedges explains that the policies of both parties give away the powers they serve. With a very small difference in preferences, they work for the largest industries in the country who spend enormous amounts of money lobbying the dominant two parties. In Hedges' words,

---

[386] Ibid.
[387] Ibid.
[388] Ibid.

> The Democrats, like the Republicans, have no intention of halting the assault on our civil liberties, the expansion of the imperial wars, the coddling of Wall Street, the destruction of the ecosystem by the fossil fuel industry and the impoverishment of the workers.[389]

Chris Hedges further reveals that Sanders supports the Democratic Party with 98 percent of his votes. For example, Sanders routinely votes for imperial wars and for the bloated military budget, supported the corporate money grab of Obamacare, and called on Ralf Nader in 2004 to abandon his presidential campaign. In 2014, when privately asked by Hedges and Kshama Savant, a City Council member of Seattle, why he wouldn't run as Independent, Sanders admitted that he didn't want to end up like Nader.[390]

Hedges clarifies that if Sanders defies the Democratic party, there will be consequences. He will be stripped from his seniority in the Senate, he will lose his committee chairmanships, and the party machine will turn him into a pariah, like Nader. Hedges adds, "Nader paid a heavy price for his courage and his honesty, but he was not a failure."[391] According to Hedges, Sanders' justification for not running as an Independent was sincere but at the same time it was also indicative of political cowardice. Therefore, Hedges concludes that Sanders secured a deal with the DNC – in return for not destroying his career, Sanders' real function had to be to lead his followers into supporting the Democratic Party, which is a dead end to progressive changes. Sanders became hugely popular because he promised millions of regular Americans a revolution, which he never delivered. In this way, Sanders' role is even more subversive because he effectively prevents a viable third party to emerge as he takes all the movement's energy and pours it into the corrupt Democratic party.[392]

Recent complacency demonstrated by Sanders includes his votes for the increased military budget in 2020, the CARES Act in 2020, which was a massive upward transfer of wealth, the Biden's Build Back Better Bill, which gutted the Green New Deal Bill, eliminated Medicare for All, and mandated vaccination that forced thousands of workers out of their jobs. In addition, Sanders goes along with the anti-Russian propaganda which challenges a

---

[389] Ibid.
[390] Ibid.
[391] Ibid.
[392] Ibid.

nuclear power country that could end up with WWIII, and always plays the partisan game – blaming the Republicans in a situation where the Democrats have majority in both Senate and Congress. Sanders repeats the claim that the repealing of Roe vs. Wade, or banning abortion was the Republicans' fault knowing that the Democrats could codify this legislation into law many times and chose not to do so.

Another prominent example of disillusionment from political representatives is Alexandria Ocasio Cortez (AOC), and the squad comprised of young women of color such as Ayana Presley, African American, Ilhan Omar originally from Somalia, Rashida Tlaib originally from Palestine. Initially, these four women made a wave and stirred hope because they primaried their opponents and won elections against establishment members of their own party.

For example, AOC defeated Joe Crowley, a twenty-year veteran and 10-teerm incumbent for NYC's 14th district in 2018. 29-year-old AOC was the new "hope and change" for America. Young people mobilized their ranks and raised money, knocked on doors, and gathered in huge crowds to support AOC. Formerly a daughter of a Puerto Rican immigrant and working as a bartender in NYC, she was the perfect representative for the underdog. It was hard to believe that a young progressive woman unseated the third powerful member of the Democratic party without the media back-up, and without corporate money.

Prior to her election, AOC said that it didn't matter if she were a one-term representative. She said that if she could make the necessary changes in one-term and be replaced afterward, it would be worthwhile sacrificing her career. She said her role was to make a ruckus in politics. As a junior member of Congress, AOC joined the Sunrise movement protest in front of Speaker of the House Nancy Pelosi's office back in 2018. AOC tweeted how she struggles to pay her rent in D.C. before she was drawing salary from the government – proof that Congress is designed for rich people. She emphasized the fact that her health insurance was much better than her insurance as a fool-time bartender.

However, as soon as AOC got settled and bestowed with privilege, her tone changed. AOC's very first vote was in support of Speaker Pelosi, who by January 2019 became "Mama Bear" to AOC. From then on, it was one betrayal after another. She voted for the CARES Act in 2020 – the greatest upward transfer of money in US history, when over $4T went to the richest corporations and billionaires, whereas a meager $2B went to regular people.

She voted for increasing the military budget to $780B the same year, for the $4B a year for Israel, the butchered New Green Deal in 2021, and the $55B aid to Ukraine in 2022. Like Bernie Sanders and the rest of the squad, she was a good solder for the establishment and never crossed her superiors.

Not only AOC voted for all these imperialistic, exploitative welfare for the rich legislations, she actively opposed Jimmy Dore's campaign for Medicare for All in the middle of a pandemic. AOC's opposition to the initiative was very vocal on Twitter and her arguments contradicted every slogan she flaunted from 2018 to 2020. For example, back on Sept. 16, 2018, AOC tweeted:

> Medicare for all costs $32T.
> Our "current" system costs more than that for less care than Medicare for All would provide.
> Medicare for All aims to cover physical, dental, and mental healthcare for less money than the current setup.[393]

Another quote by AOC from 2020, during Dore's campaign regarded a different topic but correctly described the same strategy that she later opposed:

> The whole point of protesting is to make ppl uncomfortable.
> Activist take this discomfort w/ the status quo & advocate for concrete policy changes. Popular support often starts small & grows.
> The folks who complain protest demands make others uncomfortable…
> That's the point.[394]

But when given the chance to make leaders uncomfortable, AOC defied her own advice, and started making excuses for conforming to power. Furthermore, pressed by the Force the Vote campaign, AOC tweeted,

> Problem w/ this idea is that isn't enough thought given to step 2.

---

[393] http://twitter.com/aoc, Sept.16, 2018.
[394] Ibid., Dec. 2020.

> The Dem votes aren't there yet, and with a razor thin margin the Dem Nos are more than margin. So you issue threats, hold your vote, and lose.
> Then what?

To which Dore responded,

> You are revealing that you never intended to use your leverage to fight for Med4All or cross MammaBear.[395]

This timely incident of political activism exposed at once the hypocrisy and careerism of fifteen progressive members of the Democratic party, petitioned directly by the Force the Vote campaign.[396] All fifteen members ran on Medicare for All and, despite AOC's statement, were more than the "razor thin" margin in the House, mentioned in the tweet. There was a real chance of Medicare 4ALL passing the House, even if it were killed in the Senate. However, even if it didn't pass the House, in both scenarios the opponents of the Bill would have been exposed by name and thus, their re-election seriously jeopardized. According to statistics, Medicare for All consistently is supported by 88 percent of the Democrat voters, 68 percent of independents, and 46 percent of the Republican voters, total of 69 percent nationwide.[397] During the pandemic, this number is very likely to have been increased overwhelmingly, given the recently unveiled stats that 338,000 people died in 2021 because of their lack of health insurance.[398]

As was the case with any other industry, the dreadful condition of our healthcare was exposed during the pandemic. For example, the population of the US comprises 4 percent of the world population; however, our death toll from Covid comprised 16 percent of the global deaths.[399] Furthermore, nearly 100 million Americans reported uninsured or underinsured as millions lost

---

[395] *Corporate Crime Reporter,* "Jimmy Dore Calls on Democrats to Withhold Support for Nancy Pelosi Unless She Brings Single Pair Medicare for All to a Vote," Dec. 12, 2020.

[396] AOC, Ayanna Presley, Barbara Lee, Chuy Garcia, Cori Bush, Ilhan Omar, Jamal Bowman, Jamal Raskin, Katie Porter, Marie Newman, Mark Pocan, Pramila Jayapal, Rashida Tlaib, Raul Grijalva, and Ro Khanna.

[397] Daniel Villareal, "69 percent of Americans Want Medicare for All, including 46 Percent of Republicans, New Poll Says," *Newsweek,* April 24, 2020.

[398] Mike Ludwig, "Medicare for All could Have Prevented 338,000 Deaths," *Truthout,* June 17, 2022.

[399] Ibid.

their health insurance during the pandemic.[400] Furthermore, a recent study shows that more than 100 million people are in debt due to healthcare bills, or 41 percent of the adult population.[401]

In reality, the political system is designed in the same way the media and academia are – to filter dissidents and to reward conformity. Thus, only politicians who support the status quo remain in the system. They are allowed to have the right rhetoric in order to gain popularity and support; however only cosmetic changes are possible through legislation. The few politicians who rebel against these rules and try to make real changes, are thrown out of the system. One example is Democrat Denis Kucinich, a representative from Ohio, whose 8-term service ended in 2013, when he was primaried by his own party through machinations known as gerrymandering, or changing the geographic region in order to force a politician to lose or win.[402] He also suffered media blackout during his two presidential runs in 2004 and 2008. Kucinich was anti-war, against the Patriot Act, and called for impeachment of George W. Bush and Dick Cheney for war crimes. In addition, Kucinich called Obama's air strikes in Libya "impeachment offences."[403]

Kucinich's bipartisan opposition to the Iraq war, the military intervention of Libya and Syria, regardless of the administration in power made him politically disposable. Kucinich was also the rare voice against the "deep state," alluding to the permanent bureaucracy behind the elected officials. In an interview Kucinich stated that "The political process of the United States of America is being under attack by intelligence agencies and individuals in these agencies."[404] In addition, Kucinich was opposed to NAFTA – the Act passed by Clinton and the Democratic party, which outsourced all the manufacturing well-paid jobs for Americans – political position considered suicidal because it goes against the interests of all big corporations. In the end, Kucinich was filtered out from the political system like Ralf Nader and Henry Wallace before him. A political lesson well-learned by Sanders, AOC, and the squad – if you go against the political machine, it will end your career and privileges.

---

[400] Pramila Jayapal, Congresswoman for WA-07, March 17, 2021, www.Jayapal.house.gov.
[401] Noam N. Levey, "More Than 100 Million People in the US Have Health Care Debt, Study Shows," *Truthout,* June 16, 2022.
[402] David Weigel, "Bernie Sanders Kicks off 3 Days Rallies for Like-minded Candidates," *The Washington Post,* Feb. 22, 2018.
[403] Graham Vyse, "Is Denis Kucinich Serious?" *The New Republic,* Jan. 17, 2018.
[404] Ian Schwartz, "Kucinich: 'Deep State' Trying to Take Down Trump, 'Our Country is Under Attack Within," *Real Clear Politics,* May 18, 2017.

Similarly, the mainstream media machine works endlessly to filter out the dissidents. The news anchors of the dominant political parties, Fox News for the Republicans and CNN/MSNBC for the Democrats routinely practice the principle of divide and conquer. Independent journalist Matt Taibbi discusses the artificial division imposed and maintained by the mainstream media in his 2021 book *Hate Inc: Why Today's Media Makes Us Despite One Another*.[405] Taibbi explains that Herman and Chomsky model of five filters described in their 1988 book *Manufacturing Consent* are still relevant in 21st century, with a slight correction in the fifth filter: common enemy. He enunciates:

> The news at its core is still a vehicle for advertising elite interests. Most of the filters still hold. But the model has been disrupted in one way. As Chomsky notes, the idea of anti-communism as an organized religion has gone bust.
>
> We've tried other common enemies. Islamic terrorists were serviceable for a while. Occasionally, a dictator like Slobodan Milosevic will get some air time in this role. Russia is back for a second run lately, minus the socialist black hat.
>
> None of these antagonists are close enough to home for modern audiences. This is why the biggest change to Chomsky's model is the discovery of a far superior "common enemy" in modern media: each other. So long as we remain a bitterly divided two-party state, we'll never want for TV villains. Who we hate just depends on what channel we watch.[406]

As long as the discourse is contained within a narrow scope and doesn't go beyond the artificial division of left and right, the arguments can be very heated. Chomsky explained succinctly that this performance gives the illusion of free speech while restricting a whole host of topics from the public discussion. Thomas Frank, a disillusioned Democrat wrote in 2016 *Listen, Liberal,* warning the audience that they have been abandoned by the Democratic party and this could lead to a right-wing populist like Trump. Frank also revealed the transition of a generation of journalists who belonged to the working class and represented their class to an elite class journalist

---

[405] Matt Taibbi, *Hate Inc: Why Today's Media Makes Us Despite One Another,* New York, London: Or Book, 2021.
[406] Ibid., 208.

whom Frank called "Ivy League monoculture" pundits who were urban, educated, white color and in "perpetual awe of productivity and corporate innovation."[407] Frank concluded, "By now, there are only two newspapers left, the *New York Times* and *Washington Post,* and they are identical. They say the same things: it's incredibly limited ecosystem." [408]

The rare voices, which criticize *both isles* of the spectrum are flaked and thrown out.

Taibbi summarizes the process in his book giving the example of Thomas Frank who was guilty of confronting both left and right elites:

> However, the moment his writing became too much of an indictment of the failures of the professional political class in general (read: Democrats as well as Republicans) he joined an increasing long list of people whose point of view was no longer much in demand, on TV or anywhere else.[409]

The acceptable borderline in opinions that couldn't be crossed was the bi-partisan criticism of both parties. Ironically, this proves how much in common left and right elites have with each other in contrast with the rest of the people. It demonstrates how class loyalty trumps any other factor such as race, gender, education, professional field and so on. The ersatz diversity emphasized so much in the media, academia and elsewhere did not include class. In every field especially politics, media, and academia, there were men of color, women of color, gay and trans people towing the same class line of exploitation the workers, military imperialism, and support for big pharma, Wall Street, and high-tech industries. As long as they stay within the permitted dialog and support one of the parties, they have the unconditional approval of their team members. The unforgivable offence that leads to the end of someone's career, is to criticize both parties. This puts the person in odds with the ruling class, which supports both parties' elites and is against the general population. This strict rule has been in place since the inception of the country, with the slightly more diverse media between 1830- 1930s when there were plenty of outlets that both originated from the middle and working classes and represented them.

Another prominent example of crossing the line is Academy Award

---

[407] Ibid., 184.
[408] Ibid., 186.
[409] Ibid., 184.

winning for best adopted screenplay, two times winning best director and best picture filmmaker Oliver Stone. Stone's first major recognition came with his 1986 film *Platoon*. He always has been controversial; however, since 1991 documentary *JFK* about John F. Kennedy's assassination and 2021 *JFK Revisited* the blackout of his work significantly increased. In 2016 Stone released a feature film about Snowden, therefore crossing the secret services and Silicon Valley at the same time. Stone made a number of documentaries about Latin America – most notably three films about Cuba's president Fidel Castro, and *South of the Boarder,* featuring six Latin American presidents with left leanings who resisted transforming their countries into banana republics including Venezuela, Ecuador, Cuba, Argentina, Brazil and Paraguay. For all these censored topics Stone was criticized at home but praised in Europe and Latin America. Stone also produced a series of interviews with Russian President Putin featured on Showtime in 2017. In addition, Stone interviewed Viktor Yanukovych, former Ukrainian President in 2014, and produced a documentary *Ukraine on Fire* in 2016, and another one, *Revealing Ukraine,* in 2019. Stone explains the background for the current events between Russia and Ukraine blindly ignored by the media and mainstream historians.

Stone's 1991 *JFK* won eight Oscars; however, stirred a lot of controversy. Besides shattering the shallow version of the "magic bullet," the film led to a legislation after Stone presented it to Congress. In 1992, Congress passed the Assassination Records Collection Act, which reduced the secrecy surrounding the assassination, but did not end it. Therefore, in 2021, Stone released his sequel *JFK Revisited: Through the Looking Glass* – a two-hour documentary, which did not get the same attention as the first one in the US. It was mostly acclaimed abroad and premiered in Cannes Film Festival on July 12, 2021. In an interview with Joe Rogan, Stone resisted the term "conspiracy theory" and argued that many former "conspiracies" become later indisputable facts.[410]

Stone's continuous rebellion against mainstream narratives includes his 2012 series *The Untold History of the United States.* The critical documentary only worsened Stone's stand with the mainstream media because he exposed the real motifs behind every war and the role of the military and secret services in our history. The documentary, written with historian Peter Kuznick and Matt Graham, initially was streaming on Netflix; however, was removed in November 2020. The film is accompanied by a book with the same title

---

[410] Joe Rogan, "Oliver Stone on the JFK Assassination Coverup." *The Joe Rogan Experience,* Jan.5, 2022.

written by Stone and Kuznick, and published in 2012 by Simon & Shuster. The events in the series were disputed by mainstream media critics such as historian Ronald Radosh, journalist Michael Moynihan, and filmmaker Robert Orlando. Stone defended the documentary's accuracy in an interview on Showtime program:

> This has been fact checked by corporate fact checkers, by our own fact checkers, and fact checkers [hired] by Showtime. It's been thoughtfully vetted...these are facts. Our interpretation may be different than orthodox, but it definitely holds up.[411]

Some even disputed the fact that such events were untold and claim, like Radosh, that this was the "leftist" view of the American history. Nevertheless, this version of American history is not taught in schools and it is not discussed on the mainstream news. Even when discussed, such events and interpretations were always presented as "conspiracy theories." For example, in Stone's biography page on Wikipedia most of his films such as *JFK, JFK Revisited*, and *Ukraine on Fire*, among others were dubbed as conspiratorial. Regarding Stone's hugely successful film *Platoon*, there is no mentioning of the story of the film and that it was rejected twice by the Hollywood's board of directors. The film is openly anti-war; therefore, its rejection reveals the role of the government in controlling the narrative in mainstream cinema. In an interview, Stone explains that it took ten years for *Platoon* to be released – it started in 1976, and was rejected right away, then again in 1983.[412] Finally, the film was resurrected by a British filmmaker John Daly in 1986. Stone and Daly persuaded MGM to get the Pentagon and the CIA approval, which were on the Hollywood's board of directors including secretary of State Henry Kissinger.[413]

Stone discusses the recent withdrawal from Afghanistan and its critics and compares them to the critics of the withdrawal from Vietnam. Among other things, Stone has been a solder in Vietnam in his twenties and this was his wake-up call that turned him against military intervention anywhere in the world. Much of Stone's cinematography was dedicated to the Vietnam war

---

[411] Tavis Smiley, "Oliver Stone and Peter Kuznick, Part 1," PBC, Sept. 13, 2011.
[412] Joe Rogan, "How Oliver Stone's Experience in Vietnam Influenced *Platoon*," *The Rogan Experience,* July 21, 2020.
[413] Ibid.

including his first Oscar award for directing for *The Platoon*. Stone exposed a picture of the war so authentic and shocking that changed forever public's perception about wars. Similarly, *Born on Fourth of July* raises questions about the price of the war paid by both sides.

According to Stone, iconoclastic views exhibited in his documentary do not get massive traction because mainstream media outlets do not want controversy on their programs – they want some specific type of controversy that does not provoke the kind of questions his views do.[414] For example, he noted that usually it is violence or sports that are popular in mass media, and such historian blackout causes so much ignorance when it comes to the US foreign politics. Stone's firm conviction that foreign intervention does not work, is met with opposition from the mainstream pundits. Stone talks about debacle after debacle given the examples of Mexico, Korea, Vietnam, and so on up to the current war in Afghanistan.[415] As a consistent voice against military intervention, Stone is not given a public forum on mainstream media.

Stone's counterculture films also expose Wall Street and its greed. The director's 1997 film *Wall Street* and its 2010 sequel, *Wall Street: Money Never Sleeps,* earned a huge box office success. Released soon after the 2008 financial crisis, it resonated with audiences globally, while earning him the animosity of the financial sector. Nevertheless, Stone's biggest offence to mainstream media including Hollywood, is his open support for WikiLeaks' founder Julian Assange. Stone visited Assange in the Ecuadorian Embassy in London before his arrest and criticized the smear campaign orchestrated against him. More specifically, the two films, *We Steal Secrets: The Story of WikiLeaks* (2013), and *The Fifth Estate* (2013), asserts Stone, are designed to turn the public against Assange. Moreover, the films dismiss Assange's personal sacrifice of his own comfortable life in order to alert global populations about the disturbing actions of their own governments.

With more than 50 years of successful cinematography expressed in over 50 films, Stone does not receive nearly enough credit and publicity by the media for his impressive work. The reason for this informational eclipse is his counterculture views about the American politics, especially the US foreign interventions. Although evading a complete eclipse because of his popularity abroad, and because of his multiple awards, Stone's films still do not receive adequate coverage or publicity in comparison with propaganda-friendly

---

[414] Liu Xin, "One -on -one with Oliver Stone," *The Point,* Oct 15, 2021.
[415] Ibid.

authors and filmmakers. Stone remains a controversial figure; however, his prolific and superb work is sufficient to make him an icon in both American and global cinema. As is the case with politics and academia, the most obedient representatives rise to the top and become the gatekeepers who filter out the rogue, non-conformist members in their field. The ones that fall through the cracks, are the exceptions of the rule, and they frequently pay a price for deviating from the establishment narrative's strict lines.

In addition, academia produces the necessary representatives and supplies both politics and media with trained promoters of the main goal of their education – supporting the status quo. The other important focus of the academic factory is to maintain the illusion of meritocracy by producing obedient propagandists with fancy degrees from prestigious Ivy League universities. In this way, academia fulfills two purposes: supplying willful servants to power, and providing the smoke screen of sophisticated propaganda that conceals the process. Furthermore, the media selectively make and break their heroes based on their cooperation and support of power elites. They decide whose names are well-known to the public, and whose are successfully eclipsed and forgotten.

The names that are most popularized are the conformists in every important filed. In politics, 40-50 years of loyal service to the rich and powerful, earns a systemic elevation to prominence. Familiar names from both parties such as Speakers of the House Nancy Pelosi, John Boehner, Paul Ryan, and so on are advertised on national TV. In the news media, there are anchors such as Sean Hannity, Chris Wallace, Rachel Maddow, Brian Williams, from both ends of the political spectrum. In Hollywood, there are directors Spielberg, Scorsese, Tarantino, Coppola, and so on who glorify the ruling class regardless of their party, while promoting violence. In comedy, there are Trevor Noah, Steven Colbert, and Jimmy Fallon among others who never challenge the real power and always punch down instead of up. They are all promoted by the elites and imposed on the public despite their unpopularity as a result of reporting wrong information without retraction and the ensuing loss of credibility.

One example is 34-year-old MSNBC anchor Chris Hayes, who replaced Ed Schultz, fired for insubordination in 2013, and became the youngest host of a prime-time show on a major cable news channel. In 2012, prior to his lucrative position, Hayes wrote a book, titled *Twilight of the Elites: America*

After Meritocracy.[416] While still an outsider, Hayes explained in the book the insecurity of the elites and their insatiable desire to gain access to even higher circles from which they are excluded, among other interesting ideas. Hayes had a conversation with former journalist at the *Guardian* Glen Greenwald, who also founded the *Intercept* and later left the company when he was pressed to compromise his reporting. Greenwald discussed with Hayes his new book and asked him a relevant and essential question about resisting the elites' corruption once accepted in their circles. Greenwald formulated his concern in an article in *Salon*:

> In the book, Hayes described how American elite culture is so insulated that it "produce[s] cognitive capture," meaning that even those who enter it with hostility to its orthodoxies end up shaped by – succumbing to – its warped belief system and corrupt practices. Given that Hayes pronounces this "cognitive capture" to be "an inevitable outcome of sustained immersion" in that world, I asked him what steps he is personally taking to inoculate himself against being infected now that he's highly rewarded TV personality and employee of one of the world's largest media corporations.[417]

The irony is, Hayes answered that he hasn't thought about this. Of course, Greenwald who lived through the process of his media outlet being co-opted by a corrupt but powerful culture, did not believe Hayes for a moment. Greenwald learned by experience that the only remedy to preserve one's principles is to leave the corrupt environment. Indeed, it is difficult to accept that the person who studied and analyzed the process of co-option in his book, did not arrive to some thoughts of how he would avoid corruption in the case of his acceptance. And this is the most succinct way of depicting how the culture adaptation happens when someone becomes a part of the elite power. This process occurs in every field – politics, academia, media, police and military, business and finances, and every other lucrative profession of power. For this reason alone, it is impossible to trust anyone who is in

---

[416] Chris Hayes, *Twilight of the Elites: America After Meritocracy,* New York: Crown Publishing, June 12, 2012.
[417] Glen Greenwald, "Chris Hayes on Elite Failure: Why Don't American Oligarchs Fear the Consequences of Their Corruption and How Can That Be Changed?" *Salon*, August 1, 2012.

the system, and not an outsider because of the imminent co-optation and assimilation by the system regardless of their intentions.

The alternative to succumbing to corruption is to be thrown out of the system for insubordination or leave as Glen Greenwald and others did. Many were rejected by the system because they resisted corruption– Ralf Nader, Chris Hedges, Cornel West, among others. However, most individuals remain in the system pretending that they weren't absorbed and defeated. With the help of the media, they continue their rhetoric and hope that the public won't notice their opposite actions behind the scenes. Thus, they become more dangerous to the commonwealth because they deceive their supporters. Such cases are described in this chapter regarding progressive politicians, media anchors, Hollywood directors, and academics. Inevitably, these actors would expose themselves as hypocritical, hungry for power and wealth careerists. Some of them started out with good intentions but could not resist the corruption and weren't strong enough to give up their privileges for the cause they once believed in. It is not easy to trade money, fame, and power for principles. No one actually can be trusted until they are accepted inside the elitist bubble and pass the test. Audre Lorde said famously, "The Master's tools will never dismantle the Master's house." One must be an outsider in order to destroy the system, no one can do it from the inside. Historically, it is true that power corrupts; therefore, the ultimate litmus test should be whether one is an outsider and remains an outsider or one is assimilated and rewarded by the elites.

Chapter Ten

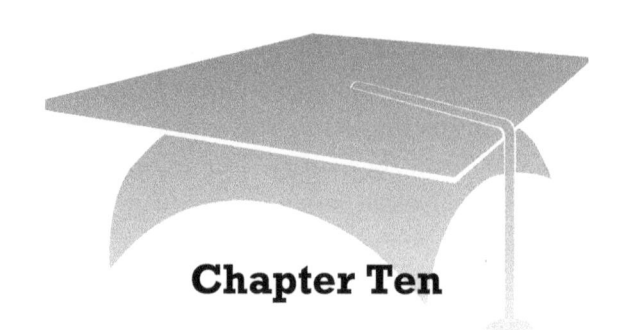

Ignorance is Propaganda's Best Friend: Challenging and Investigating The Official Narrative Is the Only Way to Educate Yourself and Others

Our number one enemy is ignorance. And I believe that is the number one enemy that everyone is not understanding what is actually going on in the world.

-Julian Assange, 2011

Obedience and conformism assure ignorance because they never challenge the conventional wisdom or the established narratives. If the population is obedient, it will not bother to investigate the orthodox knowledge or beliefs. It will not question anything studied in schools or disseminated by the news. This syllogism makes the goal of conditioning people into compliancy so important that the process starts from an early age. It is productive for the ruling class to design education to reward obedience and to punish independent thought. However, it is counterproductive if this type of conditioning is obvious, it is more effective to be subtle. If open, it would contradict the myth of freedom, democracy, and meritocracy. The task of covering up such method of producing a society of conformists is achieved through propaganda. Propaganda consistently claims the opposite of what is happening and gaslights people not to believe their own eyes. Journalist Matt Taibbi succinctly depicts the process,

> Today people are struggling and have lost so much trust in institutions that the only way to keep eyes away from the rot is by throwing the hardest propaganda fastballs. We can't allow attention to flag for even a moment because the evidence of political incompetence and corruption is so rampant and undeniable.[418]

When the process starts at an early age, it is usually ossified by the time people reach voting age and should make informed decisions. In addition, by the time some people wake up, it is often too late. They have spent half of their lives believing certain ideologies and sometimes are heavily invested in pursuing corresponding careers and lifestyles. It is very hard to throw every value instilled in you from childhood and to start all over. Caitlin Johnstone, an iconoclastic author, explained the phenomenon of human's tendency to choose cognitive ease over cognitive challenge discussed in Chapter Eight. It is the idea that most people defend official narratives because they are actually preserving their lifestyles. Since rejecting old beliefs would mean changing someone's life, people ferociously fight to defend old ideas.

Most importantly, there is the system of carrot and stick in place that strictly rewards or punishes corresponding behaviors. It is very hard to implement certain principles if the alternative leads to a lucrative and sometimes glamorous career. It is hard to go against the grain and tell the truth if the consequences are dire. Therefore, most people opt for the easier way of living and go with the flow. When the system is made in this way and is omnipresent, it is guaranteed that very few individuals will go against it. Many people will not even know about it, and will not desire to know if they sense trouble. Thus, most people remain willfully ignorant and this is exactly what the masters count on., as George Carlin explains in his monologues. Back in 2011, Assange warned us that ignorance is our enemy number one. Chomsky elaborates on the ruling class relying on people working long hours and not having the time and the energy to investigate what really is going on,

---

[418] Taibbi, *Hate Inc.*, 208.

"The general population doesn't know what's happening, and it doesn't even know that it doesn't know."

Before people start listening to the media, they go to school, and some go to kindergarten. Education is crucial for conditioning future generations. The process of inculcating ignorance and obedience is important and neatly organized. Chomsky summarizes it succinctly, "Education is a system of imposed ignorance."[419] He explains further,

> There are huge efforts that do go into making people, to borrow Adam Smith's phrase, "as stupid and ignorant as it is possible for a human being to be." A lot of the educational system is designed for that, if you think about it, it's designed for obedience and passivity. From childhood, a lot of it is designed to prevent people from being independent and creative. If you're independent-minded in school, you're probably going to get into trouble very early on.[420]

The second tool used by the ruling class – the media – is also applied widely as mass education. Indeed, the methods utilized by mass media are very similar to the ones used by education. Number one method is propaganda. In their book *Manufacturing Consent*, which reveals how mass media are tools of propaganda, Herman and Chomsky dedicate their work to Alex Carey, an Australian writer and academic, who did the pioneer work exposing corporate propaganda, according to the authors.

Alex Carey revealed that the people in the US have been subjected to an unparalleled, extensive, three quarters century long propaganda effort designed to expand corporate rights by undermining democracy and destroying the unions. Carey's unique view of US history caused him to become unpublishable and his book on the topic was released posthumously in 1995, eight years after his passing. In an interview with David Barsamian, Chomsky refers to Carey as a pioneer in this field, which "has yet to be investigated."[421] Chomsky articulates that this major phenomenon in modern world is almost unstudied. He notes that Carey's important essay, "Managing Public Opinion: The Corporate Offensive," has been circulating

---

[419] Chomsky, "Education is Ignorance." Excerpts from *Class Warfare: Interviews with David Barsamian*, London: Pluto Press, 1996, 19-23. https://chomsky.info/warfare02/
[420] Ibid., 27-31
[421] Ibid.

underground for years and was never published in his lifetime. In the essay, Carey enunciates the three most essential developments in the 20th century: the growth of democracy, the growth of corporations, and the growth of corporate propaganda as a means of defense against democracy.[422] According to Carey, corporate propaganda's main objectives are to instill in popular consciousness that free enterprise is a very cherished value, and to identify government regulations and strong unions as the enemy of democracy.[423] The techniques to achieve such objectives are called "public relations," "corporate communications," and "economic education."[424]

Carey expresses his concern that the topic of corporate propaganda has been largely ignored for over seventy years by relevant academic disciplines despite the vast scale on which propaganda has developed.[425] Interestingly, Carey claims that the idea of propaganda-managed democracy has been uniquely American and for the last fifty years the US business made great progress since 1970 in spreading it around the world including Carey's native Australia.[426] Carey urges audiences to end the long neglect of the problem of the unchallenged mass propaganda because it threatens the integrity of western democracies. Paradoxically, argues Carey, the greatest achievement of 20th century – propaganda – is persuading the public to abandon common sense in relation to propaganda.[427]

Citing Walter Lippmann from 1922, the author concludes that "the manufacturing consent has not died out" with the rise of egalitarianism; on the contrary, under the impact of propaganda, democratic values are obsolete. According to Lippmann, "it was no longer possible to believe in the original dogma of democracy," which requires any given public consent to reflect the popular will.[428] The leading American student of propaganda for the next fifty years, Harold Lasswell, echoed Lippmann's belief in 1972, arguing that the main method of social control is propaganda. Lasswell sarcastically announced, "If the mass will be free of chains of iron, it must accept chains

---

[422] Alex Carey, "Managing Public Opinion: The Corporate Offensive," *Serbian Political Thought,* Jan 2, 1996, 131.
[423] Ibid.
[424] Ibid.
[425] Ibid., 133.
[426] Ibid., 132.
[427] Ibid., 134.
[428] Ibid., 137.

of silver. If it will not love, honor and obey, it must not expect to escape seduction."[429]

Another method of propaganda, described by Carey, was big business spending millions in order to change public opinion against workers' strikes in the 1930s. The tactic was named Mohawk Valley Formula after the successful breaking of a strike against Remington Rand Corporation in 1936. A Senate Committee for investigating violations of labor rights described the tactic as follows: "The leaders of the association resorted to 'education' as they had in …1919-21…They asked not what the weaknesses and the abuses of the economic structure had been and how they could be corrected, but instead paid millions to tell the public that nothing was wrong and that great dangers lurked in the proposed remedies…"[430]

While before WWII, the methods of suppressing organized labor have been physically crushing strikes and demonstrations with the heavy use of police and military troops, after WWII the corporate elites shifted to the soft power of propaganda and passing legislations. Thus, they succeeded to achieve two main victories: the repealing of the Office of Price Administration (OPA), which regulated prices, and passed the Wagner Act, which made the pre-empting independent unions illegal.[431] President Truman, who sought to continue price control after WWII, reported the events of eliminating OPA in July 1946:

> Right after the end of the war, big business in this country set out to destroy the laws that were protecting the consumer against exploitation. This drive was spear-headed by the National Association of Manufacturers, the most powerful organization of big business in the country.
>
> …We know how the NAM organized its conspiracy against the American consumer. One of its own offices… spilled the story…after price control was killed…[He] told how his organization spent $3M in 1946 to kill OPA. The NAM spent a million and half on newspaper advertising. They sent their own speakers to make a thousand talks before women's clubs, civic organizations, and college students. A specially designed publication went to 37,000 school

---

[429] Ibid.
[430] Ibid., 139.
[431] Ibid., 146.

> teachers, another one to 15,000 clergymen, another one to 35,000 farm leaders, and still another to 40,000 leaders of women's clubs. A special clipsheet with NAM propaganda went to 7,500 weekly newspapers and to 2,500 columnists and editorial writers.
>
> …[When] NAM started the campaign against OPA, a survey showed that 85 percent of the people believed OPA was absolutely necessary. In November 1946, after the NAM campaign…only 26 percent of the people believed OPA was vital…[432]

The result of turning an overwhelming 85 percent majority into a meager 26 percent minority in favor of price control is astonishing. President Truman's free use of the terms propaganda and conspiracy is equally impressive. In addition, exposing the excessive amounts of money to indoctrinate people against their own interest is very unusual coming from a high-power politician such as president. In the course of the history, propaganda strengthened and became more overwhelming and sophisticated. It is unheard of in modern politics to speak openly about issues such as propaganda and conspiracy against the American consumer. As emphasized profusely by Assange, Chomsky, and Carlin, among others, ignorance is the worst enemy of democracy and the best friend of the ruling class. Media analyst W. Lance Bennett featured in the Herman and Chomsky's *Manufacturing Consent,* explains how the dissemination of propaganda is a one-way relationship, whose goal is to impose ignorance among the masses:

> The public is exposed to powerful persuasive messages from above and is unable to communicate meaningfully through the media in response to these messages…Leaders have usurped enormous amounts of political power and reduced popular control over the political system by using the media to generate support, compliance, and just plain confusion among the public.[433]

Confusing the public is the main breeder of ignorance. As long as people are not aware of what really is going on, they could be persuaded to vote

---

[432] Ibid., 147.
[433] W. Lance Bennett, *News: The Politics of Illusion,* Boston: Boston Beacon Press, 1980, x.

against their interests, to accept an unusual high level of corruption, and to be misled in order to remain docile workers. People are constantly being tricked to accept increasingly worse jobs with lesser pay, longer hours, and no benefits. According to Chomsky, "it is necessary to figure out ways to keep people from understanding what is happening to them."[434] Although they see their lives worsening and their slipping into poverty, they are consistently prevented from finding out the real reason because they are distracted with scapegoats such as immigrants, welfare mothers, foreign interference, and so on.

Another media analyst, Ben Bagdikian, who wrote *The Media Monopoly* in 1980, also cited by Herman and Chomsky, concludes that mass media "does not merely protect the corporate system. It robs the public of a chance to understand the real world."[435] The corporate elites rely heavily on the public's ignorance because if the people understood the actions of business corporations, they would revolt and destroy the system. Furthermore, media cooperation is required to sway the public in favor of corporate interest using scientific experts. In *Manufacturing Consent,* Herman and Chomsky refer to Judge Powell's memorandum of 1972, urging business "to buy the top academic reputations in the country to add credibility to corporate studies and give business a stronger voice on the campuses."[436] The authors conclude:

> By the sales effort, including the dissemination of the correct ideas to thousands of newspapers, it is possible to keep the debate within its proper perspective.
>
> In accordance with this formula, during the 1970s and early 1980s a string of institutions was created and old ones were activated to the end of propagandizing the corporate viewpoint. Many hundreds of intellectuals were brought to these institutions where their work was funded and their outputs were disseminated by the media by a sophisticated propaganda effort.[437]

These methods are still very useful to the corporate elite. Various studies are funded by the largest corporations in every field, most notably in medicine,

---

[434] Noam Chomsky and Marv Waterstone, *Consequences of Capitalism: Manufacturing Discontent and Resistance,* Chicago: Haymarket Books, 2021, 320.
[435] Ben Bagdikian, *The Media Monopoly,* Boston: Boston Beacon Press, 1980, x.
[436] Herman and Chomsky, 23.
[437] Ibid., 24.

climate change, and social science, shaping politics and economics to the benefit of the corporations dominating the area. The same mechanisms of propaganda are used for union-busting, outsourcing well-paying jobs abroad, and maintaining low wages. Such approaches remain unnoticed while gaslighting the public and keeping it ignorant about the real outcomes of such business actions. In the 21st century, the objectives of corporate propaganda continue to aim at shaping public opinion in favor of big monopoly and against unions, currently reduced to roughly ten percent.[438]

One of the largest global corporation, Amazon, is notorious for spreading anti-union propaganda and sabotaging workers' organizing. Amazon's corporate management interfered with the votes for unionizing and systematically advertised against unions. For example, one of the low-level managers in Amazon storage unit in NYC, Chris Smalls, was fired in 2020 for organizing a walkout to protest the unsanitary conditions and lack of safety protocols during Covid pandemic. After his firing, Smalls became a vocal activist for organizing unions in the company, and initiated an activist group called The Congress of Essential Workers. In 2021, Smalls succeeded founding the first Amazon Labor Union in the history of the company in Staten Island, NYC. This victory encouraged 50 warehouses of the digital giant to contact Amazon Labor including several overseas. Among the branches organizing a vote for unions was an Alabama warehouse, whose efforts failed thanks to Amazon's illegal interference. As a result, workers filed objections to the National Labor Relations Board claiming Amazon "created an atmosphere of confusion, coercion and/or fear of reprisals and thus interfered with the employees 'freedom of choice' to join or reject a union."[439]

Similarly, the workers of Starbucks, an international chain of coffeehouses, are organizing to form unions. As of June 31, 2022, Starbucks has succeeded to unionize 187 stores covering 5,080 workers.[440] Inversely, digital giant Apple discourages company's employees to unionize. Union organizers at Apple demand Covid safety rules, higher pay to counter inflation, and a voice on relevant issues.[441] As a whole, in 2021, the union membership in the U.S.

---

[438] "Percent of Employees with Union Membership," *USA Facts*, 2021.

[439] Annie Palmer, "Amazon Illegally Interfered in Alabama's Warehouse Vote, Union Alleges," *CNBC*, April 7, 2022.

[440] Matt Bruenig, "Starbucks Union Grows to 5,000 Workers in June," *People's Project*, July 4, 2022.

[441] Kif Leswing, "Apple Discourages Retail Employees from Joining Unions in Internal Video," *CNBC*, May 25, 2022.

is only 10.3 percent, down from 10.8 in 2020.[442] By comparison, in 1983, the union membership was 20.1 percent as reported by the Bureau of Labor Statistics.[443] The continuing decline of unionization is a direct result of the fierce propaganda and huge corporate investments in lobbying and media manipulations. In the same report of Jan 2022, the Bureau compares data and concludes that nonunion workers had median weekly earnings comprising only 83 percent of earnings for union workers. In addition, these numbers do not account for other factors such as paid vacation, health care, and sick leave among others.[444] It is obvious that unionizing only benefits workers and is against the interest of the corporations, and it requires methodical practice of confusing, distracting and gaslighting workers to keep them blindsided and ignorant.

In more recent times, in July 2022, independent journalist Matt Taibbi interviewed one of the independent reporters, Jon Farina, who worked for the *Status Coup* and became famous with his livestream footage of the January 6th Capitol Hill historic events in 2020. His footage was used by every mainstream outlet from ABC to CBS to CNN to the *Guardian* to the *Wall Street* journal to the *US Today* among others. According to Taibbi, two weeks after Jan 6, Farina was reporting on a pro-gun rally in Richmond, Virginia, and his livestream was shut down mid-event.[445] In his article, Taibbi notes that another independent journalist, Ford Fischer of *TK* partner News2Share, had the same experience during reporting from a gun rally in Columbus, Ohio. Like Farina, Fischer was told that he was in violation of You Tube's firearm policy. In addition, Fischer had later a livestream footage of January 6th removed from You Tube on similar grounds.[446] Taibbi explains in his article, "The effect of these moves is to make it difficult for independent videographers to publish controversial uncut video (or, especially, livestreams an important moneymaker for independents) unless properly contextualized by a corporate outlet."[447] Corporate propaganda affects every important aspect of life in western societies, especially issues in which public opinion contradicts the establishment's narrative. Examples include all imperialistic wars, firearm

---

[442] Bureau of Labor Statistics, *U.S. Department of Labor,* Jan. 20, 2022.
[443] Ibid.
[444] Ibid.
[445] Matt Taibbi, "Activism, Uncensored: The 'Not Calm Hearts' in Kharkiv, Ukraine," *TK News,* July 26, 2022.
[446] Ibid.
[447] Ibid.

regulations, Covid pandemic mandates, and most recently, the US proxy war in Ukraine.

The synchronized propaganda effort in support of the new military aid to Ukraine and NATO against Russia includes showing one side of the story while banning all the opposite information. Shutting down Russian news outlets in English, forbidding any historical background discussions, especially relevant Russian history, and even Russian cultural expression, are methods that should never exist in a democracy. However, they were accepted gladly and constantly promoted by the mainstream media as normal and democratic. In addition, academia also joined the effort by condemning respected scholars who deviate from the propaganda narrative. For example, John Mearsheimer, political scientist, and International Relations scholar, who has been warning since 2014 that NATO expansion at the Russian border will lead to Putin's invasion of Ukraine, is now among an official list of journalists and politicians that are dubbed Russian propagandists by the Ukrainian government. Other prominent blacklisted figures include former Representative of Hawaii Tulsi Gabbard, Senator Rand Paul, Journalist Glen Greenwald, military historian Edward Luttwak, and former marine corps intelligence officer Scott Ritter among others.

In an interview with China Global television Network (CGTN), hosted by Tian Wei, historian Mearsheimer said that the mainstream media rejects completely his theory that NATO and the US are pushing Russia into a corner, and that the outcome is not beneficial to the western countries. Mearsheimer argues that Putin drew the line back in April 2008 at the NATO Summit in Bucharest, stating that Ukraine and Georgia must not join NATO because this would be an existential threat to Russia.[448] In another interview with the *New Yorker,* Mearsheimer said that Russia does not pose a threat to the U.S., and that Putin's objective is not to occupy Ukraine, but to make a regime change and to install a Russian-friendly or neutral government.[449] Moreover, the scholar objected the commonly-agreed western view that Putin is trying to restore the pre-1991 Soviet Union, or the Russian royal empire of the 19th century. He noted that Putin actually said, "Whoever does not miss the Soviet Union has no heart. Whoever wants it back has no brain."[450] The scholar clarified that the interviewer only cited the first half of the quote, as most

---

[448] Tian Wei, CGTN, You Tube, April 16, 2022.

[449] Isaak Chotiner, "Why John Mearsheimer Blames the U.S. for the Crisis in Ukraine," *New Yorker,* March 1, 2022.

[450] Ibid.

western media do.[451] A simple notification that summarizes the way the war in Ukraine was sold by reporting selected facts out of context and especially without presenting historical background. Moreover, the crucial events that led to the Russian invasion such as the 2008 NATO Summit and the 2014 regime change in Ukraine, often emphasized in Russian reporting, were banned from the news.

Similarly, the rise of the neo-Nazi forces in Ukraine after 2014, the bombing of Donetsk and Lugansk with the support of the US were subjected to complete blackout from the news.[452] A leaked audio from 2014, shows that the US Under Secretary of State for Political Affairs Victoria Nuland is dictating to the US ambassador to Ukraine the names of officials to be installed in the Ukrainian government regardless of their own people's will and against the EU suggestions.[453] Although reported back in 2015, the leak was largely eclipsed by the news; nevertheless, popularized by 2016 Oliver Stone's documentary *Ukraine on Fire*.[454] Similarly, speeches of Putin stating historical facts and his objectives were banned from social media. In the rare occasion when the Russian president was cited, it was incomplete and out of context, sometimes reduced to parts of a sentence. As noted by Chomsky, the prevailing modern censorship is unprecedented in his lifetime, and he witnessed WWII and McCarthyism's witch hunt and hysteria of the 1950s.

As Alex Carey noted in his research, one of the main developments of the 20th century, were the growth of democracy and corporations, which contradicted each other because the corporate power was challenged by democracy. Thus, the corporate power required the growth of propaganda – the third main development of the century. Mass education became mandatory in the U.S. gradually from the late 19th century, with the first compulsory school laws in 1852-53 passed in Massachusetts and New York respectively, and completed by 1918. Such democratic measures led to the growth of democracy and with the franchise continually extended to women and people of color, the need of propaganda grew proportionally. Since then, propaganda has been promoted, developed and implemented by power-thirsty educated

---

[451] Ibid.
[452] Dan Abrams, "Are neo-Nazis Exploiting the Ukraine Crisis?" *News Nation*, March 25, 2022.
[453] Oliver Stone, *Ukraine on Fire*, Doc., "Victoria Nuland and Geoffrey Pyatt phone call," 2016.
[454] Ibid.

people who positioned themselves among the ruling class and orchestrated the inculcation of the masses.

Moreover, the intelligentsia invented and developed in the 1960s a new form of influence – the psyops – military operations aimed at influencing the enemy's state of mind through noncombative means such as commercials. However, in this case, the enemy was the American people.[455] In order to maintain the myths created in support of the status quo, an artificial division is always required. Whether it is political divide between the two elitist parties, or racial, gender, and generational division, rural vs. urban, educated vs. uneducated, the tactics always have to be in practice. Out of fear of the masses, the ruling class comes up with newer and more modern divisions among people, in addition to the traditional ones. The newest campaigns invented and escalated by the media, were the divisions between vaccinated vs. unvaccinated people; Russians vs. Ukrainians, sexual orientation and identification, among others.

These tactics are taken right from the books of dictators such as Joseph Stalin and Mao Zedong. During their reigns of terror, both insighted the division between parents and children, and encouraged the latter to spy on their parents and turn them in for not following the communist party's rules. We know from literature that Russians learned in schools about Pavlik Morozov, a youth who informed the secret services later called KGB, that his father was an enemy of the communist party. The father was arrested and later disappeared.[456] Similarly, in China during the Cultural Revolution, brainwashed children denounced their parents for criticizing Chairman Mao.[457] These are examples of the extreme lengths to which propaganda might lead as a result of rulers' artificially crafted division in order to maintain power.

Totalitarian leaders are well aware of the power of propaganda and censorship. They have been practicing information eclipse and inculcating ignorance throughout history. Back in 1792, during the French Revolution, Robespierre declared, "The secret of liberty lies in educating people, whereas the secret of tyranny is in keeping them ignorant."[458] Secrecy is the foundation

---

[455] According to Merriam-Webster dictionary, the term was first used in 1965.
[456] Yuri Druzhnikov, *Informer 001: The Myth of Pavlik Morozov,* Moscow: Moscow Worker, 1995.
[457] Tania Branigan, "China's Cultural Revolution: Son's Guilt Over the Mother He Sent to Death," *The Guardian,* March 27, 2013.
[458] Armand Carrel, *The Work of Maximilien Robespierre,* Vol 2, 1840, 253.

of all dictatorships. During the ancient times and the Middle Ages, ignorance was easily achieved because the masses didn't have access to education. Only a few landlords were literate and educated. With the implementation of mass education in the early 20th century came the need of artificial ignorance achieved by the manipulation of public opinion.

More recent examples could be drawn from the last couple of years where the public was hypnotized by fear and more susceptible to extreme influences from the media. Initially, there was the fear of dying from a respiratory contagious disease, which led to irrational behavior suggested by the media. Children's IQ dropped 20 points because of the lock-downs and missed school and social interactions. Adults voluntarily isolated themselves for months at a time. Relatives skipped gatherings on Thanksgiving and Christmas, and elderly people died alone without saying good-bye because of unreasonable restrictions. Depression was at its highest, drug and alcohol abuse increased significantly, people gained weight as they were unable to go to the gym. Cancer, diabetes, and other illnesses were unattended and their diagnoses or treatments delayed, which led to many unnecessary deaths. The damage caused by fear and mass psychosis was even greater than the damage caused by the poorly handled pandemic. As was the case with other dictatorships, ignorance was the number one enemy of people's wellbeing. The media disseminated wrong information before, during and after the pandemic. They repeated every false information without retraction, dictated to them by experts in power who were in fact sales representatives of giant pharmaceutical corporations.

Since February 2022, a new propaganda campaign emerged to deceive the public: manufacturing consent for the proxy war in Ukraine. The media had to seize their previous campaign pushing the pandemic, and to downplay the terror inflicted by the disease. They abruptly switched their focus on campaigning in favor of sending weapons, solders, and money to Ukraine. In the middle of the pandemic, Congress voted to send $55B to support Ukraine. The funds and weapons sent to Ukraine remain untraceable and unaccountable. Independent reporters informed the public that there is a black market for the weapons and that their final destination is uncertain. To some extend the media succeeded to persuade the public that sacrifices are necessary because Ukrainian children are dying, people are being displaced and starving.

As always, no tragedy goes unexploited. Oil companies doubled the prices of gasoline while blaming Putin. Food prices increased, services and digital products became more expensive, and all that caused inflation, also blamed on Putin. The war, which was preventable and could still be stopped with negotiations, was used as an excuse to loot national resources and rob the population. As was the case with the pandemic – easily preventable and poorly managed, the tragedy of the Russian/Ukrainian war was used to plunder the country. And all this was possible because people were kept in the dark. They probably suspected something was wrong in the picture presented to them by the media; however, everyone who questioned the narrative was so severely attacked that most people quickly adopted a survival mode of ignorance.

Immediately, digital networks levied a heavy censorship in the name of "fighting disinformation." When all dissent was purged, people were confused enough to act irrationally. Because it takes time to create new independent outlets, mainstream media and the digital owners used this time to further confuse and gaslight people. Conveniently, Julian Assange was arrested right before the pandemic. The journalist, who launched a war on all corrupt rulers in the world and exposed thousands of pages of government secrets to the public, was silenced forever. In fact, the secrets revealed by Assange, were all crimes against humanity. If Assange weren't arrested, he would have exposed the actual goals of the chaos and tyranny imposed on the global populations. Besides the effective silencing of the reporter who never had to retract published information, the imprisoning of a journalist had a chilling effect on the entire profession. This precedent is so severe that the damage would be experienced decades from now. The man who set out to dispel ignorance, was utterly defeated. It is hard to imagine the consequences of such punishment. The shock of such an assault on honest reporting is still rocking the world.

Of course, the continued information eclipse maintained by the media since Assange's arrest in 2019, is the reason people aren't rioting against such savagery. The activism against Assange's extradition to the U.S. is organized, promoted, and executed by independent reporters, vigilantes, and a few famous rock singers such as former Pink Floyd's co-founder Roger Waters. Rallies, concerts, and demonstrations are performed in London, where Assange is imprisoned and all over the world. Assange reveal information that changed the way people perceive power – he cracked the pedestal on which media and academia put the ruling class for our adulation. He provided evidence for the crimes, corruption, manipulation, and psyops that many suspected the elites committed but were vehemently denied. In his article at *Sheer Post*, Chris Hedges exposes Assange's prosecutors:

Let us name Julian Assange's executioners: Joe Biden, Boris Johnson, Scott Morrison, Theresa May, Lenin Moreno, Donald Trump, Barack Obama, Mike Pompeo, Hilary Clinton…Assange committed empire's greatest sin. He exposed it as a criminal enterprise. He exposed its lies, callous disregard for human life, rampant corruption and innumerable war crimes…Empires always kill those who inflict deep and serious wounds.[459]

The dark message that the executors want to send to the world with Assange, is that if anyone dares to reveal the truth and expose their secrets they will find this person, publicly torture and kill such individual. Those who shed a light on the shadowy narratives concocted by governments, would be prosecuted, imprisoned, and destroyed. Another victim of the same executors related to Wiki Leaks is Chelsey Manning, a military intelligence analyst who leaked 750,000 military classified documents to Assange in 2010. After careful redacting, Wiki Leaks published some of the data including Iraq War Logs, Afghan War Diary, and Collateral Murder in Baghdad from 2007, which went viral on the Internet. The video showed the intentional assassination and killing of 12 to 18 reporters and medical personal including two journalists from *Router*s and two children who were seriously wounded.[460] The redacted version published on YouTube by *Reuters* required the use of the Freedom of Information Act Freedom to release a copy of the video. It starts with a quote from George Orwell, "Political language is designed to make lies sound truthful and murder respectable and to give the appearance of solidity to pure wind." Furthermore, the Iraq War Logs revealed that out of 150,000 deaths between 2004 and 2009, 80 percent were civilians.[461]

Independent reporter and comedian Lee Camp dedicated a chapter to the significance of Wiki Leaks and Assange in his 2020 book *Bullet Points and Punchlines*.[462] Camp summarizes the main contribution of Assange's reporting in 18 points, outlining his most famous video from Manning's leak titled Collateral Murder. Other important reporting described in Camp's chapter include illegal detaining of innocent people hidden from organizations such

---

[459] Chris Hedges, "The Execution of Julian Assange," *The Sheer Report*, December 13, 2021.
[460] Baghdad Airstrike, July 12, 2007. www.collateralmurder.wikileaks.org
[461] "War Diary: Iraq War Logs," Wiki Leaks, Oct 22, 2010, www.wikileaks.org
[462] Lee Camp, "18 Ways Julian Assange Changed the World," *Bullet Points and Punchlines*, Oakland: PM Press, 2020.

as Red Cross in Guantanamo Bay, and the use of torture; The Iraq War Logs showing the real number of casualties not reported; Secret meetings of the Bilderberg Group of rich and powerful billionaires who make the most important policy decisions in the world; The Afghan War Diaries revealing civilian casualties and friendly fire incidents; the US State Department cables exposing Hilary Clinton's orders to spy on foreign delegations at the UN Security Council; The DNC emails showing internal corruption during the elections in 2008 and 2016 and proof that the Obama's cabinet members were dictated by Citi Bank and other financial giants; The Stratfor's emails exposing private intelligence agencies targeting activists and protesters; TPP, TISA and TTIP trade deals and their secretive, fraudulent character as well as the fact that they are literary written by corporations in order to diminish international laws for profit; the CIA operation Vault 7, designed to remotely control digital devices such as cars, smart TVs, web browsers and smartphones; Multiple foreign governments' illegal actions in China, Peru, Russia, Syria, Australia, and some African countries.[463] Camp introduces the succinct list of leaks with the idea behind the secrecy, "Ignorance is bliss," describing it as "the meditative mantra of the United States of America."[464]

Wiki Leaks' information significantly changed the public perspective of the global powers and the role of governments in manipulating public opinion through deliberate ignorance of the masses. In particular, the documents changed the public view of the war in Iraq and Afghanistan and some credit Manning for turning the global opinion against such aggression. Although Wiki Leaks strictly protects its sources, Manning confided the leak to an online acquittance, who turned her to the FBI. As a result, Manning was arrested and sentenced to 35 years at the maximum-security prison at Fort Leavenworth. After serving seven years, during which she has been tortured in solitary confinement, President Obama pardoned her. However, in March 2019, right before arresting Assange, Manning was imprisoned again and confined for another year, in addition to a fine of $256,000 for refusing to testify before a grand jury investigating Assange.

Cases such as these may seem that they belong to dictatorships like the communist or Nazis regimes; unfortunately, they happened in the US, with the cooperation of the UK, whose authorities arrested a person who had a legal refuge in a sovereign embassy in London. Manning was arrested and

---

[463] Ibid., 156-165.
[464] Ibid., 157.

175

tortured for refusing to incriminate an innocent person. Many others suffer the injustices of the western democracies, about which George Orwell warned us in the 1940s. Indeed, the totalitarian measures seem like taken out of Orwell's dystopian book *1984*. As articulated throughout the book, western democracies use different methods to oppress the masses such as propaganda, brainwashing, conditioning, using a system of reward and punishment, and keeping the public ignorant. Through a carefully designed education, which exposes students to selective information and by using very subtle censorship, the ruling elites achieve the same results as openly dictatorial regimes. As an extreme measure, the western systems use physical power of confinement and murder, and when they do, it is very public and intimidating, in order to deter further attempts of dissent.

Conclusion

The Tale of the Stairs: The Road to Hell is Full of Good Intentions

There is a wise story written by a young Bulgarian poet, Hristo Smirnenski, in 1923. He died at 24 from tuberculosis; however, in his very short life, he was a rebel against bourgeoisie exploitation and left a rich legacy of poetry and prose. With his unique lyrical style and humanistic ideas, Smirnenski inspired millions of people to rise up against social injustice. The following story metaphorically depicts the system of corruption, so ubiquitous and penetrating that is capable of overcoming even the best-intended, idealistic individuals.

The Tale of The Stairs

Dedicated to all who will say:
"It has nothing to do with me!"

"Who are you?" The Devil asked him.

"I am a plebeian by birth and all ragged folk are my brothers. How terrible the world is, how wretched the people are!"

It was a young man who spoke with his head erect and fists clenched. He stood at the foot of the Stairs - a high white staircase of rose-flecked marble. He gazed fixedly into the distance where the grey crowds of poverty stirred like the turbid waters of a swollen river. The crowds surged and seethed, raised a forest of thin black arms, thunderous cries of wrath and indignation rent the air and the echo faded slowly and solemnly like distant gun-fire. The crowds grew and grew nearer in clouds of yellow dust, single silhouettes showed more distinctly against the grey horizon. An old man approached, bent low to the ground as if seeking lost youth. A barefoot little girl clutched his ragged clothes and stared at the high Stairs with mild cornflower-blue eyes. Stared and smiled. Then thin grey figures came all in rags, singing a long-drawn funeral chorus. Someone whistled shrilly, somebody else thrusting his hands in his pockets laughed loud and harshly and insanity blazed in his eyes.

"I am a plebeian by birth and all ragged folk are my brothers. How terrible the world is, how wretched the people are! But you there, you at the top there..."

It was a young man who spoke with head erect and fists clenched in menace.

"So, you hate those up at the top," the Devil asked, and slyly leaned forward towards the young man.

"I shall have my revenge on those nobles and princes. I shall cruelly avenge my brothers - my brothers whose faces are as yellow as sand and who groan more bitterly than the blizzards of December. See their naked bleeding bodies, hear their groans! I shall avenge them. Let me go!"

The Devil smiled: "I am the guardian of those at the top and without a bribe I shall not betray them."

"I have no gold. I have nothing with which to bribe you... I am poor, a youth in rags... But I am willing to give up my life..."

Again, the Devil smiled: "O no, I do not ask as much as that. Just give me your hearing."

"My hearing? Gladly... May I never hear anything anymore, may I..."

"You still shall hear," the Devil assured him, and made way for him. "Pass!"

The young man set off at a run and had taken three steps in one stride when the hairy hand of the Devil caught him.

"That's enough! Now pause and listen to your brothers groaning below."

The young man paused and listened.

"How strange! Why have they suddenly begun to sing happy songs and to laugh light-heartedly?..." Again, he set off at a run.

Again, the Devil stopped him. "For you to go three more steps I must have your eyes."

The young man made a gesture of despair. "But then I shall be unable to see my brothers or those I go to punish."

"You still shall see them..." The Devil said. "I will give you different, much better eyes."

The young man rose three more steps and looked back.

"See your brothers' naked bleeding bodies," the Devil prompted him.

"My God, how very strange! When did they manage to don such beautiful clothes? And not bleeding wounds but splendid red roses deck their bodies..."

At every third stair the Devil exacted his little toll. But the young man proceeded, willingly giving everything, he had in order to reach his goal and to punish the well-fed nobles and princes. Now one step, just one last step remained and he would be at the top. Then indeed he would avenge his brothers.

"I am a plebeian by birth and all ragged folk..."

"Young man, one last step still remains. Just one more step and you shall have your revenge. But for this last step I always exact a double toll: give me your heart and give me your memory."

The young man protested.

"My heart? No, that is too cruel!"

The Devil gave a deep and masterful laugh: "I am not so cruel as you imagine. In exchange I will give you a heart of gold and a brand-new memory. But if you refuse me, then you shall never avenge your brothers whose faces are the color of sand and who groan more bitterly than December blizzards."

The young man saw irony in the Devil's green eyes.

"But there will be nobody then more wretched than I. You are taking away all my human nature."

"On the contrary, nobody shall be happier than you. Well, do you agree: just your heart and memory?"

The young man pondered, his face clouded over, beads of sweat ran from the furrowed brow, in anger he tightened his fists and through clenched teeth said: "Very well, then. Take them!"

…And like a swift summer storm of rage and wrath, his dark locks flying in the wind, he crossed the final step. He was now at the very top. And a broad a smile suddenly in his face, his eyes now shone with tranquil joy and his fists relaxed. He looked at the nobles reveling there and looked down to the roaring, cursing, grey ragged crowds below. He gazed, but not a muscle of his face quivered: his face was radiant, happy and content. The crowds he saw below were in holiday attire and their groans were now hymns.

"Who are you?" the Devil asked in a low sly voice.

"I am a prince by birth and the gods are my brothers. How beautiful the world is and how happy are the people!"[465]

This profound allegory epitomizes so well the stories of many activist leaders, movements, and politicians who set out to change the world and ended up overwhelmed by the mechanisms of power. Because as many found out, one cannot change the system from within. This applies to the media, academia, the political sphere, and any other powerful institution. All dissidents understood this. As feminist Audre Lorde taught us, "The masters' tools will never dismantle the master's house," we learn from the tale that the way up is the wrong way. Scholar Noam Chomsky provocatively articulated to a young British journalist that he has no doubt that the journalist believes every word he says; however, Chomsky also was convinced that the journalist

---

[465] Hristo Smirnenski, "The Tale of the Stares," 1923, www.slovo.bg.

wouldn't be sitting where he was if he didn't. A century ago, young poet Smirnenski understood the simple truth that in order to climb the hierarchical ladder one must trade his heart, memory, eyes and hearing. Thankfully, they shared their experience and wisdom with us; therefore, the blow wouldn't be a great surprise when leaders we trust betray us.

Fortunately, there are philanthropic idealists who choose not to climb up the ladder. They stayed down on earth with their brothers and sisters who suffer immensely. These individuals are the ones who can lay the foundation on which we can build a better society. They are in every field – independent media, academia, grassroots movements, the arts, and so on. The only place they cannot be found is at the top of the hierarchical ladder or in high places of power. If they accept high-paying positions, or rub shoulders with famous and powerful people, they don't have a chance, like the pauper-prince from the Tale of the Stairs. In the media, they are the struggling independent journalists, filmmakers, and reporters. In academia, they are among the 76 percent contingent faculty. They couldn't be found in politics either because the system is created in a way that even the politicians that are at the bottom of the stairs must make trade deals with the devil. Otherwise, if they refuse to sell their souls, the system rejects them.

The lesson to be learned here is that selling out is a slow, incremental process, and it is easy to be delusional about it. Sometimes, it encroaches on people gradually. It is not a great glamorous sudden deal when they shake hands with Satan; although it could happen this way too. Usually, however, like awakening, it happens slowly and often unremarkably, little by little. It is up to individuals, nevertheless, to choose their direction. Moreover, it is up to all of us to support strong persons who refuse to sell their souls, because they are not trying to climb the corporate ladder. Such people stay with the general population where it is safe for their souls and where they fight from below as outsiders. Some of these people are described in the chapters; however, their list is too long to be completed. Moreover, there are so many anonymous activists, community leaders, and fighters for justice that work tirelessly in the name of the oppressed. They fall and get up; they get flaked and do not give up. They lose their jobs; they lose friends and love ones over principles; they lose privileges and wealth to preserve their hearts and minds. They see, hear, and feel through the prism of the common good. They sleep well at night because they didn't trade their consciousness. They work long and hard to find the truth. To these heroes, known and unknown, I dedicate this book.

Finally, in a pseudo-democracy, where propaganda prevails in education, media, and academia; nevertheless, information is still available, autodidacticism is the best way to learn. Through trial and error, the heuristic method that accompanies self-education, is truth-seekers' most valuable option. Then, there is the hermeneutic method, which is interpretative and explanatory. Both methods are widely used in academia; however, to pursue meaningless objectives that don't benefit humanity, only profiteers. Therefore, it is harder to study within the official system, where the facts are suppressed and drowned in a sea of deliberate misinformation. However, knowledge is still possible thanks to the brave truth-tellers who risk everything to report hidden events and powerful secrets, which should be open sources in real democracies.

Bibliography

Abrams, Dan. "Are neo-Nazis Exploiting the Ukraine Crisis?" *News Nation*. March 25, 2022.

Alba, Davey. "The Latest Covid Misinformation Star Says He Invented the Vaccines." *The New York Times*. April 3, 2022.

"Alyssa Milano's #MeToo Tweet on Sexual Harassment Gets Thousands of Replies." *Sky News*. Oct 17, 2017.

"Amazon – 25 Year Stock Price History." *AMZN-Macrotrends*. https://www.macrotrends.net>charts

Anderson, Monica; Skye Toor, Lee Raine, and Aaron Smith. *Pew Research Center*. July 11, 2018. "2. An analysis of #BlackLivesMatter and other Twitter hashtags related to political or social issues". Pew Research Center: Internet, Science & Tech

Apatow, Judd and Michael Bonfiglio. Dirs. *George Carlin's American Dream*. Doc. May, 2022.

Arnold Amanda and Claire Lampen. "All the Women Who Have Spoken Out Against Joe Biden." *Mass Central Media*. Facebook. April 12, 2020.

Arnove, Anthony. "Introduction to the 35th Anniversary Edition of *A Peoples' History of the United States*." New York: Harper Perennial Modern Classics. 2015.

Andrzejewski, Adam. "America's Colleges and Universities Awarded $12.5 Billion in Coronavirus Bailout – Who Can Get It and How Much." *Forbes*. May 5, 2020.

Arkin, William M. *The Generals Have No Clothes: The Untold Story of Our Endless Wars*. New York: Simon and Schuster. 2021.

———. "Must Flee TV." *Harpers Magazine* March 2019.

Baroud, Ramzy. "Not a Justification but a Provocation: Chomsky on the Root Causes of the Russia Ukraine War." *Counterpunch.* June 28, 2022

Baer, Brett. "Lawmakers Consider Linking Ukraine and Covid Funding." Billable Hours. *Fox News.* May 2, 2022.

Baghdad Airstrike. July 12, 2007. www.collateralmurder.wikileaks.org

Bagdikian, Ben H. *The New Media Monopoly: A Completely Revised and Updated Edition with Seven New Chapters.* Vienna, Torino, Bari, and Oldenburg: Beacon Press. May. 15, 2004. First published in 1983.

BBC News. "Edward Snowden: Leaks that Exposed US Spy Programme." July 1, 2013.

Bennett, Lance W. News: *The Politics of Illusion.* Boston: Boston Beacon Press. 1980.

Bernays Edward. *Propaganda.* "Introduction by Mark Crispin Miller." Brooklyn: Ig Publishing, 2005.

Bernstein, Carl. "The CIA and the Media." *Rolling Stone.* June 27, 2007.

Blumenthal, Max. "Corporate/national security state censorship operation @ NewsGuardRating is preparing to blacklist several anti-imperialist sites including @TheGrayzoneNews." April 27, 2022. https://twitter.com/MaxBlumenthal/status/1519359169287147520

Blumenthal, Max Aaron Mate, and Martina Fucks. "Fifty Shades of Truth." *Collision Tech Conference.* Toronto. June 21, 2022. https://www.youtube.com/watch?v=qcGlc3mw8lk&t=3s

Brand, Russel. "You've Been Lied to About Why Ukraine War Begin." *Under the Skin.* March 27, 2022.

———. "It's a Big Club and You Ain't' in It – How the Game is Rigged." *Under the Skin.* June 30, 2021.

Branigan, Tania. "China's Cultural Revolution: Son's Guilt Over the Mother He Sent to Death." *The Guardian.* March 27, 2013.

Browning, Oliver. "Noam Chomsky Calls for Unvaccinated to Be 'Isolated' from Society in Resurfaced Clip." *Independent.* Nov., 2021.

Brueck, Hilary. "The Rise of Robert Malone, the mRNA scientist, Turned Vaccine Sceptic Who Shot to Fame on Joe Rogan's Podcast." *Business Insider.* Feb 27, 2022.

Bruenig, Matt. "Starbucks Union Grows to 5,000 Workers in June." *People's Project.* July 4, 2022.

Brussat, Frederic and Mary Ann. "Film Review of Planet of the Humans." *Spirituality and Practice.* April 21, 2020.

Buchanan, Larry. Quoting Bui and Jugal Patel. "Black Lives Matter May Be the Largest Movement in US History." *The New York Times.* July 3, 2020.

Bureau of Labor Statistics. U.S. *Department of Labor.* Jan. 20, 2022.

Camp, Lee. "18 Ways Julian Assange Changed the World." *Bullet Points and Punchlines.* Oakland: PM Press. 2020.

Canova, Timothy A. "The Role of Central Banks in Global Austerity." *Global Legal Studies.* 22. No 2. Summer 2015. Bloomington: Indiana U Press.

Carrel, Armand. *The Work of Maximilien Robespierre.* Vol 2. 1840.

Carey, Alex. "Managing Public Opinion: The Corporate Offensive." *Serbian Political Thought.* Jan 2, 1996.

Carlsen, Audrey, Maya Salam, Claire Cain Miller, Denise Lu, Ash Ngu Jugal K. Patel, and Zach Wichter. "#MeToo Brought Down 201 Powerful Men: Nearly Half of Their Replacement Are Women." The *NYT.* Oct. 23, 2018.

Carson, E. Ann and Elizabeth Anderson. "Prisoners of 2015." *US Department of Justice, Bureau of Justice Statistics.* December 16, 2016.

Chomsky, Aviva. "A Brief History of the Green New Deal (So Far)". *Lit Hub.* April 25, 2022.

Chomsky, Noam. *Requiem for the American Dream.* New York: Seven Stories Press, 2017.

———. The *Common Good.* Odonian Press: *Open Library.* 1998.

———. "Education is Ignorance." Excerpts from Class Warfare: Interviews with David Barsamian. London: Pluto Press. 1996. https://chomsky.info/warfare02/

Chomsky, Noam and Marv Waterstone. *Consequences of Capitalism: Manufacturing Discontent and Resistance.* Chicago: Haymarket Books, 2021.

"Chomsky is Citation Champ." *MIT News on Campus and Around the World.* April 15, 1992. https://news.mit.edu/1992/citation-0415

Cirucci, Johnny. "CIA Subsidized Festival Trips: Hundreds of Students Were Sent to World Gatherings." *The New York Times.* Feb. 21, 1967.

Collins Michael. "The Abandonment of Small Cities in the Rustbelt." *Industry Week.* Oct. 10, 2019.

Conger Kate, and Rachel Shorey. "Examining the Allegation Against Joe Biden." *The New York Times.* Oct 28, 2020.

Corporate Crime Reporter. "Jimmy Dore Calls on Democrats to Withhold Support for Nancy Pelosi Unless She Brings Single Pair Medicare for All to a Vote." Dec. 12, 2020.

CQ Transcript Wire, Nov.4, 2008." Sen. Barack Obama's Acceptance Speech in Chicago." *The Washington Post,* Nov. 5, 2008

Creamer, Mathew. "Obama Wins!...Ad Age's Marketer of the Year." *Advertising Age.* October 17, 2008.

"Dark Winter," John Hopkins, Bloomberg School of Public Health, Center for Health Security. https://www.centerforhealthsecurity.org/our-work/events-archive/2001_dark-winter/about.html

Davis, Ian. "The New Normal & the Civil Society Deception." *Unlimited Hangout.* http://i-this-together-com

"Declassified documents show security assurances against NATO expansion to Soviet leaders from Baker, Bush, Genscher, Kohl, Gates, Mitterrand, Thatcher, Hurd, Major, and Woerner." *National Security Archive.* . https://nsarchive.gwu.edu/briefing-book/russia-programs/2017-12-12/nato-expansion-what-gorbachev-heard-western-leaders-early

DeSanctis, Alexandra. "Alysa Milano Ties Herself in a Knot." *National Review.* April 30, 2020.

Detmer, David. *Zinophobia: The Battle over History in Education, Politics, and Scholarship.* London: Zero Books. September 28, 2018.

Devereaux, Ryan. "How the CIA Watched Over the Destruction of Gary Webb." *The Intercept.* Sept 25, 2014.

Dore, Jimmy. "Pentagon-Backed "Newsguard" Threatening You Tube's Anti-War Voices." *Rokfin.* May, 2022.

———. "You Tube Host Silenced for Challenging U.S. Gov on Ukraine." *The Jimmy Dore Show.* July 14, 2022.

———. "Kelly Carlin on Growing Up with George, Interview with Jimmy Dore. *The Young Turks.* 2016.

———. "Hilarious Hit Piece on Jimmy Dore by Democratic Rag," *The Jimmy Dore Show.* 2021.

Dorfman, Zack, Sean D. Naylor, and Michael Isikoff. "Kidnapping, Assassination, and London Shoot-out: Inside the CIA Secret War against Wiki Leaks." *Yahoo News.* Sept 26, 2021.

Druzhnikov, Yuri. *Informer 001: The Myth of Pavlik Morozov.* Moscow: Moscow Worker. 1995.

D'Souza, Deborah, Sierra Murry, and Kristen Rohrs Schmitt, "The Green New Deal Explained." *Investopedia.* May 28, 2022.

Eley, Tom. "Citigroup Chose Obama's Cabinet, WikiLeaks Document Reveals." October 15, 2016. https://www.wsws.org/en/articles/2016/10/15/wiki-o15.html

Elliot, Larry. "Greece's Bailout Is Finally at an End – But It Has Been a Failure." *The Guardian.* Aug. 19, 2018.

Ewell, Audrey, Aaron Aites, Lucian Reed, Nina Krstic, Katie Teague, Peter Leeman, Aric Gutnick, Doree Simon, and Abby Martin. Dirs., *99%: The Occupy Wall Street Collaborative Film,* Doc. 2013.

"Fact Sheet: The Bipartisan Infrastructure Deal Boosts Clean Energy Jobs, Strengthens Resilience, and Advances Environmental Justice." *The White House Briefing Room.* Nov. 8, 2021.

Faludi, Susan. "Facebook Feminism, Like It or Not." *The Baffler.* No. 23. August 2013.

Farrow, Ronan. *Catch and Kill.* Boston: Little, Brown, and Co. Oct 15, 2019.

Feffer, John. "What Remains of the Green New Deal?" *Foreign Policy in Focus.* May 5, 2022.

Foner, Eric. "Acclaim for Howard Zinn and A People's History of the United States." *A People's History of the United States.* 3rd edition. Oxford: Routledge. 2015

Forlano, Julianna. "Chris Hedges on The Reason He Lost His Job at The New York Times." *Act.TV.* Oct. 29, 2020. https://www.youtube.com/watch?v=Dnee-FGcT4s

Flitter, Emily and James B. Steward. "Bill Gates Met with Epstein Many Times Despite Past." *The New York Times.* October 12, 2021.

Florida, Richard. *The Rise of the Creative Class: And How It's Transforming Work, Leisure, and Everyday Life.* New York: Basic Books. 2002

France, Lisa Raspers. "#MeToo: Social Media Flooded with Personal Stories of Assault." *CNN.* October 16, 2017.

Frances, Megan Ming. "The Price of Civil Rights: Black Lives, White Funding, and Movement Capture." *Law and Society.* Jan. 29, 2019.

Gay, Kathlyn. *American Dissidents: An Encyclopedia of Activists, Subversives, and Prisoners of Conscience.* Sept., 2018.

Gibbs, Jeff. Director. Michael Moore. Producer. *Planet of the Humans.* Huron Mountain Films. July 30, 2019.

Gilens, Martin and Benjamin I. Page. "Testing Theories of American Politics: Elites, Interest Groups and Average Citizens." *American Political Science Association.* Vol 12 No 3. Sept, 2014. https://scholar.princeton.edu/sites/default/files/mgilens/files/gilens_and_page_2014_-testing_theories_of_american_politics.doc.pdf

Gleicher, Nathaniel and Oscar Rodriguez. *Facebook Newsroom.* October 11, 2018.

Goldenberg, Suzanne. "Why Women Are Poor at Science, by Harvard President." *The Guardian*. Jan.18, 2005.

Goodman, Amy. *Democracy Now*, "Legendary Talk Show Host Phil Donahue on the Silencing of Antiwar Voices in U.S. Media." Nov. 11, 2014. https://www.youtube.com/watch?v=Ac7S-QHekio

———— and Gonzales. "How False Testimony and Massive US Propaganda Machine Bolstered George H.W. Bush's War on Iraq." *Democracy Now*, Nov. 30, 2018.

———— and David Moynihan. *The Silenced Majority: Stories of Uprising, Occupations, Resistance and Hope*. Chicago: Haymarket Books. 2012.

Greenwald, Glen. "Chris Hayes on Elite Failure: Why Don't American Oligarchs Fear the Consequences of Their Corruption and How Can That Be Changed?" *Salon*. August 1, 2012.

Guccione, Bob Jr. "The Outsider." *SPIN*. Jan 17, 2022.

Halas, Susan. "Orwell Values Soar as Dystopia Closes In." *Rare Book Monthly*. Nov., 2016.

Harari, Yuval Noah. "How to Survive the 21st Century." Davos. Jan., 2020. https://www.youtube.com/watch?v=gG6WnMb9Fho

Haselby, Sam and Matt Stoller. "It's Time to Break Up the Ivy League Cartel." *Chronicle of Higher Education*. May 28, 2021.

Hayes, Arthur S. *Press Critics Are the Fifth Estate*. Westport: Praeger Publishers. 2008.

Hayes, Chris. *Twilight of the Elites: America After Meritocracy*. New York: Crown Publishing. June 12, 2012.

Hearing Before the Committee of Finance, United States Senate, First Session of the Nomination of Larry Summers to be Under Secretary of the Treasury for International Affairs. March 18, 1993.

Hedges, Chris. "The Chris Hedges Report," *Scheer Post*. March 17, 2022. https://scheerpost.com/2022/03/17/the-chris-hedges-report/

————. *Academic Dictionaries and Encyclopedias*.

————. *The Sanctuary for Independent Media*.

————. "Bernie Sanders' Phantom Movement." *Tikkun*. Feb. 14, 2016.

————. "The Execution of Julian Assange." *The Sheer Report*. December 13, 2021.

Heer, Jeet. "At Liberalism's Crossroads." *The Nation*. Issue October 19/26. Oct. 6, 2020.

Herby, Jonas, Lars Jonung, and Steve H. Hanke. "A Literature Review and Meta-Analysis of the Effects of Lockdowns Covid-19 Mortality-II." *Studies in Applied Economics*. No 210. May 20, 2022.

Herman, Edward S., and Noam Chomsky. *Manufacturing Consent: The Political Economy of Mass Media,* New York: Pantheon Books. 1988.

Holmes, Aaron. "Protesters Set Up a Guillotine Outside Bezos' Mansion and Demanded Higher Wages for Amazon Workers after the CEO's Net worth Surpassed $200 Billion." *Business Insider*. Aug. 27, 2020.

hooks, bell. "Dig Deep: Beyond Lean In." *The Feminist Wire*. Oct 28, 2013.

Hope, Justus R. MD. "Dr. Malone Headwind Interview." *Desert Review*. April 12, 2022.

House Hearing. 116 Congress. "Examining the Oil Industry's Efforts to Suppress the Truth about Climate Change." Hearing Before the Subcommittee on Civil Rights and Civil Liberties of the Committee on Oversight and Reform. Oct 23, 2019.

Jackson, Janine. "Jeff Bezos Fake News in the Newspaper He Really Owns." *FAIR*. June 4, 2021.

Jacobsen, Mark Z., Mark A. Delucchi, Guillaume Bazouin, Zack A.F. Bauer, Christa C. Heavey, Emma Fisher, Sean B. Morris, Diniana J.Y. Piekutowsky, Taylor A. Vencill, and Tim W. Yeskoo. "100% Clean and Renewable Wind, Water, and Sunlight (WWS) All-sector Energy Roadmaps for the 50 United States." *Energy & Environmental Science*. No. 8. 2093. 2015. https://web.stanford.edu

Jankowicz, Nina. "You Can Just Call Me the Mary Poppins of Disinformation." *Twitter*. Feb. 17, 2021. https://twitter.com/wiczipedia/status/1362153807879303171

Jay, Paul. "Chris Hedges on Russia and Ukraine." *The Analysis News*. April 21, 2022.

Jayapal, Pramila. Congresswoman for WA-07. March 17, 2021. www.Jayapal.house.gov.

Johnstone, Caitlin. "The Most American Thing That Has Happened." May 10, 2022. www.caitlinjohnstone.com

———. "People Who Defend Empire Narratives Are Really Just Defending Their Worldview From Destruction." June 1, 2022. www.caitlinjohnstone.com

———. "Society Is Made of Narrative: Realizing This is Awakening from the Matrix." *Caitlin's Newsletter*. July 13, 2021.

Kaplan, J., S Gimbel, and S Harris. "Neural Correlates of Maintaining One's Political Beliefs in the Face of Counterevidence." *Scientific Report*. 6. No 39589. 2016.

Kennedy, Robert F. Jr. *The Real Anthony Fauci: Bill Gates, Big Pharma, and the Global War on Democracy and Public Health*. Delaware: Skyhorse Publishing, 2021.

———. "Epstein and Bill Gates with Whitney Webb." *RFK Jr. The Defender – Audacity*. May 22, 2021. https://www.audacy.com/podcasts/rfk-jr-the-defender-podcast-55171/epstein-and-bill-gates-with-whitney-webb-386014851

King, Larry. "CNN Official Interview: Colin Powell Now Regrets UN Speech about WMD." Nov 15, 2020.

Kirell, Andrew. "Cornel West: Obama a 'Republican in Blackface.' Black MSNBC Hosts are Selling Their Souls." *Mediate*. Nov. 12, 2012.

Kisin, Konstantin. "Jimmy Dore: They Won't Let the Great Unwashed Have a Voice." *Trigonometry*. Feb., 2022.

Kolewe, Julia. "Pfizer Accused of Pandemic Profiteering as Profit Double," *The Guardian*, Feb. 8, 2022.

Korecki, Natasha. "'Manipulative, Deceitful, User': Tara Reade Left a Trail of Aggrieved Acquaintances." *Politico*. May 15, 2020.

Koss, Jeff. "Senate Rejects Green New Deal as Marathon Voting Begins." *E&E News*. August 10, 2021.

Kurion, Tomas. "Update on Google Cloud's Work with the Government." *Inside Google Cloud*. Nov. 11, 2021.

Lang, Chris. "Planet of the Humans (Part 1): Blood and Gore." *Redd*. April 29, 2020.

Lauria, Joe. "Julian Assange Wins 2020 Gary Webb Freedom of the Press Reward." *Consortium News*. Feb. 10, 2020.

Leswing, Kif. "Apple Discourages Retail Employees from Joining Unions in Internal Video." *CNBC*. May 25, 2022.

Levey, Noam N. "More Than 100 Million People in the US Have Health Care Debt, Study Shows," *Truthout*. June 16, 2022.

Long, Heather. "The Federal reserve Has Pumped $2.3T into the US Economy. It's Just Getting Started." *The Washington Post*. April 29, 2020.

Ludwig, Mike. "Medicare for All could Have Prevented 338,000 Deaths." *Truthout*. June 17, 2022.

Luscombe, Richard and Vivian Ho. "George Floyd Protests Enter Third Week as Push for Change Sweeps America." *The Guardian*. June 7, 2020.

Macleod, Alan. "Documents Show Bill Gates Has Given $319 Million to Media Outlets to Promote His Global Agenda." *Grayzone*. Nov. 21, 2021.

———. "With Bezos at the Helm, Democracy Dies at the Washington Post Editorial Board." *Mint Press*. June 18, 2021.

Malone, Robert W. MD, MS. *Lies My Gov't Told Me and the Better Future Coming*. Sept. 27, 2022.

Martin, Abby. *RT America* on Jan. 13, 2014. https://www.youtube.com/watch?v=NKI0j18Ylpg

Martinich, Jeremy and Allison Crimmins. "Climate Damages and Adaptation Potential Across Sectors of the United States." *Nature Climate Change*. Vol. 9. April 2019.

Mate, Aaron. "At UN, Aaron Mate Debunks OPCW's Syria Lies and Confronts US, UK on Cover Up." *The Grayzone*. April 18, 2021.

Mathews, Mark, Nick Bowlin and Benjamin Hulac. "Inside the Sunrise Movement (It didn't Happen by Accident)." *E &E News*. Feb. 19, 2019.

McGreal, Chris. "Big Oil and Gas Kept Dirty Secret for Decades. Now They May Pay the Price." *The Guardian*. June 30, 2021.

McMenamin, Lexi. "Sunrise Issues a Memo to Democrats Calling for Green New Deal Commitments." *Teen Vogue*. March 17, 2022.

Milano, Alysa. "Living in the Gray as a Woman." *Deadline*. April 29, 2020.

Murakawa, Naomi. *The First Civil Right: How Liberals Built Prison America*. Oxford, 2014. Kindle Edition.

Nakataviclute, Jomile. "What Is Net Neutrality: Its History and Importance." *Nord VPN*. April 26, 2022.

Norton, Ben. "CNN and 60 Minutes Host Anderson Cooper, a Scion of the Vanderbilt Oligarch Dynasty, Worked in CIA Headquarters for Two Summers." *The Gray Zone*. Feb. 25, 2020.

Novet, Jordan. "Pentagon Asks Amazon, Google, Microsoft and Oracle for Bids for New Cloud Contracts." *CNBC*. Nov, 19, 2021.

Olson, Emily. "Antifa, Boogaloo Boys, White Nationalists: Which Extremists Showed Up to the US Black Lives Matter Protests?" *ABC News. Australian Broadcasting Corporation*. June 27, 2020.

Omachonu, John O. and David Schultz. "Media Concentration." *The First Amendment Encyclopedia*. 2009.

Open Secrets: Following the Money in Politics. "2020 Top Recipients." https://www.opensecrets.org/2020-presidential-race

Orwell, George. "The Freedom of the Press." *The Times Literary Supplement*. Sept. 15, 1972.

Palmer, Annie. "Amazon Illegally Interfered in Alabama's Warehouse Vote, Union Alleges." *CNBC*. April 7, 2022.

Penny, Laurie. "We Are Not Done Here." *Longreads*. Jan 2018.

"Percent of Employees with Union Membership." *USA Facts*. 2021.

Perry, Audrey. "Fairness Doctrine." *First Amendment Encyclopedia*. 2009.

Peterson-Withorn, Chase. "How Much Money American's Billionaires Have Made during the Covid 19 Pandemic," *Forbes,* April 30, 2022.

Poverty.umich.edu "Poverty Solutions." University of Michigan. http://data.oecd.org/inequality/poverty-rate.htm

Raza, Zain. "Noam Chomsky and Peter Kuznick – The Untold History of the United States." *AcTVism*. Feb. 5, 2019.

Reade, Tara. *Left Out: When the Truth Doesn't Fit In*. Los Angeles: TV Guestpert Publishing. 2021.

Real, Evan. "Rose McGowan Rips NYTimes, Claims She was the First to Speak Out in #MeToo Movement." *The Guardian*. July 1, 2019.

Redman, Janet. "Report: Trump's 'Energy Dominance Plans Rely on Billions on Fossil Fuel Subsidies." *Oil Change International*. October 3, 2017.

Rogan, Joe. "Oliver Stone on the JFK Assassination Coverup." *The Joe Rogan Experience*. Jan.5, 2022.

———. "How Oliver Stone's Experience in Vietnam Influenced Platoon." *The Joe Rogan Experience*. July 21, 2020.

Rohle, Stephanie. "George Carlin's Daughter Kelly and Judd Apatow on the Legacy of Comedian George Carlin." *MSNBC*. May 20, 2022.

Rosado, Emanuel. "The History Behind Orwell's Animal Farm Unpublished Preface." *Medium*. Sept. 16, 2019. https://medium.com/lessons-from-history/the-history-behind-george-orwells-animal-farm-unpublished-preface-bf3b64496463

Savranskaya, Svetlana and Tom Blanton. Slavic Studies Panel "Who Promised What to Whom on NATO Expansion?" *Briefing Book #613*. Dec. 12, 2017. . https://nsarchive.gwu.edu/briefing-book/russia-programs/2017-12-12/nato-expansion-what-gorbachev-heard-western-leaders-early

Scahill, Jeremy. Interview. "Noam Chomsky and Jeremy Scahill on the Russia-Ukraine War, the Media, Propaganda, and Accountability." *The Intercept*. April 19, 2022.

Schneider, Matt. "Wild Shoutfest between Al Sharpton and Cornel West on Obama and Race." *Mediate*. April 11, 2011. www.mediate.com.

Schultz, Julianne. *Reviving the Fourth Estate*. UK: Cambridge U Press, 1998.

Schuyler, Samantha. "Noam Chomsky on Higher Education," *Generation Progress*. November 13, 2013.

Schwartz, Ian. "Kucinich: 'Deep State' Trying to Take Down Trump, 'Our Country is Under Attack Within." *Real Clear Politics*. May 18, 2017.

Senate Committee on Natural Resources. August 10, 2021.

Sherman, Carter. "How Time's Up Failed Sexual Survivors and Cozied Up to Power." *Vice News*. Sept. 1, 2021.

Sheryl Sandberg. *Lean In: Women, Work, and the Will to Lead*. New York: Alfred Knopf. 2013.

———. "Larry Summers' True Record on Women." *Huffington Post*. December 8, 2008.

Sinclair, Upton I. *Candidate for Governor: And How I Got Licked*. U of CA Press. Dec. 16, 1994. (First published in 1934).

Singh, Kanishka. "CIA Sued Over Alleged Spying on Lawyers, Journalists Who Met Assange." *Reuters*. August 15, 2022.

Smiley, Tavis. "Oliver Stone and Peter Kuznick. Part 1." *PBC*. Sept. 13, 2011.

Smirnenski, Hristo. "The Tale of the Stares." 1923. www.slovo.bg

Snowden, Edward. *Permanent Record*. New York: Metropolitan Books. 2019.

Steward, Jon. "Jon and Judd Apatow on Why George Carlin Still Resonates." *The Problem with Jon Steward* Podcast. June, 2022.

Strozewski, Zoe. "Ten Percent of Americans Don't Believe in Climate Change, 15 Percent Unsure: Poll." *Newsweek*. Oct. 26 2021. https://www.newsweek.com/10-percent-americans-dont-believe-climate-change-15-percent-unsure-poll-1642747

Stone, Oliver. *Ukraine on Fire*. Doc. "Victoria Nuland and Geoffrey Pyatt Phone Call." 2016.

Sykes, Stefan. "8 Million Americans Slipped into Poverty amid Coronavirus Pandemic, New Study Says." *NBC News*. Oct. 16, 2020.

Taibbi, Matt. *Hate, Inc: Why Today's Media Makes Us Despise One Another*. New York,
London: OR Books. 2021.

———. "Sweeps Week on FBI TV!" *TK News by Matt Taibbi*, Aug. 16, 2022.

———. "Activism, Uncensored: The 'Not Calm Hearts' in Kharkiv, Ukraine." *TK News*. July 26, 2022.

The Joe Rogan Experience # 950. Abby Martin. April 25, 2017.

The White House. Office of the Press Secretary. "Remarks by the President at the 50th Anniversary at the Selma to Montgomery Marches." March 7, 2015.

The *American Political Tradition,* RHP, Box 3.

Thijmen Spakel. "Noam Chomsky on the Russia-Ukraine War, the Media, Propaganda, Orwell Newspeak, and Language." *Edukitchen.* Podcast from the Netherland. April 26, 2022.

Timpane, John. "'Caged': How 28 Inmates' Tales of Prison and Poverty Became New Jersey's Must-See Play." *The Inquirer.* May 2, 2018.

Thomson, Alex. "Exxon Mobil Lobbyist Reveals Company's Involvement with 'Forever Chemicals.'" *Channel 4 News.* July 1, 2021.

US Bureau of Labor Statistics.

Vernay, Du. Director. *Thirteenth.* Doc. 2016.

Villareal, Daniel. "69 percent of Americans Want Medicare for All, including 46 Percent of Republicans, New Poll Says." *Newsweek.* April 24, 2020.

Vyse, Graham. "Is Denis Kucinich Serious?" *The New Republic.* Jan. 17, 2018.

Walker, Joseph L. "Global Science Communication: Action Plan." April 3, 1998. http://www.sourcewatch.org

"War Diary: Iraq War Logs." *Wiki Leaks.* Oct 22, 2010, www.wikileaks.org

Webb, Gary *Encyclopedia Britannica.*

Webb, Whitney Alyse. *One Nation under Blackmail: The Sordid Union between Intelligence and Crime that Gave Rise to Jeffrey Epstein.* Barnes & Noble. July 22, 2022.

———. "Invisible Enemies: Parallel between the Anthrax Attacks and Covid 19." *Unlimited Hangouts.* Oct. 2021.

Wehman, Ben. "6 Reasons Why Planet of the Humans is a Disaster." *Films for Action.* April 29, 2020.

Wei, Tian. "John Mearsheimer: Great Power Politics on Ukraine." *CGTN. You Tube.* April 16, 2022.

Weigel, David. "Bernie Sanders Kicks off 3 Days Rallies for Like-minded Candidates." *The Washington Post.* Feb. 22, 2018.

West, Cornel and Tricia Rose. "Tight Rope Final Episode: Reflecting on a Year of Love, Wisdom, and Fortitude." *You Tube.* September 9, 2021. https://www.youtube.com/watch?v=clFVKr-rtxs

Williams, Maxine. "Facebook 2018 Diversity Report: Reflecting on Our Journey." July 12, 2018.

Wolfgang, Ben. "Hilary Clinton says She Has Both a Public and a Private Position on Wall Street." *The Washington Times.* October 8, 2016.

Wolinsky, Howard. "The Crash Reaches Universities. The Global Financial Crisis Threatens the University Funding in the USA and Europe." *EMBO Reports.* 10 (3) March 2009.

Xin, Liu. "One-on-one with Oliver Stone." *The Point*. Oct 15, 2021. 40 Years Comedy. *HBO*. 1997.

https://searchengineland.com/wp-content/seloads/2011/09/Eric-Schmidt-Testimony.pdf

https://thepressproject.gr/person-of-the-year-julian-assange/

https://www.youtube.com/watch?v=l5ef856QHdQ

https://web.archive.org/web/20150627195622/http://humanrightsaward.org/past-honorees/

http://www.abi.org.br/abi-homenageia-defensores-da-liberdade-de-imprensa-e-de-informacao/

http://www.newyorkfestivals.com/winners/2013/pieces.php?iid=444956&pid=1

http://imaginepeace.com/archives/19347

https://bba.winstonsmith.info/bbai2012.html

http://libertyvictoria.org/node/172

https://www.walkleys.com/board-statement-4-16/

http://www.marthagellhorn.com/previous.htm

http://sydneypeacefoundation.org.au/peace-medal-julian-assange/

http://www.cbsnews.com/news/julian-assange-given-press-freedom-award/

http://www.digitaljournal.com/article/301727

http://samadamsaward.ch/julian-assange/

http://newsfeed.time.com/2010/12/13/julian-assange-readers-choice-for-times-person-of-the-year-2010/

https://www.theguardian.com/media/2009/jun/03/amnesty-international-media-awards

https://www.indexoncensorship.org/index-on-censorship-awards-archive/index-on-censorship-award-winners-2008

https://www.linkedin.com/feed/update/rn:li:activity:6926391630958661633/

www.challengepower.info

https://rokfin.com/unlimitedhangout

https://info.scoop.co.nz/Caitlin_JohnstoneCaitlinjohnstone.com

https://www.centerforhealthsecurity.org/event201/about

https://climatechampions.unfccc.int/davos-2022-what-to-expect-from-this-meeting-like-no-other/

https://www.youtube.com/watch?v=34LGPIXvU5M

https://www.youtube.com/watch?v=7RPt7hRfr8I

www.cornelwest.com

https://www.statista.com/statistics/585152/people-shot-to-death-by-us-police-by-race/

https://www.statista.com/statistics/319246/police-fatal-shootings-england-wales/

http://www.ipcc.ch/2018/10/08/summary-for-policymakers-of-ipcc-special-report-on-global-warming-of-1-5c-approved-by-governments-ipcc

http://www.ipccch/report/sixth-assessment-report-working-group-ii

www.sunrisemovement.org

https://planetofthehumans.com

https://en.wikipedia.org/wiki/Jimmy_Dore

www.Forcethevote.org

Lightning Source UK Ltd.
Milton Keynes UK
UKHW010042291122
413021UK00013B/231/J

9 781665 575270